D1600883

The Black Foster Youth Handbook

50+ LESSONS I LEARNED TO
SUCCESSFULLY AGE-OUT OF FOSTER
CARE AND HOLISTICALLY HEAL

Ángela Quijada-Banks

ISBN: 978-1-7357842-0-5

DEDICATION

This book is dedicated to all the young people currently in foster care. I hope you find this helpful to navigating your experience in foster care and beyond. You're not alone and you can be successful! You can heal! You can be all that you desire to be. Trust the process and lean into your purpose.

HOW TO USE THIS HANDBOOK:

YOUTH

My best advice is for you to come to this book with an open mind and with an expectancy that you will learn atleast one thing from reading it.

It will be very helpful for you to use a journal and pace yourself. I have a #selfreflection journal that you can find and download from my website for free.

Throughout this handbook, I will challenge you to take a look at your own life right now and decide if you'd like to keep going the way you are or if it may be time to tweak a few things to be in alignment to your divine purpose, fulfillment and freedom.

Statistics say, that less that 4% of foster youth graduate college, lead successful lives after foster care and many never get to live a life without the molds of their trauma. Within this book, I am challenging that narrative. That means, it won't be a bunch of information you've already heard before. It won't be everyday things people say because I chose a different way to live my life than what the statics pushed me toward. And you too, can choose another way to realizing your full potential and creating a life far beyond your wildest imagination.

I recommend that you take your time with this book, but hold yourself accountable. Maybe find a buddie that will read with you and go through each phase in this book together. It is time for you to move forward from your trauma and step into who you are called to be. It is time to heal and shed the pain of your past from affecting your future success. You got this. I believe in you.

ADULT SUPPORTER

Feel free to make this a community experience. Perhaps, even make a book club out of it to immerse yourself, your young people and others who may benefit from this book in this journey.

Although, my experience is of a young person of color who experienced foster care, I have also met with many supportive adults throughout the nation and have heard what they deem as problems. I have listened and thus added fostering success tips in hopes to support what they are already doing to help young people in foster care's success outcomes.

I know that to an adult supporter; it can be very challenging to navigate the complexities of fostering or adopting a young person. So, take this handbook and read it with your young person. Pace yourself and have your own journal to reflect in as well. This will not be a comprehensive guide with each and every scenario in foster care – however, it will provide some clear answers to questions or thoughts that are not usually spoken on.

BOTH

Throughout this book, you will see: #IAmSuccess Questions, #FosteringSuccess tips and Chapter exercises.

Please keep in mind that these are my 50+ lessons that I learned and everything here is a suggestion meant to aid you on your own personal journey. I implore you to think outside of the box and not to rush the process. This book is not mean to be read at once, in one sitting. It is meant to be read in sections and for you to take time to reflect then apply something from what you have learned. Be open. Be ready and I look forward to connecting with you on the other side on your journey to success, healing and soulful liberation!

The Black Foster Youth Workbook is meant to be supplemental to this handbook.

It provides space to dive deeper into the #IAmSuccess Questions, Chapter Exercises and #FosteringSuccessTips.

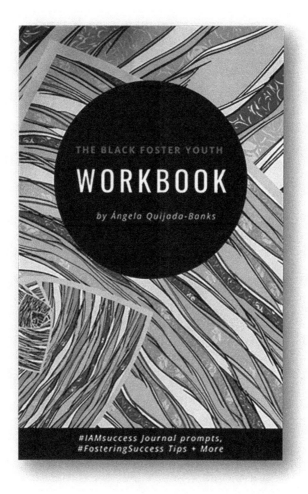

You can download the free e-book at
www.blackfostercareyouthhandbook.com

TABLE OF CONTENTS

Chapter Three: The Mindset to Success

Phase Two: Envision

Chapter Four: Evolving Definitions

Chapter Five: Building Your Success Team

Chapter Six: Maintaining a connection to your culture

Phase Three: Ascension

Chapter Seven: Your Existence Matters

Chapter Eight: Protecting Your Spiritual Connection

Chapter Nine: Level Up, Level Up, Level Up

Phase Four: Liberation.

Chapter Ten: Your Voice Matters

Chapter Eleven: Cultivating and Sustaining Inner Peace

Chapter Twelve: Be In a Constant State of Transformation

Conclusion : Life is Feedback to What Frequency we are Vibrating on

ACKNOWLEDGEMENTS

First, I'd like to acknowledge the divine creator and my ancestors who have paved a way for me to learn the English language, and write this book.

In the journey of this book, I have come across and been blessed with the support of so many individuals who wanted this dream to come into fruition.

Thank you and it would not have been possible without your help.

The following individuals have shown me so much love and belief in my vision, they went above and beyond to make sure my book was the best that it could be .

My entire Dream Team, they helped to make sure the work was shared with everyone they knew it could help. They encouraged me and helped me make executive decisions about this book.

Portia Harger, who was once my personal yogi instructor and has morphed into my sister in this struggle to liberation. She cut a lot of the fat in my rough draft edit and influenced the piece of what it is today. She supported me as I went through some emotional spells dealing with my past.

Cheryl Bunn, my aunt on my dad's side of the family. She has been an incredible support for me since we reconnected and pushed me to root in my why of this book. She has helped me process alot of the painful memories that have come up.

Liza Weidle, my guardian ad litem-now aunt has shown me so much love and support from the beginning of this journey and made space when I felt overwhelmed about particular life events during this process.

Jenifer McClafferty, was an incredible motivator and predicted that this book would be a national best seller! Love her so much!

Victor Sims for his feedback and support through the launch of this book.

Melissa Gutierrez, my colleague for her feedback and review to further the reach of this book.

Jeffrey Bunn, my dad and good friend who rooted me on even in the times when the world felt heavy and I began to feel the grief of not having my mom...

Amal Amoora & Michael Stroud for sharing and combatting with trolls about the importance of this book aside from politics. For reiterating to strangers who were committed to putting anything with the word, "BLACK" in it down that this book is imperative for young people's success in foster care.

Toni Contini, my soul sister who is always showing up for me. She helped me navigate harder pieces of my story and process the heaviness that came up so that I could continue writing. She has not waivered not one time with her commitment to our sisterhood and this book.

Tamisha Macklin, my friend that I met at the National Foster Youth and Alumni Policy Council who took time to reassure me how much this book is truly needed.

My Editor, Teshia Harding who ensured that I made my deadlines and showed so much grace and care for my manuscript throughout the process.

My life partner and best friend, Michael Banks Jr. There is so much to say, but I want to thank him for his support. For cooking when I felt tired and making sure I wasn't staying glued to my computer. I want to thank him for being there when hard emotions and memories came up or an event would come up and try to distract me. I want to thank him for being on this journey of decolonization and healing alongside me.

PROLOGUE

I still remember the day I met Angela Quijada-Banks, the summer of 2013. I was a clinician in North Carolina, working as an outpatient therapist, and I had been assigned to work with this young woman. She was living with her foster parent s in a situation where she was described as, "a ward of the state". The mere sound of that phrasing felt diminishing, almost as if a young person was held captive by no wrongdoing of their own. As a clinician, I was new to working with foster care youth during that time. However, I would soon discover that young people in the foster care system not only experience several systemic, educational, social, and emotional barriers; but they must also attempt to shed the labels that are inadvertently and unfortunately placed upon them as a result of being in the foster care system.

During one of our first counseling sessions, I remember asking her what she believes the future holds for her. Being a senior in high school, I wanted to know from her purview what her plans were after graduating high school. At that moment, Angie expressed to me that she had no future plans, what she desired for herself was peace; to be left alone from the chaos that encompassed her life in the foster care system, filled with social services, family disruptions, high mobility, and separation from her siblings. She expressed her life, at the time, was overwhelming, chaotic, and emotional, and she wanted the roller coaster ride to end. I soon found out that since she had been in foster care, she had spent very little time thinking about her future and what she wanted it to look like.

Prior to being placed in the foster care system, around the age of 13, Angie did have very high hopes and dreams for her future. But this positive outlook on life was diminished after the struggles she had been through prior to entering foster care. Angie had lost all hope in what life would be like for her upon reaching the age of 18. I knew then that I must make it my mission to turn this aspect of her life around, to help her to visualize her future, and start making plans. To understand that the time is NOW.

I knew in order for this to happen that I had to go above and beyond my role in two ways: 1) I needed to earn her trust, and create a therapeutic relationship with her based on honesty, empathy, and emotional safety. To do this, I had to create a space for her to be vulnerable, and engage in a certain level of disclosure that allowed her to work through the traumas and emotional hardships of her past and present. 2) I had to transcend beyond my role as a therapist, which was already a meaningful and valuable component of helping any youth in foster care successfully accomplish adult self-sufficiency.

During the time I was working with Angie, I was a doctoral student in the Counseling and Counselor Education program at North Carolina State University. A huge component, if not the component of the Ph.D. program was to conduct high-level research as a budding scientist practitioner. In this regard, I was to contribute to the body of knowledge in the counseling field through scholarly research, and if possible, fill gaps in the body of knowledge in the counseling literature. As I sat there, contemplating what would be my contribution to the field, and what can I do to further advocate for something within the field that I strongly believe in, there was only one research focus that came to mind. I reflected on the meaningful work that I had accomplished with Angie.

Mind you, by this time, I had worked with and seen Angie grow in numerous ways over several years. After serving as her therapist while she was in high school, I would then go on to serve as a transitional living specialist at another agency, and to my surprise, was assigned Angie as a client that I would then go on to help with her college transition. I did not know Angie was being served at this agency because during this time she had gone off to college and we stopped working together in the therapeutic capacity. I was so delighted that we could continue to what we started years prior, and that I can see her enter her next phase of life, her college years! I remember one favorite moment when I had a video project for a course where I had to focus on a topic related to social justice advocacy. I decided to focus mine on advocating for foster youth. I asked Angie if she would allow me to come to campus to interview her and do a documentary on her journey over the course of a few days.

I remember walking around campus and sitting and having her reflect on her past, share her passions of the present, and candidly map and outline her future. I still have that video I created for that class. In viewing the video today, it is so amazing to see her living out the very dreams she talked with me about on that bench in the middle of campus all those years ago. At the same time, I see how much we have both grown as people, and how much our kinship and connectedness has grown as well. The video not only left a lasting impact on me, but to the peers I shared it with in that room that day as well. It gave us all hope. In reflecting upon this previous and continued work, and the impact Angie had on me over the years, I knew that my doctoral research needed to focus on the career and college readiness of adolescents aging out of the foster care system. My secondary focus is on the adult self-sufficiency of youth aging out of foster care. My adaptation of my research agenda during this time would soon prove to be massive in years to come. It has allowed me to fill a gap in the body of knowledge in counseling, and extended my advocacy efforts from the local level to a national platform such as publishing op-eds in Youth Today, the only independent, national, and digital media publication that is read by thousands of professionals in the youth service field.

Today, I serve as a counselor educator at a historically Black college and university (HBCU), where I proudly train the next generation of culturally competent social justice counselors. Through my position as a faculty member, I teach students pertinent counseling advocacy skills centered around the multicultural and social justice counseling competencies (MSJCC's), as well as continue my research and work focused on advocating for youth in the foster care system. And as a co investigator on a grant funded project, I focus on campus support programs for foster alumni in Texas as well as training foster caregivers regarding their roles in the support networks of the foster youth they serve.

My work, my passion for supporting youth aging out of foster care, is deeply rooted in the experiences I had supporting Angie and seeing her grow into the adult that she is today. She has pushed me to utilize my voice, and minimal place of influence, to advocate on behalf of individuals who truly need me. This has stretched me in a number of ways, more so that I am beginning to see myself as a budding expert as it relates to the educational needs and outcomes of adolescents in foster care. This is a position that I do not carry lightly, as there is still much work to be done.

Fast forward to today, seven years after I met Angie, and I see a completely transformed person, one filled with joy, hope, and a certain zest for life that I did not quite see in the 17-year-old version of herself.

I see a woman who has reached a level of success beyond even her own wildest dreams. She has taken her own story of hopelessness, despair, and disruption, and re-wrote her narrative to teach others how to live in joy and success. This was no small undertaking. This took much work on Angie's end both mentally and emotionally, but for her, it was more than that. It was a matter of survival. To create a life both worth living and for living. Did I also mention that she is now Mrs. Quijada-Banks?! One of my most fondest moments was witnessing Angie marry the absolute love of her life, Michael. I was honored to watch her marry this most amazing person and see the rest of their lives begin. I remember my daughter saying, "Wow, a princess!!" when she saw her walk down the aisle.

Indeed, that is how she made us all feel. I felt honored that I was asked to say some words on her behalf at her reception, and I wiped back tears as she danced with the love of her life, reflecting on how far she had come, and seeing her exude pure love and joy made me so happy. Little did I know was that she would move away to California and become hard at work advocating for foster youth in the most amazing ways. Following her California journey has instilled in me even greater hope for the future of our youth, but also pushed me to better use my voice to advocate on behalf of those who need it. In this way, I have seen the student now transition into the role of teacher, as Angie has taught me how to better stand up for what I believe in, be a voice for the voiceless, and do it all while leading in peace and love.

One of things I have been most proud of Angie over the years is her ability to advocate for youth in foster care, particularly for Black youth in foster care. She has a natural desire to help others navigate through the muddy waters she experienced as a young person aging out of the foster care system. Angie has made it her mission to help shed light on that plight that these youth face on a local, regional, and national level, even interfacing with politicians and has influenced passed legislation that will help better facilitate the needs of youth in foster care. Angie wants to help all youth, with a focus on those who look like her, in foster care to successfully reach adult self-sufficiency and self-actualize their dreams because she knows first-hand what it's like to lose hope. She understands the intersectionality of being young and Black, and recognizes just how far the odds can be stacked against Black youth aging out of the system. Furthermore, her professional credentials as a scholar, coach and holistic wellness practitioner further add to her body of work in revolutionizing systems, holistically healing communities, all while uplifting the work of her ancestors, elders and colleagues. As a purpose coach, best-selling author, spoken word artist, and founder of the Soulful Liberation (a publishing company and podcast), Angie is empowering communities across the nation and helping individuals uncover their divine purpose, redefine success for themselves and begin to heal. To see her flourish in her work, while advocating for some of the most disenfranchised communities, is something that is to be both appreciated and celebrated.

In this regard, her most recent project, The Black Foster Youth Handbook, is her best effort to capture all the tools, resources, and nuggets of knowledge and inspiration that she could give to Black youth who also desire to successfully navigate their way out of the foster care system , while building a support network to accomplish this goal. In this handbook, Angie includes a model inspired and built from the inspiration of Maslow's Hierarchy of Needs and African & Indigenous spiritual systems as a conceptual foundation, which details how Black foster youth and supportive adults can work towards success and healing while also sharing anecdotes that allow readers to relate to Angie's own experiences. As a clinician and counselor educator, I can attest that the Black Foster Youth Handbook is the most ideal resource for helping professionals in their work with young people in foster care. It is also the best resource for the young people in foster care themselves. Mrs. Quijada-Banks utilizes her knowledge, skills, and expertise to not only speak to the experiences Black youth in foster care face, which includes personal anecdotes from her own life experiences, but I have found her 50+lessons, tips, detailed explanations related to foster care and the child welfare systems, and her writing activities as tangible ways practitioners can successfully facilitate the needs of youth navigating the foster care system. For me, Ms. Quijada-Banks' handbook took the guesswork out of how I can both adequately understand and support these youth in their holistic healing. It was all right here in this book, and I feel that it would be a great resource for you in your work as well.

I believe that you will find this handbook both enlightening, fulfilling, and real, because it comes from the perspective of a person who has not only been there and done that, but truly cares about the future of our Black youth aging out of the foster care system. I know that it will help me in my work with Black youth in foster care, and that it will strengthen my advocacy efforts even further. I hope you join the journey that Angie has set forth here in this handbook, and allow your wildest dreams to take flight. Angie, I am so proud of you. You are my sister, you are my kindred spirit, you are what this generation needs right now. Continue to wear your crown with pride, Queen, and shine like the sun.

With Love,
Regina Gavin Williams, Ph.D., NCC, LCMHC

The Black Foster Youth Handbook

INTRODUCTION

Just the other day I was talking with a friend about how big I would dream as a child, and how as I reached my teenage years that inner knowing to dream big began to disappear. Instead, those big dreams began to turn into strong, elaborate, and even monstrous nightmares. It seemed as though it didn't matter whether or not I was asleep or awake, because somehow and in some way life would feel suffocating. As I approached graduation in my senior year of high school, I feared that I may not make it. I couldn't see myself living past eighteen years old. The reality I lived in for so long clouded my vision of all the future possibilities. I was sure I would be dead before becoming an adult.

And since I wasn't dead, what was I to do? Was college really still an option for me? What about entrepreneurship? After so many unhealthy relationships, was marriage a jump beyond my reach? As the weight of the world, loved ones' expectations, and my own limiting beliefs began to speed up their pace, I pushed on in hopes of one day achieving grand success.

For many years, I felt lost, confused, hurt, angry, and unloved. That part, I knew was not supposed to be normal, but the way they showed up for me was difficult to decode at times. Some days, I felt happy. (After knowing now what the state of joy is, I equate what I experienced as happy back then to pleasure; a short-term stimulus that inevitably runs out. After which you will need a new stimulus to help you prolong the sense of "happiness", even if it's just for a few more moments.) In this state of happiness, my mind would always bring up ideas as to how it wasn't going to be long before that feeling expired. And, soon enough, it would. Just like I predicted. Then, I'd go on a whole rant about how the universe was BS, asking why did God hate me so much, and why did this always happen to me.

What I failed to realize, was that I had choices. I could choose to no longer allow my environment, past trauma, people in my life, and negative thoughts to control me.

When I was a child, I had little control over my circumstances. I couldn't just get up one day, pack up all my clothes, and move out at 6 years old without there being real problems that I would have to face. Like, where would I go, and how was I going to get there? And of course, I wouldn't leave my siblings behind, so where would we sleep? How would we eat? Was I going to have to get a job to take care of us, at six years old?

No, there are child labor laws in place now.

And more importantly, I don't even have to stay in that state of mind because I'm not six nor in that space anymore. For a long time, I became accustomed to having one traumatic event happen after the other, non-stop. I was constantly reliving my past, catastrophizing my next moves, living in a perpetual state of survival mode. And I would put up a fight to stay there, although I craved more. I wanted to travel the world, to be genuinely full of joy, and feel unconditional love without the prerequisite of pain first. I wanted to experience eating delicious, well-balanced meals with a clean bill of health and circles of amazing friendships. I desired a life that filled me up inside. A life that I didn't need a break from. And I knew it existed. Perhaps, somewhere in the cosmos, or in an alternate dimension.

I just didn't know how to get there.

From Pain to Power

The Black Foster Youth Handbook is a compilation of over 50 out of the many lessons I learned from my personal experience as a young person of color navigating a life that included trauma, foster care, and racism. I have acquired many bumps and bruises along the way, and yet I am still here. And hey, so are you.

When I was a freshman at North Carolina Central University, I took a sociology class that taught me about Abraham Maslow's hierarchy of needs. This concept stood out to me. Abraham Maslow was an American psychologist that wrote a paper in 1943 named *A Theory of Human Motivation*. In this paper is a pyramid shaped figure that outlines the foundation of basic human needs as the figure's base, and self-actualization as the narrow tip of the pyramid.

Over the years, I've done in depth research on my heritage of Indigenous and African descent, as well as the history of institutional racism in America, and more recently, within foster care. Why is it that after decades upon decades of the child welfare system being in place, with the intention of catering to the well-being of young people, that the success rate among these same young people remains so low? Why is it that less than 3% of the foster care population actually graduate from a four-year university across the nation? What are the common variables between the very small percentage of young people that make it through the cracks? And lastly, how can we begin to actively prepare young people within the foster care system to successfully navigate through with competence, a strong support system, and confidence that their own dreams (no matter how big) have the ability to become a reality? Once I made the decision to write this book, I knew I would be taking a holistic approach. I planned to break it down into tangible steps that can be applicable through foster care and beyond.

I have broken this concept down into four main phases. I call it the R.E.A.L success model. Each part has three chapters, for a total of 12 chapters filled with life lessons I've learned to help you and supportive adults understand and successfully navigate through foster care together.

PHASE 1 IS (R)OOT.

To help you and your adult supporter(s) gain understanding of some of the basics of foster care, and how you can begin to understand everyone's role and who to contact when your needs are not being met. After you gain that understanding, we kick off with grooming your mind to prepare you for the remaining chapters of this book.

PHASE 2 IS (E)NVISION

To help you and your supportive adult(s) understand the importance of working together. You will learn why you need healthy loving relationships around you and how to begin acquiring them.

PHASE 3 IS (A)SCENSION

Each chapter in this phase helps you build your self-confidence and further root and envision your life far beyond foster care. This phase will support you and your supportive adults' understanding of the next steps, and help you begin to actively seek out what you need in order to ensure your success.

PHASE 4 IS (L)IBERATION

In this last phase of this book, you will have understood the foundations of where you are in your life and where you want to go. You will have begun putting systems in place to support your big vision. You will know who you need in your life, and who you will need to release in order to achieve your version of success. You will also begin to uncover your divine purpose, do what is needed to achieve freedom from your past, and accelerate into soulful liberation.

At the end of the day, these 4 R.E.A.L success phases can only support you in your journey if you are open to it, and ready to do the work. Nothing in this life worth acquiring will be "easy", at least not at first. Sometimes, when learning something new or starting a new habit, it can feel overwhelming until you get into the flow of your new reality. The best part about a new paradigm shift is you actually get to choose. You get to choose if you'd like to hold on to your limitations. You get to choose if you will make it a priority to heal and release generational curses from your family's lineage. You get to choose if you are ready and willing to achieve holistic healing and R.E.A.L success. Keep in mind that with every choice there are consequences and rewards. Choose wisely.

As the title states, this handbook is purposely geared toward Black and brown youth, yet it is also beneficial to anyone reading these lessons who desires a deeper knowledge and understanding regarding the foster care system and institutional racism in America.

Foster care is a global enterprise complicated by often-conflicting agendas of stakeholders in spite of a common concern for the overall well-being and care for young people. Any institution involving billions of dollars is bound to require periodic assessment, accountability, and reform. Perhaps even a revolution. And, as I've learned over the years, these things take time. As we continue to focus on the advancements of these systems in place, I believe that the holistic well-being and success of young people in foster care is something we need to support now! Well, yesterday, but we will settle for now!

(Table A)

Timeline of Foster Care and Legislation:			
Date:	Entity or Legislation:	Purpose:	Potential Impact:
1500s	English Poor Laws	Placement of orphaned children into indentured service until adulthood in England	Model for origins of Foster Care in the United States
1636	First documented Foster Child in US	Benjamin Eaton, seven year old male, is first foster child on record in the nation	"Foster-Servitude"
1825	NY House of Refuge	Specifically addressing children of neglect from poor families unable to provide care	Pioneered boarding of juvenile delinquents based on reformatory ideology justifying child labor force
1853	Free Foster Home (Orphan Train) Movement	Orphaned children were sent to live with families in rural areas via New York Children's Aid Society initiative directed by Charles L. Brace	Offset urban homelessness of neglected children

1912	US Children's Bureau Created	First federal department established to address welfare of children	Create funding and policies
1935	Social Security Act	Established federal regulations of child welfare services necessary to receive funding under Title IV-B;IV-E (AFDC) and Title XXX	Consisted of federal funds for child welfare services
1977	Court Appointed Special Advocate (CASA)	CASA/gal programs began to emerge	Assigned volunteer advocate on behalf of foster child
1977	The Indian Child Welfare Act (ICWA)	Prohibit removal of children from reservations to boarding schools	Cease the cultural colonization of Native heritage
1980	Adoption Assistance and Child Welfare Act	Provided a structure of guidelines for policies and practices in determining reasonable efforts to maintain kinship placement children in need and provide the necessary federal funding	Implemented the CPS court system to regulate compliance of policies and practices
1986	IV-E Amendment	Section 477: Independent Living Program implemented	to assist youth emancipated from foster care program
2018	Family First Prevention Service Act	Restructure IV-E amendments of group and institutional care with incentives for children in crisis to remain at home by reducing use of congregate care	Implementation of mental health, substance abuse prevention and home based parent skill programs

Although history can be a clear indicator of how far foster care legislation has been pushed by its constituents and allies to provide benchmarks to ensure necessary care is possible, the element of implementation of this legislation is where things can get fuzzy. To help bridge the gap between unpassed, passed, and implemented legislation,

I believe more stories from those directly involved must be shared and elevated. Whether that is a young person currently in or an alumni of the foster care system, foster/resource parents, social workers, guardian ad litems, and others. This will also help those of us that are actively seeking to support young people with what they need.

What is deemed appropriate to meet the needs and care of one individual person may not appropriately meet the needs and care of another. It is difficult, if not impossible, to provide a blanket approach to address the needs and care for all young people in the foster care system. Too often, young people are placed in unsafe home environments with foster parents who are non-nurturing and lack the understanding and guidance of what is required to support a young person who has endured very traumaticevents.

Through further education, perspective, patience, and preparation, I believe that these issues among others can be alleviated. In spite of policies and practices proposed by legislation throughout the history of foster care and child welfare services, refer to table A, very few state or federal laws earnestly address the immediate or long term effect of Adverse Childhood Experiences.

Black and brown youth in foster care experience a disproportionally higher percentage of traumatic events classified as ACEs, according to a 2018 ChildTrends study.

The demographics of children placed in foster care stretches across the spectrum of all societal categories, and the reasons requiring placement into foster care can easily be argued as too broad to even categorize. Yet, perspective is imperative in order to approach such a daunting task of creating a roadmap of success for young people in foster care.

My perspective is that of an empowered woman of color with an unshakeable sense of purpose, unapologetically refusing to be silent while knowing firsthand the hardships faced by young people in foster care. I know what it is like to feel silenced by the pain of apathy and ignorance. I know what it is like to feel neglected, abandoned, isolated, and marginalized. I have been in difficult seasons of life not knowing where to turn, who to trust, or what steps to take in order to combat dire circumstances seemingly beyond my control and definitely not of my choosing. I know that the plight of young people of color in foster care is a microcosm, reflecting the systematic racial injustices within the infrastructure and daily social indoctrination of American society. And I know how hopeless it all can seem.

However, I also know that I stand with the strength of my ancestors who have come before me, who have fearlessly endured the most horrific of circumstances throughout history without defeat. I did not come this far just to be shut down when the fight for justice and freedom gets brutal.

The lessons compiled in this handbook emerged from a necessity to survive, and have evolved into a voyage filled with a greater understanding and desire to answer the divine call. We must first ground ourselves in our foundation, then make our way to sustaining an ever evolving transcendence with an unshakable life mission.

Despite the most unfavorable of circumstances, I have found myself joyfully married to an incredible human being, prioritizing my own healing, giving back to my communities, and leading a life that I am proud of. I emerged with the memories of my past carrying the intention to ignite *self-reflection* and *soulful liberation* in young people currently experiencing foster care. I want them, and you, to know there can be a prosperous life after foster care. In previous years, I have openly advocated and advised child welfare stakeholders, politicians, and university staff alongside constituents regarding the betterment of these systems.

We need more people talking about these issues in order to continue in this fight! We need more prevention and solution-oriented action plans. We need more recognition, and accountability, for what is not working and the negative impacts those mistakes have created.

We need to continue to educate and empower youth of color in foster care to embrace adversity from a perspective of opportunity.

Each chapter in this handbook encourages you to trust your own life journey while providing you with the opportunity to learn lessons from someone who has experienced similar struggles and is doing the work every single day to challenge indoctrinated narratives, contradict current statistics about our race, class, definitions of success, and holistically heal from childhood trauma and generational colonization.

Your mission in this life, if you choose to accept it, is more powerful than just what you believe. It is an inner knowing that you must pick up and choose to dwell only in the possibilities of a future beyond any limitation of your past. My hope is that through this handbook, you will have some form of guideline to support you on your own journey of success. I hope to help you establish within your life, a strong over standing of your current state of reality and a discernment about keeping unhealthy vs healthy circles of people. I hope to help you cultivate a high sense of self-esteem, strengthen your resilience muscle, and encourage you to look at the future with a smile, embodying an inner knowing that everything will work out as it should.

After all, if our ancestors survived all that they were made to endure, so can we. It is time to step out into the world of opportunity and live abundantly in your purpose without the shame or pain of your past paralyzing your next steps.

THE R.E.A.L SUCCESS MODEL

PHASE 1

ROOT

Analyzing what you are currently rooted in. Assessing what may need to shift in order for different results. Recognizing what your current systems, routines and every day duties are.

Being clear on who are the current people in your life- are they bringing you quality support, authentic love and or guidance or is it time to shed some dead weight?

*Does the soil need to be changed? Do the roots need more water?**

PHASE 2

ENVISION

"What would life look like outside of the bubble I've placed for myself?"

How do i want to move forward despite my past trauma and pain to a vision bigger than what I previously accepted?

Dream big, don't concern too much on being "realistic".

Being focused on building your success team and identifying healthy relationships in your liner circle.

What am I growing into?

PHASE 3

ASCENSION

Take it a step forward and identify the people who can help you realize your goals and dreams. Write your goals, the skills and habits needed to achieve your wildest dreams.

Begin to look at what is the legacy you wish to realize for your life.

**What am I choosing to water?? Who do I choose to become and how am I showing up in this way? **

> ❝ Whether you believe you can or believe you can't, you're right. ❞

PHASE 4
LIBERATION

Liberating self (system) into defining a clear divine purpose, striving in awareness toward holistic health, growing community of success team players and giving back to communities we come from.

What is the quality of the fruit that I (or the system) is baring?

Liberation

Ascension

Envision

Root

The Black Foster Youth Handbook, Ángela Quijada-Banks © 2021

This model illustrates the inspired Maslow's Hierarchy of Needs triangle expanded with African and Indigenous spiritual systems and the representation of a "being" or "system". This is a visual representation of how this book is taking you from Root to Soulful Liberation. Before you begin your journey, take a moment and send an email to mrs.banksofficial@gmail.com with the SUBJECT LINE : " I AM COMMITTED TO SOULFUL LIBERATION! " The truth is we are more likely to follow through with our commitments if we 1. Write it down and 2. Tell at least one friend See you on the other side !

STILL HERE...

BY ÁNGELA QUIJADA-BANKS

Let us never forget our roots,

nor who we have become.

WOur origin is of stardust

Revolution is our legacy

United through bloodlines of royalty,

I must profess.

For our people will always rise

seeking progress.

Nothing can hush our pride

Or slow the stamina of our stride

Our heritage flows with gold and honey

From lands of wealth in jewels and money

Oh, how we have endured the trials of our past.

Yet, When all else has diminished,

this resilience will last

For it is written in the cosmos eons beyond us

We are divine

And without fear.

And above all, we are still here.

Phase 1
Root

CHAPTER ONE

THE BASICS TO UNDERSTANDING THIS NEW REALITY

"You might be temporary in their lives or they might be temporary in yours. But there is nothing temporary about the love or the lesson."

-TONIA CHRISTLE

"With guidance and support from a caring adult, children and youth in foster care are resilient and are capable of realizing their fullest human potential."

- FERNANDO SERRANO

Change is not easy. Even if the change is for the better, it is still hard. I still remember my first day in foster care. My siblings and I, after years of hiding our holistic instability from routine visits from child protective services (CPS), finally decided enough was enough. We finally told the truth of what was happening in our lives. As a result, after many hours waiting in the social services building and overhearing the confusion of where the fate of our lives resided, we were placed with my aunt and uncle on my dad's side of the family.

What made me withhold the true nature of our family dynamic in the first place? Well, looking back it was for several reasons. One reason was wanting to be with family. I didn't want myself nor my siblings to be with strangers or in a worse off predicament. There's a saying that goes, *We prefer known hells over unknown heavens,* and that was certainly the case for me. Regardless of the pain and suffering or how horrible it was, there was the familiarity of it all. Secondly, I had become comfortable with the uncertainty of living... (which is a very depressive state to be in). Thirdly, I had a need to be loyal to my parents. I was told to always "obey" my mother and father even when things they'd ask me to do may have been questionable. In the case of withholding information, my parents had warned all of us about not discussing matters that had to do with the family... *or else.* That "or else" was enough to keep all of our mouths shut.

"You keep those people out of our business," they'd tell me, referring to anyone other than them, including teachers, concerned school counselors, and other parents.

For a long time, keeping my head up in conversations, making eye contact, or looking at anything above the ground was not something I'd do. When I walked, I'd stare at the ground, anxious to look up and catch some form of criticism or an insult. "You know better than to be walking around here looking all miserable." they'd say. Except, it wasn't just a look. I really was miserable.

Before being in the system, I saw foster care as a scary place that the most unfortunate of children went through. My parents would say, "If you do this... or if you do that, we are going to send you away to be with some other family to take you and do what they will." Except, unbeknownst to them, that's exactly what I wanted. I remember days where I'd be in the back seat of the car, trying to make a "dead-looking" appearance so that possibly, maybe a nice, warm, and loving family would inquire about my well-being from the windows of their car. Maybe they'd signal for my dad to stop the car and suggest I come stay with them for a few days. Maybe they'd take me in. Seem too far-fetched? Yeah... maybe. A kid can dream, right?

The cool thing about dreaming is that it is where the most amazing inventions, ideas, and multibillion dollar industries all begin... with a dream. I mean look at the founder of OWN. That kind of success did not happen overnight. It began with a single dream. Think about Martin Luther King Jr. and his ideas around racial integration. One single dream, grown and nurtured into a massive dream, carefully calculated into a plan, applied with daily action, can produce the most astounding results even if it seems completely unreasonable or illogical at the time. In those moments of pain, confusion, and dysfunction, I'd dream to live a happy life, have a warm bed, a loving family, and delicious food.

My first day in foster care was a mixture of feelings. We ended up in kinship care, which I thought was going to be amazing since I was still with family and not with strangers. I thought, *YAY! We made it! We are away from the craziness, but not with totally random people.* I didn't hate my parents, per say, I just didn't want to live with them. I never truly felt safe with them. Nothing ever seemed stable.

At the time that we were removed, I was sixteen years old and I had little, if any, hope in a bright future. I knew that if my siblings and I continued to stay there, that we would not have made it another year alive. I know what you're thinking. And no, I'm not exaggerating.

I am the oldest of four siblings that I grew up with. From the age of seven, I fed, bathed, clothed, read to, and protected them as if they were my own children. We had a very strong bond at the time. From the eldest (me) to the youngest, 5 years old I believe, we had each other's backs and told each other everything. The first day that we were removed was unexpected. After finally making it to our aunt and uncle's home, I hoped that maybe after a decade and a half of torment, my life was going to make a 180.

My sister and I shared a room, and my three brothers shared a room. Our rooms were across from each other with our doorways facing each other. After dinner, our aunt and uncle told us to head upstairs to take our showers before heading to sleep. We all rushed up the stairs. My youngest brother exaggeratedly acted as if he was falling down the stairs, playfully grabbing our legs as we all bum rushed to our rooms.

We giggled and laughed until we heard my uncle yell, "Stop running around up there!"

I thought nothing of it as I slowed my pace and took off my back pack and took out my science book. "I'm sleeping on this side of the bed", I announced, marking it with my book.

"Fine, well, I guess I'll take this side," my sister said in her snarky tone. Excitedly and full from dinner, my sister and I wanted to see what our brothers' thoughts were about everything that happened that day. We decided to go to their rooms to talk with them.

We rushed over to their room, which was less than 5 feet away from ours, only to be interrupted by our uncle. "Umm.., where do you two think you're going?", his voice began to raise. "Anddd didn't I say not to run in this house?" I was stunned by this reaction. Why was he so upset? What did we do wrong? Afterall, all we wanted to do was talk to our brothers.

My sister was the first to break the silence, "We were just going to talk to the boys. And I didn't think we were running."

"It was more like fast walking", I said, "And-"

Before I could finish, he interrupted me. "So now y'all are liars, too. I see we have a lot of work to do. Well, let this be a lesson to everyone." I was confused. Let what be a lesson?

He began to take off his belt, gesturing for us to turn around. We kept staring at him. I was in disbelief. "No running in this house! No boys are allowed in the girls' room! And no girls are allowed in the boys' room!" I began to cry as he was yelling. What was happening? Were we going to be safe?

Before we dive into my lessons, I want to take some time in this chapter to provide you with some solid information that will prove helpful throughout your journey in foster care.

The fundamental goal of foster care is to provide a safe environment for anyone under the age of eighteen who is not able to live with and be cared for by their biological parents.

In this chapter, we take a look at the infrastructure of foster care, explain the role of key constituents involved (i.e foster parents, social workers, case managers), and introduce common terminology so you can begin to understand when it is used and become an active participant in your case plan. This will allow you to become involved in important conversations about your safety and quality of life. I will explain where to gather resources that may prove helpful in clearing up confusion generated by this sudden change in your life.

For me, it was often the unknown that made changes during my time in foster care more confusing, and even scary. I sometimes became frustrated and fearful of not knowing what to do or how to tell someone when something was wrong. When I was first placed in foster care, I had little hope, and felt trapped within my own mind, body, and past. I didn't see the value in trusting others, because it was hard to look past what I already been through. Today, I realize that this was the wrong way of looking at life.

Why? You may have great intentions of protecting yourself; however, you can do more damage to people who are placed in your life to help you. You can begin working against your own success and actually block your own blessings. Looking back, I could have been more open to the people and opportunities that were presented to me. So many people could have been a part of my success team (we will talk about this in later chapters) along the way, but I had no idea how to have a healthy relationship with another human being. I didn't even know how to have a healthy relationship with myself.

Our lives and experiences may be different in nature, nevertheless, we were still placed in foster care, and I know how alienating that can feel. How your sense of "normalcy" can be displaced, and even nonexistent. In these moments, it's important to ask yourself and others around you questions to gain clarity about where you are and what that means for you. Ask yourself, *what is normal*? *What can support me in feeling a sense of normalcy in foster care at this time?* Begin to paint a clear picture for yourself in what that means, whether in a drawing, a poem, or a letter to your social worker and foster/resource parent. This will help them understand where you are coming from and open conversation.

Everyone, regardless of age, gender, race, religion, or lack of, can make it out of even the most difficult of experiences. How do I know? Haha... you will piece together the answer throughout this book. Besides me, millions, if not billions, of people across the world have already done it. Did you know that Malcolm X was a foster kid? I had no idea, and he has been one of my role models since I was a child. How about Alonzo Mourning, a famous basketball player? Eddie Murphy, Cher, Louis Armstrong, Ice-T, Colin Kaepernick, Les Brown, Tiffany Haddish, the founder of the shade room, Angelica Nwandu, and even Harry Potter.

Yep, Harry Potter was a foster kid, too. Don't believe me? Rewatch the movie. Bet you'll fall in love with it in an entirely new way.

Another piece of good news is we all have the same 24 hours. None of us have more or less time than the other on any given day. Although, it may not seem like it, time is an illusion, my friend. I found this to be true multiple times throughout my life. At one point, when I was fresh out of foster care, I ended up in a very unhealthy relationship. Well, let's face it...*all* my romantic relationships prior to this one with my husband were pretty unhealthy.

In this particular relationship, I convinced myself that I would work four jobs, pay all the bills for the both of us, and then have the audacity to complain that I had no time. However, my ego didn't really care about that. I was having too much fun, posting on snapchat and flashing $20 dollar bills in the camera with the hashtags #4jobs #selfmade #independent #hustler.

The truth was, the only thing being hustled was me. Fourteen to sixteen hour work days, unhealthy eating habits, no exercise, a face full of pimples, barely any support, and a not so great, one-sided relationship. Can you say *tragic*?

How we use our time is our choice. We all have the ability to cultivate within ourselves the understanding of how to shape our lives into what we want them to become despite what our past has been. Sometimes, we get lost along the way and become blinded by the ideas and advice given by well-meaning family and friends that don't really know the answers themselves. They may have just winged-it their entire lives.

For over a year, I stayed in that toxic relationship because I didn't know my own self-worth, and family advised me that we were just having a rough patch and that I needed to suck it up and be strong for my boyfriend at the time. I'd call my family in tears, yelling about how scared I was while locking myself in my car flinching as my ex-boyfriend would be pounding on the car windows with his fits threatening to kill me if I didn't come out.

My family would tell me to just wait it out, and that obviously he needed my support so he could get himself together. I was told to pick up another job when I had two already, and yet another after acquiring the third. I was advised to drop out of school to focus on how I could support him and myself. I was told to do anything to make it work as if it only takes one person to have a healthy, loving relationship.

I loved these people who were giving me this advice, but I've learned that just because you love someone doesn't mean you have to listen and apply what they say, especially if they aren't where you want to be in life. Why was I modeling my life after people who could barely make their rent every month, had toxic or flaky relationships, and complained about almost everything and everyone in their circle? Maybe it was time to stop listening to people who clearly didn't prove great results. Did I love them any less? No. But I didn't want their results, so why follow their formula?

Life is a sum of seasons. Some seasons are long, and some seasons are short. But every season has a start and an end. And every season in life is going to be different. Some are beautiful, and some can be absolutely terrifying. Maybe you have already experienced some terrifying and unnerving seasons in your life. Perhaps that's now, being in foster care. And that's okay. We are most terrified about things we do not understand. Know that this is a temporary feeling, and you have the ability to transition out of that fear.

Being in foster care is a season in your life that can be thought of as just temporary. At some point, it will end.

So, how will *you* use this time while you are here? How will *you* endure this season? How will you make the most of this experience and prepare yourself for the wealth of experiences to come?

For a long time, I couldn't wrap my head around what life could mean beyond my troubled childhood. Then when in foster care, I couldn't see past seventeen.

I remember turning seventeen like it was yesterday.

My sister and I were in a foster home. It was our second foster home, the one we were placed in after being removed from my uncle and aunt's house. My siblings and I were separated by gender, and sent to live with complete strangers. Before foster care, if I was around my grandma (nana) or uncle Rey, that meant my birthday was going to be amazing and memorable. I'd feel love and excitement! I was going to have a good time.

The night before my seventeenth birthday, I remember crying myself to sleep. Although I had my sister with me, I felt alone. Since being separated from our brothers months before, we had both dealt with it in different ways. It hurt to even think about them, since we were unable to call or see them. That's all I wanted for my birthday.

I had spent weeks before pleading with my social worker about having a sibling visit for just one day. To no avail, the night before had come. My foster parent (we will call her S) decided that we were going to merge my birthday with her daughter's baby shower. I tried to stay optimistic, but when my birthday finally came, I was emotionally burnt out. We arrived at the park fifteen minutes early to help set up and clean the table area outdoors. After guests began to pile in to the party, my sister and I were asked to stay out of the way of pictures.

I held my tears in front of everyone as I wondered what my brothers would be doing in that moment. Could they be laughing and enjoying themselves? Were they okay? Were they safe?

Luckily, although dealing with our own turmoil, I was able to talk with my sister. We joked about what was going on at the baby shower and I felt a lot better about the whole situation. This was just another time where we had to see the humor in it all and laugh it out.

Situations such as these are what have pushed me to write this book. I'm not going to sugar coat it, life in foster care can be extremely challenging. It's a whole other world that people know little about, especially if you aren't experiencing it firsthand. So, when the going gets tough, know that you have people that are rooting for you. You are not alone. And together we will navigate this drastic change in your life using the information and exercises available in this handbook to increase your knowledge, expand your awareness, and equip you with tools needed to navigate foster care successfully and the great future you have beyond it.

WHY AM I IN FOSTER CARE?

Children and youth come into foster care for many reasons. The majority of those reasons are abuse and neglect. Of course, this is only the surface level answer, but it is a start. To determine why you were placed in foster care, you may have to think back to your living situation prior to being in foster care. What was it like? Who were you around?

If you are still unsure, ask your siblings, your foster/resource parent or social worker. They will know what was documented as the reason for your placement in foster care.

WHAT IS FOSTER CARE?

It is a temporary placement of a person or people with the intent of reunification with the biological family.

As defined by Annie E. Casie Foundation:

"**Foster care** is a temporary living situation for children whose **parents** cannot take **care** of them **and** whose need for **care** has come to the attention of **child welfare** agency staff."

What does foster care mean to you in your own words? (Min. 5 words)

_____

_____

_____

_____

Keep this with you, and periodically come back to it and write a new definition. You may be surprised at the ways your views of foster care change as you learn more about it and familiarize yourself with your next steps for your specific case plan while you are in foster care and beyond.

TYPES OF FOSTER CARE PLACEMENTS

There are many types of placements in foster care. Here is a list of the most common.

a. Kinship/family
b. Group home
c. Non-relative Home
d. Supervised Independent Living
e. Behavioral Health facility
f. Pre-Adoptive Home
g. Adopted Home
h. Respit

My four siblings and I were placed with family members initially, which is known as kinship care. After that didn't work out due to abuse in the home, we were separated by gender and relocated to foster family homes.

What type of foster care placement are you in?

_____

_____

AM I ALONE IN FOSTER CARE? AM I THE ONLY ONE?

Nope. Actually there are over 400,000 foster youth in the U.S alone, and according to NFYI (National Foster Youth Institute), **More than 250,000 children are placed into the foster care system in the United States annually.** And that's just in the United States. There are young people being placed in foster care all over the world!

So you are far from alone, and the likelihood that you have a foster youth in your neighborhood is actually pretty high. When I first found out that I wasn't alone, it opened a whole new world for me. It was 2015, I was a YV Scholar with Youth Villages and on a scholars trip to Memphis. This was the first time I met young people who understood what I had gone through and was still going through in foster care. We went to the Dr. Martin Luther King Jr. museum, and I felt a sense of pride.

Do not think you are alone, because you really aren't. At the end of this chapter and throughout this book, you will see resources for you to look up and reach out to with a trusted adult, or on your own. As I've traveled the world and met some incredible alumni of the system, I have learned there are hundreds of thousands of organizations to support young people in foster care, especially in the United States. Many of us just don't know they exist.

I WANT TO BE WITH MY SIBLINGS, WHAT CAN I DO?

Sibling groups entering foster care are often separated, and they can be moved between anywhere from ten to over hundreds of miles away from each other. This can happen for many reasons, and is definitely a point of concern for many in the foster care system.

If you have siblings, it is important for you to know that foster youth all over the nation have been advocating on your behalf so that you can speak out when your rights are not being honored. When I was in foster care, my siblings and I were separated by gender, and we did not know when or how we would be able to see each other.

You now have a *Sibling Bill of Rights*. Your foster parent or social worker may not know of these rights, so try to exercise patience if they don't know what they are talking about. You learning about your Sibling Bill of Rights will help you and your siblings advocate on each other's behalf, and educate the supportive adults in your circle.

Your Sibling Bill of Rights is as follows:

Siblings have a right to:

- Be placed with each other when possible to remain a family.
- Give adult siblings a chance to be a foster parent, adoptive parent, or to gain custody over younger siblings in order to keep families together.
- Be placed in homes close by each other, if they cannot be placed together, to facilitate frequent and meaningful contact, including phone, internet, social media, FaceTime, skype, etc. Siblings will be provided with a phone number, email, and/or address, and access to updated photos by email or mail.
- Be actively involved in each other's lives if they choose. Share celebrations including: birthdays, holidays, graduations and other school events, extracurricular activities, cultural customs, including speaking their native language, and other meaningful milestones.
- Be informed about changes in each other's placements, including being notified of discharge from placements, new placements, as well as discharge from foster care. Siblings will be allowed to maintain contact with other siblings who remain in care. Every effort should be made to ensure contact among siblings in care and those not in care.
- Predictable and regular visits that shall not be withheld as a behavioral consequence. Unless verifiable safety concerns exist, siblings should not be kept from each other. Visits can be monitored, but should not be supervised unless there is a safety risk. Youth, caregivers, caseworkers, and parents are all responsible for ensuring that siblings have contact. All parties will coordinate dates and times, transportation, and other accommodations to ensure contact occurs. This should be outlined in their service plan. Due to the normalcy provision,

caseworkers do not need to give permission for visits or possible sleepovers, but foster parents should still communicate with and inform caseworkers that these activities are occurring. The judge should also be updated on sibling connections at every hearing.

- Be included in permanency planning decisions relative to siblings. They should know what expectations are for continued contact when a sibling is adopted or custody is transferred to a relative. For questions or complaints, contact the Office of Ombudsperson for Families by mail, phone, or email. Provide the following information:
- Name, address and telephone number
- A description of the situation
- Names and dates of birth of children involved in the case
- Tribal affiliation of children, if applicable, and
- Names and contact information of caseworkers and other agency or service providers.

Take some time to research more about Siblings Bill of rights in your own state, and make sure to have a copy with you in a safe space.

Minnesota's Bill of rights

https://www.dhs.state.mn.us/main/groups/county_access/documents/pub/dhs-305844.pdf

Rhode Island

http://www.dcyf.ri.gov/documents/rds-portal/RDSPortal_SiblingsBill.pdf

WHAT IS A FOSTER/RESOURCE PARENT?

An adult to support and help you navigate life and foster care. Foster parents must be licensed by a foster care agency or the Department of Social Services, or by their state or country's respective department.

ARE FOSTER PARENTS PAID TO TAKE ME IN?

Yes, Foster parents are paid to ensure your wellbeing, however they must be financially stable prior to having you in their home. Funds must be supplemental to supporting your needs while you are living with them.

WHAT IS A CASE MANAGER OR SOCIAL WORKER?

They are paid by the state to enforce state laws. They are man-dated reporters which means they have to report anything that is illegal or a harm to you and others. They work with judges, biological families and anyone in connection to you to keep you safe.

WHAT IS A GAL / CASA?

GAL: Guardian Ad Litem

CASA: Court Appointed Special Advocate

They are appointed by judges to advocate on your behalf. Be sure to keep a steady line of communication with your GAL/CASA. If you do not have one, or are unsure, reach out to your social worker and ask.

Be clear on your needs with your Guardian Ad Litem. Voice your concerns and thoughts around your current placement. Let your CASA/

GAL know about your goals and what you are looking to accomplish. Let them know how you feel about your future, and what you are looking forward to having in your placement. Be sure to vocalize things that are going well.

When I was placed with my aunt and uncle initially in foster care, I withheld information from my Guardian Ad Litem because I was afraid of what would happen to me. I was living in a kinship placement and it was the first time I was away from my parents for an extended period of time. I was unsure about how to voice how distressed I was. I became afraid of what my uncle and aunt might do. Plus, I did not want to be separated from my siblings. At the same time, I knew that the abuse we were enduring within the home was not conducive to any of our well-being. It was a difficult choice to make.

Months went by, and with yet another severely traumatic event, I eventually mustered the strength and clarity of choice to run out of the home, go to a neighbor's house, and report what was happening.

I urge you not to allow anything to fester and prolong the difficult choice of getting out of a life-altering or life-ending situation. If you notice something is wrong or something is bothering you, as clearly as you can, tell your CASA/ GAL, foster parent, or any trusted adult. Let them know how you feel about it.

Think about how you would want this issue to be resolved. Would you like for there to be a conversation with support? Would you like to continue staying within this placement? Why or why not? How do you feel about being with your guardians? Do you feel safe? Why or why not?

You can ask yourself these questions so that when you're speaking with your GAL/ CASA, you can ensure the communication is clear and direct. You have taken time to think about what you want to say and how you can answer their potential questions. It is by no means EASY, but it is important to begin to understand why these relationships with supportive adults are important to have, and how they can help provide you the best support they can.

INDEPENDENT LIVING COORDINATORS

There are independent living coordinators all throughout the states. Coordinators help to support youth in foster care's transition into adulthood.

In North Carolina, one of these programs is called LINKS. Independent Living programs, such as LINKS, provide support to young people in foster care by helping develop skills so you can live on your own confidently without the presence of foster care officials. These programs are usually geared at youth thirteen to twenty one years old.

I FEEL SAD AND ALONE, WHO CAN I CALL?

When there is something that goes on regarding my foster parent, who can I contact?

Make a list of trusted adults. Be sure to include an ombudsperson, family members, friends, and other trusted supports to be sure that when the time comes when you need them, you have their contact information on hand.

If there is anything that bothers you, you will need to speak up. No matter how big or small the situation is. No one will know you need help or how to support you if you just act like everything is okay.

In one of my foster homes, I had a situation where my foster parent spent all of the money she was given to care for me, on clothes for herself and her dog. All that was left in her house for me to eat was already expired meat and canned goods dating 3 to 5 years back. I was mortified. My foster sister, who was newly placed in the home was upset and decided to throw all of the old food away. I didn't think it was my place to remove the old, molded food, but I could understand her frustration.

There was no financial accountability. There wasn't anything in place to make sure the funds she was given for me were actually used for me. Unfortunately, a year prior my Guardian Ad Litem had been removed from my case. I could not call my social worker, because she'd retired two weeks ago. I wasn't speaking up about any of the situations that were going on prior to this one, so there was no record of the gradual negative circumstances. I didn't want anyone to get in trouble, but I knew that this as well as the other events were not supposed to be going on.

We must advocate upon these matters within the system to ensure the best possible outcome. We must speak up as soon as we notice something may be off.

AUTHOR'S NOTE:

Where are the receipt logs to ensure that the funds within the foster home are being managed and allocated responsibly?

The foster/ resource/parent(s) are human too. They can make mistakes.

And so can social workers. All constituents within the foster care system are more than capable of lying or withholding information. We are all human. And we need more systems in place to ensure the safety and optimal well-being of youth in foster care.

WHAT DO I SAY WHEN PEOPLE ASK ABOUT MY FAMILY?

You do not have to tell them anything, until you are ready... if ever. In fact, most people had no idea that I was in foster care. I called my foster parents my aunts or uncles, and my social workers family friends. I never shared with anyone I was in foster care.

Why? Because I didn't know if I could trust them and if they were mature enough to keep it to themselves. I had previous experiences with giving too much information to the individuals that didn't have good intentions.

Whether or not you decide to tell others about being in foster care, it is important to think it through a bit. How would you feel if the relationship went sour? Would you be okay with them saying certain things about you? I wasn't. So, I did not share that I was in foster care or any of the events taking place in my case.

WHAT DO I SAY WHEN PEOPLE ASK TO COME OVER?

No. Or you can say that your parents said no.

DID YOU KNOW THAT YOU MIGHT BE ELIGIBLE FOR HEALTHCARE UNTIL 26?

Check with your social worker to make sure you have this information with you. Keep a digital copy in your google drive files or screenshots in a private fb album so you can keep track of documents that you may need later.

SPECIAL IMMIGRANT JUVENILES

http://www.uscis.gov

LIST YOUR EMERGENCY CONTACTS HERE:

Foster Youth Bill of Rights

All of things you have rights to do and not do. Foster parents cannot take your stuff, it is an invasion of privacy. You have a right to privacy and your own items and material possessions.

If you'd like more information, it can be found on the child welfare website:

https://nfpaonline.org/page-1105707

And this one is from Sayso *For You Guide Book*:

As a youth in foster care, you have the right* and responsibility:

- **To know your rights in foster care, to receive a list of those rights in written form, and to know how to file a complaint if your rights are being violated.**
- **To be told why you came into foster care and why you are still in foster care.**
- **To live in a safe and healthy home where you are treated with respect, with your own place to store your things and where you receive healthy food, adequate clothing, and appropriate personal hygiene products.**
- **To have personal belongings secure and transported with you.**
- **To have caring foster parents or caretakers who are properly trained, have received background checks and screenings, and who receive adequate support from the Agency to help ensure stability in the placement.**
- **To be placed in a home with your brothers and sisters when possible, and to maintain regular and unrestricted contact with siblings when separated (including help with transportation), unless ordered by the court.**

- To attend school and participate in extracurricular, cultural, and personal enrichment activities.
- To have your privacy protected. You can expect confidentiality from the adults involved in your case.
- To be protected from physical, sexual, emotional, or other abuse, including corporal punishment (hitting or spanking as a punishment) and being locked in a room (unless you are in a treatment facility).
- To receive medical, dental, vision, and mental health services.
- To refuse to take medications, vitamins, or herbs, unless prescribed by a doctor.
- To have an immediate visit after placement and have regular ongoing visits with biological parents and other relatives unless prohibited by court, or you don't want to visit.
- To make and receive confidential telephone calls and send and receive unopened mail, unless prohibited by court order.
- To have regular contact from and unrestricted access to social workers, attorneys, and advocates, and to be allowed to have confidential conversations with such individuals.
- To be told by your social worker and your attorney about any changes in your case plan or placement, and to receive honest information about the decisions the Agency is making that affect your life.
- To attend religious services, activities of your choice, and to preserve your cultural heritage. If possible, your placement should be with a family member or someone from your community with similar religion, culture and/or heritage.
- To be represented by an attorney at law in administrative or judicial proceedings with access to fair hearings and a

court review of decisions, so that your best interests are safeguarded.

- To be involved, where appropriate, in the development of your case plan, and to object to any of the provisions of the case plan during case reviews, court hearings, and case planning conferences.
- To attend court and speak to a judge (at a certain age, usually 12) about what you want to have happen in your case.
- To have a plan for your future, including an emancipation plan if appropriate (for leaving foster care when you become an adult), and to be provided services to help you prepare to become a successful adult.

* Unless restricted by law or otherwise restricted by the court

Be sure to take a moment to print out a copy of your Bill of Rights. Keep it with your other important documents. Share it with your foster parent/resource parent. Then both of you sign the bottom of the rights to have a mutual observance and understanding of your rights.

My aim is to get us acquainted with this kind of information, and to provide some ways to address and alleviate the effects of ignorance of this information. Alleviation may not happen overnight; however, through continuous application and consistent accountability, I know you will find my suggestions to be helpful.

What to do when your Bill of Rights are not honored:

- Step back from the situation and clearly map it out in your head. If it's hard to think through this, call your therapist, foster parent, teacher, school counselor or a trusted adult.

- ○ If you do not have anyone that you can think of then call the Ombudsperson. You can reach them at:
- Talk to your social worker.
- Document what is going on and think about what you would like to have happen. Write that down too. Or record a video and send it to yourself on a social media platform so if your phone or anything gets confiscated that you have a record of the events.
- Talk to your GAL or CASA.
- If your social worker and GAL are unable to assist you, write a letter to the foster care supervisor and copy it to the agency director.
  - ○ (Ask for your social worker's supervisor's information)
- The truth is if you are speaking and are very emotional, adults may not fully listen to what you are trying to say. If it's a very emotional topic, then by all means cry, stutter, spit, but get it out.

In my personal experience, I learned that when I was very angry or sad, many adults were less likely to listen to what I had to say because I wasn't just stating the facts and ideas without emotion. It was difficult to understand at first that most adults will take you more seriously if you have something written and can speak clearly about a possible solution.

This is something I believe needs to be changed within the system. You shouldn't have to restrict your emotion so that you can be heard. You shouldn't have to limit your tears to appear more "professional" about a tough situation to voice. Of course, this isn't the case for all youth, but I do want to share what is possible and prepare so that you understand how others may perceive your approach.

- At the end of the day, although you have guardians available to you, much of the footwork will likely be done by you. They are there to support your safety and success. If this is not being met, speak up and call on your support.

As a former foster youth, I never thought life would be what it is for me today. I never would have thought I would experience weeks and months in a chain of blissful existence. I hadn't thought about what being successful truly meant to me.

How could I, when there were traumatic situations happening one right after the other, making me believe it would never end? Eventually, I made the decision to investigate my past, my ancestors' past, and to take stock in where I currently was in life and why I wasn't happy. Who did I want to become?

After many years of intense research into the history of Indigenous people on my mother's side and African people on my fathers' side, I realized that I was navigating many elements of what it meant to be a multiracial youth within America's foster care experience.

I had to make a decision to release the trauma I endured in the past, and stop allowing it to take over several layers of my life including my platonic and romantic relationships, my health, and my finances. It took over my ability to experience joy, cultivate inner peace, and embrace the connection to my culture. As I traveled across the nation from one coast to the other, advocating, leading discussions, and speaking to hundreds of young people with the experience of foster care, foster parents, social workers, and other constituents of the foster care system... it left me with questions found in this chapter and those sprinkled throughout this book.

I didn't research much about what foster care truly is until after I was kicked out of the system due to reporting feeling unsafe in a foster home. Yeah... you'll learn more about that later.

In this chapter and the next two chapters, we are building a foundation. Many people with or without foster care experience skip this step in life and wonder why, after having so many accomplishments and/or money, feel unfulfilled and empty inside. A strong foundation consists of meeting all of your basic needs emotionally, spiritually, physically, financially, and mentally. Not just the physical. Not just the financial. Not just the spiritual.

I've talked with people who attempt to replace this need with being extremely spiritual or religious while still experiencing ongoing financial hardships or physical dis-ease. I've also talked with people who are fixated on being rich and physical wellness, but feel at a loss about their true purpose in life and lack a connection culturally and spiritually. I think we need a balance of both spectrums, and in return will come to achieve different avenues of holistic wellbeing. A mix of what Abraham Maslow describes as self-actualization and what you will come to know in this book as soulful liberation.

It is imperative to establish a foundation in *who you are* and *who you would like to become* in this life. Part of being able to understand this is analyzing your current environment. In this chapter, we have taken a step in knowing *where* you are right now and what resources you have available to dive deeper in learning about your new reality in foster care. At this very moment, your reality is not what it was before. Therefore, we cannot use old ways to support us. Those old ways may have served a purpose at that time, but they have now expired. We may need new thought processes, habits, and systems to adapt to this new way of life.

The information within this chapter is not a comprehensive list, rather a starting point for you to dive deeper if you choose and understand the fabrics of this new reality, your new "normal".

I know that this can be a very confusing and scary time. You may have many many questions, thoughts, and concerns. I was there, but remember you do not have to navigate this on your own. There are people, organizations, and resources in place to help you along the way.

After each chapter you will find a chapter exercise to guide you to understanding yourself and your journey through foster care and beyond.

After you complete this chapter's exercise, move on to chapter two where we will be diving deeper into what it takes to successfully transition out of the foster care system.

FOSTERING SUCCESS TIP:

(Fostering success tips are for the supportive adult(s) that may be reading this book alongside you. It will help them to understand how they can support you during or after each chapter in this book.)

Print out the #FosteringSuccess Scavenger Hunt that you can find at the end of this chapter or you can visit www.blackfostercareyouthhandbook. com

Fostering
Success

Scavenger Hunt

Name of
players:

Have a tour of new place	Knows Home rules	Knows when and how to access food/water	Has signed Agreement of responsibilities	Has created a Vision board for the year
Has completed the 21 day mind challenge	Is on track with school studies	Has found their ideal therapist and is going regualarly	has created a resting routine they absolutely love	Knows the status of their case plan
Has begun researching scholarships and grants for post-secondary education	Has created a mind map of their ideas	Has been writing in their journal for over 60 days	has had 3 really hard days but decided each time to make it a good one	Has been learning more about how to take care of their hair
Knows the role of the CASA/GAL	Has created a rising routine that gives them energy	has been drinking atleast 5 glasses of water daily	Has shut their negative self talk up with positive self talk	Knows the role of their social worker
has been taking steps to strengthen their spirituality	has ten people they deem as part of their success team	has uncovered their divine purpose in this life	has tried something new that they enjoy	knows the role of their foster parent
has been taking steps to love themselves just as they are	knows what to do and who to call when they do not feel safe	has been challenging themselves to do things outside of their comfort zone	has spoken up about something that bothers them	knows all of their foster youth bill of rights

CHAPTER TWO

REDEFINING YOU

*"Be good to people for no reason. Not because they speak English
well. Not because they look well put together. Not because they have
a vast vocabulary. Not because you like the way they did their hair.
Not because they have expensive shoes on. Not because they look like
they have money. Not because they have something to offer you. Not
because you may feel sorry for them... Not because you think you'll be
blessed later. Just be a decent human being to others. Does that seem
too hard?"*

- ÁNGELA QUIJADA-BANKS

*"When you're in a dark place, you sometimes tend to think you've
been buried. Perhaps you've been planted, bloom."*

-UNKNOWN

After reading through chapter one, I'm sure you have tons of
questions. Think for a moment then write them in the space
below. You can come back to them whenever you'd like. Some
of your questions and thoughts may even prepare you for your next
meeting with your social worker.

On top of the everyday racial injustices and mental anguish we endure, some of us also have to try to hold our chests just to catch a breath in foster care. It means having to turn heavy traumatic situations into some form of humor to not be crushed by the weight of it. It means over-analyzing each level of success we do acquire and measuring it up to others, who have 100x more resources and support. It means willingly partaking in episodes of amnesia to feel joy and a glimpse of peace. Otherwise, reacting in a way that others may not be committed to understanding.

To be a Black person in foster care is to constantly be in search of who you are. Sometimes, you may feel lost amongst all the trauma, multiple places you've had to live, people you've had to please and attempting to gain an understanding of why it has all happened to you in the first place. It is continuing to awaken while in survival mode to the fact that your childhood was the sum of actions from caregivers who were doing the best they could with their own unhealed childhood trauma or undiagnosed mental illness(es). It's deciding whether the damage that has been done is repairable and longing to be in connection with those you share blood with. It is filtering through belief systems that have been shoved down our throats. It is struggling to find a way to truly live a life of stability while keeping our head afloat to prevent ourselves from drowning in poverty, toxic relationships, our own negative internal dialogue, or health complications. It is searching for community and not knowing whether they'll accept you so deciding to not even try. It is yelling at the top of your lungs that you won't be like the ones that have hurt you and then checking yourself to make sure you aren't lying.

The question is, what can we really do about all of this? Do we have to do it alone? No, of course not. We do not have to do this work to dismantle systems and change the entire world all by ourselves. We can, however, begin with ourselves. Looking at the man, woman, or gender non-conforming individual in the mirror and being honest about where we are and where we want to go in life. It is our responsibility to start with ourselves, our own biases, ego, and self-sabotaging narratives, before we can begin to correct our mindset and behaviors around ourselves' and others' well-being and success.

Responsibility - to own the ability to control your response.

LESSON I

PRIORITIZING A RELATIONSHIP WITH YOURSELF

"Plot twist: YOU are the bag. Secure yourself."

-UNKNOWN

SECURE YOU

BY ÁNGELA QUIJADA-BANKS

Secure your happiness & joy.

Secure your spiritual connection.

Secure your peace of mind!

Secure your prosperity.

Secure your home and loving nature.

Secure your soul family that holds value to you.

Secure your mind and flip your mindset until it begins to benefit all that you are striving towards.

Secure your education to make sure you're not just blindly and ignorantly following behind the masses of BS.

Secure your foundation.

Secure your history of who you are, who your ancestors are ,what your culture is.

Secure the essence of what sets your soul on fire in passion.

Secure your life's purpose.

Secure your well-being in all forms: mind, body and spirit.

Secure the bag.

Secure you.

This is where our power lies.

WHAT IS THE FIRST STEP IN REDEFINING YOUR-SELF?

Becoming aware of yourself, this world and your current reality.

Becoming familiar with your current state of mind.

What are the stories you tell yourself about your past, present and future?

Do you KNOW who you are?

Have you ever stopped to think about it?

Do you love who you are?

Your name, your smile, your hair, your waist?

Do you care about your mental health?

Do you make sure you put yourself in positive environments?

For a long time, I did not love myself. Not my facial features, smile, body, voice, or much of anything. I subconsciously felt disgusted by my Blackness, let alone being a woman because of what I was told that meant.

Unfortunately, I had subscribed to society's toxic ideas of what "Beauty" and a "Black" body meant. I was confused and constantly entertaining my defiled and broken illusion with negative self-talk. I grasped on to my childhood trauma as a part of my identity. I merged my pain with being who I was. I defined myself as *Angie... the girl that had horrible things happen to her, period.*

As I became an adult, it really didn't stop. It began to transform under a protective umbrella of "false self-love" that crippled my productivity, health, and chipped at my own ability to choose things in my own best interest. It created a barrier between me and other people. Instead of being on time to that meeting, my self-sabotaging inner voice that disguised itself as "self-love" would say, "No, sleep in... you're too tired to go, and you deserve more rest". All while creating anxieties around a situation that most likely was false!

Even if it was valid, I know now-I had to go anyway! Deciding to push myself in spite of being told otherwise... even if it was by myself... was so difficult. It was habitual programming that I had to let go of in order to grow and elevate my life.

Throughout my childhood and during my time in foster care, I had developed many coping mechanisms to help me survive very strenuous, stressful situations. One coping mechanism was to self-isolate so that I was not a bother, among other reasons. As I grew older, this coping mechanism showed up in other areas of my life, including really big opportunities. The negative self-talk became way too loud, and I felt like I was drowning in it. I couldn't tell the difference between my intuition and self-sabotage. So, I believed the voice when it told me not to do something or when my gut feeling was to not finish applying to an incredible poetry venture.

One time, I applied for a position with congressman G.K Butterfield in North Carolina. Someone called me back for an interview, and at the end told me to write a letter with specific requirements. She told me that once I had completed the letter, I would have the position.

At first, I was ecstatic! I was well on my way in my political endeavors! Then, within hours, a voice in my head and a feeling within my body began to magnify. "What am I doing? There is no way I'll be able to keep up with an opportunity like this. I have no support, so what if something goes wrong?" I began telling myself about all the ways things could go wrong. Vivid images of "what if" failures began to play out in my mind.

At this time, my dad had recently been diagnosed with kidney failure, and was living with me in an apartment in Raleigh, North Carolina.

It became a huge mental, financial, and emotional strain on me and I tried to reach out to others for help. I reached out to my therapist who told me to get a job at the local grocery store to alleviate my $3,000 immediate financial obligation.

She told me that if I really wanted the problem to be solved, I'd apply there or at a fast food joint.

I had already expressed to her how against these businesses I was due to their poor food quality and ethics in previous conversations. She was also well aware of my lack of transportation options. This was a new financial obligation that was due within the week, and I still had to figure out my dad's medicine.

I reached out to my dad's side of the family, and not one person would have a conversation with me or come to see me. At that point, I was alone in my room, in the middle of the day paralyzed in bed, just crying, completely overwhelmed with anxiety and stress. I feel like if someone would have come and given me a hug, showed that they cared, or just talked with me through some ideas... I would have felt 1000x better. Even though some people did go visit my dad at the hospital, no one came to visit me. Not one person, although they comforted my dad with the lies that they would.

At the time, I had many poor quality people around me, so I didn't get much help at all. I felt alone, again. My mind spiraled into dark places. A few days went by and I had missed the deadline to send in the letter for this political internship. I rationalized by telling myself that, "If it was meant to be then it would have happened". A cute cop out for my own lack of self-discipline, low self-esteem, and self-sabotaging inaction. Later that day I received an email. It was from the hiring manager.

"I'm very disappointed to have not received your assignment", the first sentence read. I didn't know why at the time, but I felt that disappointment right in my chest. I continued to read on, and to my surprise, she had been looking forward to working with me. She wrote how she'd been impressed by my poise and professionalism, but I never sent in the letter.

I quickly replied to the email and said how I wasn't sure if I'd have a steady ride, and went on about my situation with my dad. I thought to myself, *yes, she should understand that it's been hard for me and I cannot have this job right now. I do not want another chance. I just need her to understand why I cannot continue.*

Later that evening she responded with, "...if you needed accommodations, we could have worked something out. All you needed to do was send in that letter, and you did not. I would have made some phone calls and you could be at a closer office to your home. You have to stop sabotaging your opportunities. I wish you the best in your future, and maybe one day we will cross paths. Have a great week!"

Sheesh! I was all over the place. I thought to myself, *Surely, she just doesn't understand how much stress I'm under. I don't have to prove to her how hard this has been for me. What am I sabotaging?*

I didn't know it at the time, but this email made me look at myself and my life through the lens of self-sabotage. How did things end up this way? And why was there always something dramatic happening in my life? Who and what were some of the common sources of this turmoil? What role did I have to play in all of this?

Was I one of the sources of my own anguish?

This is one issue I am very passionate about, helping others understand and overcome. During my #selfreflection series, on YouTube, I touch on and unpack these areas.

Every episode, there is a new focus of looking within and being in that vulnerable state to understand ourselves better! In my Purpose coaching program, we dive deeper in finding the root of the stagnation for individuals, which empowers them to redefine who they are with what they've been given, and discover how they can show up more authentic and rooted in purpose. Sometimes, they realize that certain situations are repeating because what they've been lacking is accountability and consistency. We cannot say we value something and everywhere in our life, it shows the complete opposite.

That inconsistency is creating a space for lack of fulfillment, productivity, confidence, and joy. It is stifling our growth leading a purposeful life.

IAmSuccess Questions are questions that you will find at the end of some lessons. These questions are included to help you dive deeper into the lesson on your own or with a supportive adult. It will be of best interest to complete all questions before moving on to the next lesson since each lesson builds upon the previous one.

Take some time to check out the 16 personalities test. I love it. It gave me tons of insight into things I enjoy, strengths and weaknesses I possess, and where to move forward in a career path. I took it for the first time when I was 18, again when I was 20, and most recently, when I was 23. I'll likely take it again at some point, to see if anything has changed.

www.16personalities.com

FOSTERING SUCCESS TIP:

Make taking the 16 personalities quiz a fun, household activity. Have everyone take this test and compare results. When my husband and I took it in 2018, we were shocked to find out we had the exact same personality type.

As I dove deeper into my own personality, I was simultaneously learning more about him.

LESSON 2

LIVE IN THE MOMENT AND CAPTURE THE MEMORIES

"If you are living in the past you are going to be depressed because you are rehashing things that happened to you that are not going to happen again. If you are living in the future, you are going to be anxious, because you are anticipating what's coming, or you are wishing for things that aren't happening yet. Being in the present is where the gold is. Being in the present moment is where you will have the greatest control, where you will find the most at ease and where happiness flourishes."

-MEL ROBBINS

As a youth experiencing foster care, it can be difficult not to think about the horrific moments in your past. In fact, even as I am now 23 years old and writing this, I still find my mind drifting towards thoughts of my past. I've experienced severe trauma, and I used to think that I'd have to live with extreme anxiety and panic attacks for the rest of my life. I thought that being deeply sad was possibly how the rest of the world had to deal with things. I began to normalize my trauma, and it slowly began to take over my life. Over the years, after lots of havoc had been wrecked, I decided to entertain a thought that perhaps there was more to life than one filled with pain. Perhaps I could be amongst those that did not feel the pain so heavy every single moment of the day. Maybe I didn't have to be consumed by my thoughts, dragging me back to yet another unfortunate circumstance that happened to me.

Was there a way to do this? How would I navigate the pain of my past when it does come up?

How do I minimize it coming up at all? I haven't found the answer to completely relieving myself from having self-sabotaging thoughts, painful and horrific memories, or emotional outbursts from time to time; however, I can share with you some skills you can use and apply to your life that will help you alleviate the frequency of them and redirect your mind to become more present.

In chapter one, we briefly talked about creating a foundation. In lesson one, we spent time talking about awareness and how pivotal it is for you to practice this as often as you can. They say it takes 60-90 days to make something a habit. I've known people to have 200 and 400 day streaks on snapchat, so don't give me the whole "I don't think I'm disciplined enough to become more aware". We are disciplined enough to do the things we believe and know matter to us.

How much does living a life of peace, love, purpose, and pure joy matter to you? I can't answer that for you, but for me, it means everything. If that is something that matters to you, or intrigues you as a possibility, then read on.

1. BECOME MORE CONSCIOUS OF YOUR PHYSICAL BREATH-ING.

Are you stress breathing with your chest?

You can feel that you are stress breathing if when you take a deep breath, you are moving your chest up and not inflating your diaphragm. Your shoulders may feel tight and be high up toward your ears. Lower them.

Take a moment to take a deep breath.

Relax your shoulders.

Unclench your jaw.

Smile.

Don't pay attention to your thoughts. Focus your attention on your breath.

Take another breath.

In for four seconds.

Hold.

Slowly release your breath with the count to eight.

Smile.

You may notice that you stress breathe often with your chest, and do not breathe with your diaphragm. No worries. Pay attention and whenever you notice that you are stress breathing, gently smile, and begin actively breathing through your nose, relax your shoulders, put a hand on your abdomen and unclench your jaw. Then breathe using the above method as many times as you desire. Make sure to brush your teeth, or your attention may be focused on holding your breath or how you should have used that Listerine on your sink.

2. PRACTICE GRATITUDE.

- You can start a Gratitude journal.
- Make time to be more grateful for your current circumstances.

Slow down and savor your joyful moments. Literally, pause in the middle of it and take it in. Find the joy in the little things. Even if it seems ridiculous at first.

When I was at North Carolina Central University, I'd go on 21 day smile challenges with myself. No matter if it was raining outside, or everyone else seemed to be having a bad temper, I told myself for (x) amount of time each day I will smile and find things to be genuinely happy about.

So, I'd complete my rising routine then I'd grab my keys for my dorm room. As I was locking my door to head out, I'd remind myself to smile and find something to be grateful about. At that time, I'd choose to be grateful for having a place to lay my head. I was grateful for myself because despite the wildest of odds, I made it to college. I'd beam with joy as I was making my way to class at a prestigious, historically resilient university. As I'd pass by others, I'd find something to compliment or greet them with a "Hello!"

Some would respond back, but many would not. I didn't take it personally. Not everyone is an 8a.m. person.

• Give more compliments to others.

When you like someone's hairstyle, don't just let the thought bounce around your head... go out of your way to compliment them with a smile.

If you see someone doing something out of their comfort zone, cheer them on and compliment their efforts.

When you are outside, just think to yourself of all the reasons you could be happy. Maybe even start with, "Wouldn't it be nice if..." and fill in the blank with a positive statement. Then carry out the emotion as if it is true. "Wouldn't it be nice if I was happy right now?" Then daydream about it. What would that look like? Picture what happiness looks like to you.

When you first rise up as the sun is coming up and you realize that you aren't feeling so good, begin to think of ways that you will take control of your day. What are the things that you are happy about?

Ex. I'm happy that I have a warm bed. I may not have my own room, but I have a clean place to lay my head, at least one person who cares about me, and a place to shower.

Don't just allow a bad mood to take over your day. Instead, make gratitude a part of your attitude.

3. NOTICE WHAT YOU DO NOT LIKE, AND BEGIN TO BRAIN-STORM HOW YOU CAN IMPROVE OR CHANGE IT.

While you are going through your day, begin to recognize the things that you are not so happy about. Then write them down and mark from a scale of 1-5, how excited this event/ person or task makes you feel.

Then determine the level of necessity it has in your life currently.

What would happen if you removed this person/activity/ task/ thing out of your life?

Would it make it better? Worse? Neutral?

Ex. Brushing my teeth when I wake up.

I will rate it a 3, because it's not the most exciting task, but it is important that I do it. If I removed brushing my teeth once I woke up, I would have stank breath and end up as a meme without any friends.

Now, it's your turn.

Think about what you do from the time that you wake up, until the moment that you lay your head to rest.

What tasks, people, and events could you live without? What do you desire to do instead?

Of course, these things may not be possible to have a drastic change overnight, but recognizing what you enjoy vs. the things you could do without will help you determine your next steps today and on the path to a future of success, joy, and healing.

4. ENGAGE ALL OF YOUR SENSES WITH INTENTION AND RELAXATION

Begin to activate your senses with asking questions.

Begin to mindfully self-reflect periodically.

This takes time, honesty, and patience with yourself. It took time for certain unfavorable habits to develop and it will take time to unlearn these habits. It will take time to recognize different behaviors that you find no longer serve you in your voyage to a life transitioning from a mode of survival to a mode of thriving.

If you want to take it up a notch... make it a 30 day challenge where you ask others for feedback on how you can be a better friend, sister, brother, or colleague.

Ask people to notify you when you are expressing a behavior you'd like to remove, and replace with something more pleasant and helpful on your path toward success.

Many times, we are more compassionate with others than we are with ourselves. Notice the ways you speak to yourself in your head. Be more compassionate with yourself and know that it is all a part of the process.

The fact that you are even taking time to do some work within yourself, says a lot about how you feel about your own personal development. You are making it a priority, and you should be proud! Keep it up!

5. WHAT MEMORIES ARE WE CHOOSING TO RELIVE?

When we go through traumatic events, it may begin to become a habit of only remembering the bad times, especially if those situations were happening during times when we were young. These horrific memories become the foundation to our world. In order to live a life of joy and active enjoyment of our success we must begin to acknowledge our past memories as what they are, memories from the past. We are no longer there. And we deserve to begin to actively create, store and relive positive and exciting ones instead.

When I was in foster care, it felt impossible to relieve myself of the pain and unfortunate events I endured before coming into the system. I'd sometimes be walking down the steps and have a flashback of something that happened and literally miss a step and fall all the way down. At first, I'd dismiss it as being clumsy. As I've tuned in further to being more accountable for myself, I've learned that the mental anguish I carried would constantly manifest itself to physical pain.

The amazing thing about that realization is that the same can be done with mental positivity manifesting itself to physical pleasure. Immediately, I began to put my theory to the test. I decided to only choose memories of joy and to relive them within my mind. I'd close my eyes and really feel that happiness and harness its energy with a smile perhaps even a chuckle. I noticed a shift in my reality and the quality of people I began to meet. I was raising my vibration within my body, mind, and spirit.

How about you, what memories are you choosing to relive? Are they good ones or mainly sad, painful ones?

Is this something you need to focus on healing? Why is it important for you to do this?

#IamSuccess Questions:

- Am I living the moment?

_____

_____

_____

_____

_____

- Who am I becoming with the path that I am on right now?

_____

_____

_____

_____

_____

- What is the way that I am living really saying about me?

_____

_____

_____

_____

_____

⎮LESSON 3

BEING ACCOUNTABLE FOR YOUR ACTIONS

"Stop making excuses. Stop being a victim. Take personal responsibility."

-DAVID GOGGINS

During my entire time in foster care, I had a really hard time expressing to others when something was wrong. I guess I was just tired of there always being something wrong. I didn't want to be the person who had a problem. I wanted everything to be smooth sailing and for everyone to get along. I wanted to be understood and supported in my various endeavors.

At one point, while attending North Carolina Central University I was moved from one foster care placement to the other. The new foster parent greeted me at the door and told me how excited she was for me to be there. I wasn't nearly as excited. I was more worried about how I'd get to my classes, since we were over forty-five mins away from my school, and if she'd be willing to take me. I struggled with obtaining my driver's license since it seemed every year I moved and didn't have a permanent residence. My foster parents never allowed me to use their car to take the driver's test. I kept going in a circle of trying to get my license so that I could make it to a job consistently. However, I needed car insurance before I could get my driver's license. And I needed a job to afford car insurance. And I couldn't be reliable at my job without a car. Every one of my foster parents would express being scared to allow me to drive their car. Some of them let me test drive with their supervision, and realized I was actually a pretty safe driver. They still felt that I'd have to figure things out on my own, though.

Within that new foster home, while attending college I recognized a lot of red flags. The first night I stayed there, she told me she loved me and it made me extremely uncomfortable. I replied with, "Thank you for caring" as I cringed my way to bed. I tried to tell myself not to think too much about it. Maybe she is just excited, reading my file and wanting to be welcoming. A few months went by and she started calling me her daughter, which I expressed made me uncomfortable. I mean, she barely knew me! She became glued to whatever success I acquired without her presence. She would make statements like, "You are so smart. I'm so glad you are here and that I've gained another daughter! Now, you will be even smarter with my help." I cringed. When we went out and someone complimented the way I carry myself, or the way I articulate my ideas, she'd take credit for it. "Thank you. I've done my best to raise her right."

As the months passed, I began to try to assimilate with her lifestyle and family. It was very difficult. I did not want to move again, but maybe I didn't have a choice; we were just so different. I was just turning twenty years old and she would urge me to "loosen up", go to parties, and drink alcohol with friends. I guess for many people my age, that was a normal thing. But to me, it wasn't. I was never interested in partying, drinking alcohol, or any of the other "mainstream" activities. I expressed that to her countless times. One day, to appease her, I agreed to her request to go out with some friends to a 21st birthday party late that night. My main concern was transportation, but she agreed to pick me up at 11pm that night (which, by the way, was way beyond the bedtime I set for myself).

After arriving, I instantly wanted to leave, but she made me promise to stay for at least an hour. As I approached the house, I heard loud music and people screaming in excitement. I knew others were having fun, but it affirmed to me that I should not have come. It just wasn't my scene. After going into my friends house, my friend immediately asked me to take three shots of alcohol with them. My friend reminded me that it was his birthday and I had to partake in the party rules. Standing in the kitchen, my friend looked absolutely wasted.

I laughed and said, "You know I don't drink."

Within minutes, over twenty of the birthday party guests began to chant to encourage me to drink. "Take a shot! Take a shot! Take a shot! Take a shot!"

My friend looked over to me after scanning the room of people, "Come on Angie... you don't even have to do three okay? Just one."

"I'm a light-weight... haha I'm good everyone. Thanks, though." I left the kitchen area, moved into the living room, and plopped myself on the couch. With a sigh, I began to contemplate why I convinced myself to come in the first place. I peered at the watch on my wrist, to discover that only eight minutes had passed. As I searched my mind for a way out of this, my phone started ringing. It was my other friend who happened to live just a few blocks away. Thank god!

I excitedly answered the phone. We made plans to hang out at the nearby park. I handed my birthday friend their gift and told them I had to head out, but I'd see them in class. A wave of relief rushed over me as I closed their front door behind me.

I knew that I had gone against my own values and beliefs. I did not honor my own needs and boundaries. I would need to reassess why I made that decision and minimize unwanted interactions like that to be accepted. What was the cost of trying to appease my foster parent?

The more that I am beginning to become aware of my own accountability with my success, the more self-awareness and dedication to self-love that I understand I have yet to master.

It takes ignorance to believe that you have mastered self-love, because self-love is a lifelong journey. There's never a cap on how much you love yourself, especially within the accordance of gaining new experiences, perspectives, ideas, and values as you withstand your own biological clock. Through each year, we are expanding our consciousness through our surroundings, knowledge of self, people that accompany us, various skills we decide to pursue, and lessons that are learned. One thing that I've been learning is to take responsibility for my own happiness, by any means!

Another thing I've struggled with was seeing people for who they truly are versus who they've shown themselves to be. This distorted perception of reality has wreaked havoc in my life. As time after time, I'd break my own heart. The truth is, no amount of positive thinking could change another person's way of life, how they treat me or others, and it definitely cannot help them see their faults as toxic. However, I have learned that it is not my job to help them see their faults-it is only my job to assist myself and find ways to correct my own faults.

Through discarding the idea that it's my responsibility to "help" others become better human beings at the expense of my own well-being and peace of mind, I have grown into a better understanding of what it truly means to continue my path in self-love. The truth is you can only focus on controlling your mind, behavior, and responses to people and situations. And you can't be super trusting to every single person. You can't tell everyone your next move. You can't tell everyone who you like or love. You can't tell everyone your biggest dreams and desires. And truth be told, everyone does not deserve to know.

I've come across many people who were miserable without wanting to do anything to alleviate their misery. And that's fine. If someone wants to stay miserable then that's their prerogative. The problem is misery seldom is satisfied being alone. Misery loves company. So don't be naïve, and believe that just because someone is curious about what you're up to or who you've decided to be in this life that you should now trust them with your holy grail of thoughts, ideas, and values.

Sometimes it's not a good idea to follow your heart, especially if you haven't trained your heart to be dependable in choosing people, events, and opportunities in your own best interest. That being said, situations in your life will continue to arise until you have come to a realization that which you have overlooked in the past. If you aren't learning from your mistakes, they will repeat until you do.

Be mindful! Take responsibility! Regardless of the situation, at the end of the day, it is your life! You can choose to go around making excuses as to why you couldn't achieve all that you know you are meant to be. Just know that when it's all said and done, your hair is gray and you're almost hitting three digits in age, you will realize the truth. It was the people you chose to surround yourself with, the mentality that you chose to keep, and toxicity that you refused to release that has kept you from achieving your greatest accomplishments and becoming the best version of yourself.

So why not start now? Will it be easy? Maybe not. Be present in the moment and take charge of your circle or square... whatever floats your boats. Ultimately, you are in control of who has access to you .You are in control of your happiness, regardless of what has happened to you in your past. The past may have felt out of your control. But, what about your present? What about your future?

The game of life is continuously at play, but now the ball is in your court. Get to dribbling and WIN WIN WINNNN NO MATTER WHAT!

#IAmSuccess Questions:

- What is something that has happened to me in the past that I believe will hold me back from being successful in the future?

_____

_____

_____

_____

- What do I believe could come up and be in the way of my happiness in the future?

_____

_____

_____

_____

- What can I do to minimize my exposure to or completely eliminate this blockage?

_____

_____

_____

_____

- If I had three wishes to use on my path toward success, what would they be?

_____

_____

_____

_____

LESSON 4

TRAUMA DOESN'T DEFINE MY FUTURE

"You act like I'm supposed to just get over it! How the hell am I supposed to move past the abuse and abandonment issues all because of her actions?! And on top of that, she acts like she doesn't even care!" I yelled over the phone.

This was during a conversation with my dad, who usually would understand when I'd vent about matters concerning my mother. He was telling me to calm down and that I shouldn't allow the lack of a mother-daughter relationship to affect me... But I was not trying to hear it.

"You don't understand! You aren't a woman, and your mother loves and adores you! Mine hardly recognizes I exist! So, if I want to be mad at her forever, I will!"

He paused and said, "...but that's the point. Why waste your time with that? Your life has to move on. You have to move on. You need to get past it so you can be happy, Angie. You're resilient, smart, funny, and a beautiful young lady. Stop letting this hold you back. Keep your head up. Remember, no matter what-You've got to strut."

It's been six years since this conversation, and I still remember how it made me feel. Open. I felt open to the possibility that my trauma didn't have to define my future. I felt open to the idea of healing past all the anger and pain I felt. Growing up, my relationship with my dad was very strained. It wasn't until I was nineteen and reached out to him while in college after not hearing from him anymore once his parental rights were removed that we were able to build a new relationship.

When we reconnected, he told me about his depressive episodes and how hard he tried to get us back. As an adult, our relationship has grown into a harmonious friendship without limits from our past. We have talked through painful memories, accountability addressed, and apologies exchanged. One contributing factor to this has been acknowledging the true power of managing expectations. If I expected him to make a complete 180 and be a super present dad then I would be setting myself up to be disappointed. I recognize and see him for who he is and how he functions.

My dad is a great emotional supporter and if I expect him to be anything more or less, I will be disregarding who he is and how he functions. This perspective takes a lot of understanding, empathy, accountability, honesty, and resilience. Resilience plays a key role in many areas of life, especially when dealing with dysfunctional relationships. You have to assess whether or not falling down and trying again with that individual is truly worth it in order to find and maintain harmony between the both of you. Resilience will help you see ways the relationship may become functional, even if it is out of the specific title a person carries.

Seeing the power of resilience as part of my own superpower in my toolbox of life, allows me to identify times when I need to pull it out and continue in the same path. Other times, it's time to change paths. For instance, if someone slaps you in the face repeatedly, you do not need resilience to stay in that same spot. You need resilience to do something differently. Perhaps get out of the way. If the slapper doesn't stop, or even follows you, maybe it's time for them to get slapped as you remove yourself from that space all together. I had to heal my inner child in order to see resilience as a tool and not just a surviving behavioral pattern. What was my inner child craving and yearning for? How could

I help the younger me transition into a supportive, productive, and reciprocal human being and shed the weight of my childhood?

My husband describes a "toolbox of life" as a place within you that you store all of the positive and strengthening qualities you see from yourself, other people, and experiences that you can tap into when you need them. See resilience as one of those tools in your toolbox.

Below is an article I wrote when I was 21. The beginning was changed when it was published, which caused some inconsistency within it's message. However, this is the original text. I was asked, "What does resilience mean to you?"

Resilience, to me, is the constant quick bounce-back to the best ability of a being regardless of any or every situation that exerts a significant amount of physical, mental, emotional and/or spiritual stress.

Some of us are born with resilience and others can learn it. There are some that have a genetic connection to it followed by the constant experience that life gives them to continue to exercise the craft.

I'm not quite sure if I was born with it, but I do know that I have it. There are many ways to harness and master the art. One way to understand more about resilience is to find out what your ACE Score is.

What Are ACES?

An ACE assessment is a test that measures an individual's Adverse Childhood Experiences.

After taking the assessment, which ranges from scores of 1-10, you will be able to understand yourself more in depth and see which coping skills work best to heal in all areas. Personally, I had resilience long before taking the ACE assessment, however, it helped me to understand myself better and why I would be or act a certain way towards others or specific situations.

As a former foster youth, my ACE score ended up being a 9/10 which was alarming at first, however, you must remember that information is inherently a good thing. It's what you do with that information that counts. How can you address something if you have no idea it exists? It's kind of like being oblivious in a toxic relationship. You have no idea what a healthy blueprint of a relationship looks like so you just endure the high toxicity until you find out on a show, with a friend or on the internet that being yelled at and passively aggressively shoved etc is not a conducive relationship. With that information, you are able to then seek assistance. In the case of this scenario, couples counseling or learning how to effectively communicate would be helpful in the solutions. This leads to the next extremely significant way one can build resilience: being honest with yourself. In different situations, it may be hard to understand or accept the reality of your current situation. As a youth who has experienced several adverse childhood traumas before, during and post foster care, I can say that it was difficult ,at first, to fully acknowledge all of the events that led up to who I am today.

It's important to be honest with yourself every step of the way. You have to really understand who you are and what makes you upset, angry, frustrated, excited, joyous, ecstatic etc. It matters because after you recognize and understand this then you can heal.

Being resilient means being patient with yourself, persisting even if you don't get something right the first time or second...or third, and to persevere through all obstacles.

Find your purpose. Look deep within and ask yourself who or what is your motivation? What's keeping you going or who are you doing it for?

Remember to always take care of yourself. Self-care is one of the most undermined qualities anyone and everyone should learn to obtain.

Things like yoga, reading a book, poetry, meditation, taking deep breaths and creating a garden are a few hobbies that can get your mind off of everything for a few moments. This will help you reassess what or how you're thinking about something and help you build resilience!

Now, get out there warriors and start perfecting the art of your own resilience!

Resilience is me.

Resilience is YOU.

Resilience is us.

#IAMSUCCESS QUESTIONS:

◆ What does resilience mean to you?

_____

_____

_____

_____

◆ What other tools can you add into your Toolbox when life gets hard again?

_____

_____

_____

_____

◆ What ways can you begin to be aware of your inner child and nurturing that side of you?

_____

_____

_____

_____

◆ What have you been avoiding that needs your attention?

_____

_____

_____

_____

LESSON 5

THE IMPORTANCE OF A RISING AND RESTING ROUTINE

A rising routine is a "morning routine"; however, due to my love for studying etymology I prefer to use "rising" instead of morning. I am very careful with my words and am intentional with what I say to the best of my ability. So, I call it a rising routine, aligned with what rising means. It is more empowering. And a resting routine is a ritual that helps your mind and body signal that it's time for bed.

A great rising routine is one that energizes you for the day and prioritizes your relationship with self through either meditation, journaling, yoga, dancing, or something else that connects you to your inner self/soul. It is intentional consumption or refrain from consumption of food/drink/media/people and so on. It is a ritual that allows you to take control of the spirit of your day. I personally cannot tell you what a perfect routine for you is because I am not you .That is for you to discover; however, I can say that mine currently has shifted throughout different seasons of my life and what matters most to me at that time.

Summer 2019 my rising was:

5:00 am - Awaken and Shower (with chanting / listening to Affirmations)

5:15 am - Wash my face/ brush my teeth in robe

5:30 am - Light Work out/ yoga w/ motivational speech or podcast

5:45 am - Meditation and journal insight, intentions, and gratitude for the day

6:15 am - Talk to my fiancé who was in Japan

6:30 am - Make up and get dressed while listening to hype music

6:50 am - Drink 3 glasses of warm water with lemon

7:00 am - Be ready for the day ahead

I hope this helps and gives you loads of ideas on how to craft your own rising routine. Also, it is important to know that your rising and resting routine may take at least a couple of months of consistency to become a normal part of your day.

For most of us, this will not happen overnight. Give yourself grace if it doesn't. It doesn't have to be the end of the world if you don't complete something by a specific time bracket that you have prescribed for yourself (unless you'd like to challenge yourself to be disciplined).

On harder days, when it was time to get out of bed, I'd count down from 5 in my head and on 2 or 1 I would play music and push myself to get in the shower, wash my face, and brush my teeth. I always felt 10x better when I did. Shout out to the artists that I will list below, their craft motivated me to keep moving forward.

SONGS FROM MY PLAYLIST I LISTENED TO GET ME THROUGH FOSTER CARE EACH RISING :

I Smile by Kirk Franklin	*In the middle of it* by Isaac Carree
Crooked smile by J. Cole	*Wanna Be Happy* by Kirk Franklin
Roar by Katy Perry	*Pretty Girl Rock* by Keri Hilson
Suit and Tie by Justin Timberlake	*Forever* by Chris Brown
#Beautiful by Mariah Carey ft. Miguel	Ordinary People by John Legend

Power Trip by J. Cole	*Day N Nite* by Kid Cudi
Sure Thing by Miguel	*Gimme that* by Kirk Franklin ft. Marli
Whatever You Like by T.I	*Live Your Life* by T.I ft. Rihanna
Beautiful by Akon	*Moment 4 Life* by Nicki Minaj
Nobody's Perfect by J. Cole	*Cocoa Butter Kisses* by Chance the Rapper
Knock You Down by Keri Hilson ft. Neyo & Kanye	*Juice* by Chance the Rapper
Brown Skin Girl by Chris Brown	*Roses* by OutKast
Just the Way you are by Bruno Mars	*Miss Independent* by Neyo
Countdown by Beyonce	

(Not in any particular order)

There are so many others, it alone would probably take 50+ pages of this book, but I hope with these you can make some additions to your own playlist.

When we experience trauma, sometimes it can be difficult to focus on all the good times in life. Another way that you can begin to take control of this narrative is by taking some time at the end of every month to reflect and record the highs of that month. You can take out your journal and answer the following:

#IAMSUCCESS: NEW MONTH PREPARATION

Previous month:

- Describe the previous month in three words
  Example: July was.... Electric, different, stressful.

  _____

  _____

- What were the best moments of the previous month that you always want to remember?

  _____

  _____

  _____

- What was one lesson you learned this previous month?

  _____

  _____

  _____

- What is one thing you are proud of from this month?

  _____

  _____

  _____

- What is one thing that you did not like that happened this month and how will you improve this in the future?

  _____

  _____

  _____

Take control of your reality. Set intentions for the next month. Repeat this process with each new month.

New month:

◆ Set your intentions for this new month in three words or less. Example: August is vibrant and exciting!

_____

_____

◆ What are your top 3 goals that you want to accomplish in this month?

_____

_____

_____

◆ How do you want to feel this month?

_____

_____

_____

◆ What will you put into place this month from what you have learned in the previous month?
Example: In the previous month, I learned that I need to learn how to set strong boundaries between my friends and myself. I will be asking others how to do this, reading books, and watching Youtube videos on how to effectively protect my space so that what happened last month does not happen again.

_____

_____

_____

LESSON 6

BLACK HISTORY IS STILL RELEVANT TODAY

*"For as long as I am Black... I am historic. I do not need a month...
I exist for a lifetime"*

-KARL BURROW

Well, there is so much to know and so little space on paper. This is something I can dive into all day, but alas, I will keep it short. Many people think that Black history is no longer relevant because it has already passed. However, the past teaches us so much about the future if we take time to understand it. Much can be learned by examining the different perspectives, and taking the time to grasp the lessons it can teach us.

For instance, let's take the word black. The word "black" is often a way we, as people of color, describe ourselves. This concept gets misconstrued, and I have noticed that the lack of information around this word and it's internalized perception can create identity issues within our communities. Many people struggle between using "African-American" "Indigenous" or "Black" when referring to people in relation to the African diaspora, among others, and I only wish to empower you to dive deeper into the concepts I will touch on in this lesson.

Throughout history, the word "black" has been used to describe a certain genotype of human beings that have evolved over time. From "moor", to the n-word, to "colored", to "negro", to "Afro-American", and of late, the interchanging of the words "Black" and "African-American". Black was used for primarily two reasons after the enslavement of people of African descent and Indigenous origins. One, to separate the ones who would receive societal privileges from those deemed ineligible. And two, to erase the true tribal and cultural history of our enslaved ancestors.

Notice that I used the word "enslaved" as opposed to slaves. What's the difference? One is a descriptor, and the other is an identity. Our ancestors were not slaves. They were human beings that were stolen from their native land and/or (for our Indigenous brothers and sisters) had their land stolen from them. The term "black" is still serving these purposes today, whether or not we would like to acknowledge these facts. It has become an umbrella term to describe people with certain genotypes, phenotypes, mannerisms and even levels of class that do not have access to certain basic human rights, known in today's society as "privileges". At one point, it was a "privilege" to be considered human, to be treated with respect and dignity. It was a privilege for your life, as a person of color to be honored and considered valuable past slave owner's monetary compensation for it. How do you think that affected our people from generation to generation?

Many years ago, Kenneth B. Clark, an African-American psychologist, social activist, and educator, and his wife, Mamie Clark who was also a social scientist, decided to research the self-consciousness of young Black children. They conducted the well-known "doll experiment". The doll experiment measured children's self-esteem by allowing them to choose which dolls of various skin colors were considered beautiful, nice, or smart. Children were asked to choose between dolls with a lighter complexion with blonde or red hair and dolls with a darker complexion with black or brown hair. Lastly, they were given the option of which doll carried better physical and personality traits to reflect their own image. Overwhelmingly, the majority of children-regardless of race-chose the dolls with a fair complexion to have encompassed positive physical traits and desirable personality traits. This study concluded that children of all ethnic backgrounds identified a fair complexion with being a good person, and a darker complexion encompassing dark features with being a bad person with bad traits.

How are Black people depicted in the media? How about in history textbooks? How are Black people talked about without any Black people around? When I was growing up, I barely saw positive images of Black people. And barely any images of Indigenous people, besides having a spear in hand or big feathered headdresses, dancing in circles and uttering the infamous "how" as a greeting.

Nowadays, I would say that I've seen significantly more and increasingly positive images of people of color throughout the years. I am happy about that, but it's not just about that. From my various research of my people, following my family's lineage and travels across the nation, and my conversations with many women and men of color, I see that there is much more to be done than just positive images and depictions of Black people.

Many of us have come to believe that "Black" is an ethnicity or nationality. It has become a way we identify ourselves without the desire to look further in our roots. Many of us have settled for "Black" to be our only identity. It is our birthright to go deeper than this umbrella term to uncover our true context. If we know we are of African descent, then that's a start! Africa is a whole continent with over fifty countries. Which country did your lineage of people come from? What language did they speak before being forced to learn English or Spanish (speaking to my Mexican brothers and sisters, we will talk about this in further chapters)? What tribe did your ancestors belong to?

What do I mean? When I ask a "white" person what their heritage or ethnicity is, they will say things like, "Oh, my mom is Irish and that's where I get my name from." Or, "My father is German, and that's why we visit Berlin once a year to celebrate our great history and where my great-great-grandfather took his last breath." When I ask a Black or brown person, specifically Indigenous or of African descent, it will go something like this:

Me: "What's your ethnicity?"

Brotha from anotha motha: "Who me? Oh... I'm just Black."

Me: "What do you mean *just Black*? Black is just a color. Where are your parents from? Or great-grandparents from?"

Brotha from anotha motha: "Uh, Georgia? And I don't know about my grandparents..."

Me: "So, then you don't know where you're from, or your ethnicity...?"

Brotha from anotha motha: "Nah... I guess not. I just know I'm Black and my auntie said somewhere down the line I'm mixed with Indian or something since I got *good hair*, but I don't know."

I've had hundreds, if not thousands of these types of conversations with people, not just in the United States, but other countries as well. This deeply disturbs me. How can we, as people of color, fully bond to ourselves without some bias of what beauty, success, or a prosperous person resembles if:

1. We do not have a clear idea of where we come from and the cultural values we, as a people, embodied way before slavery?

2. We are in a constant mental battle of surviving in a predominantly white favored society?

3. We are having to relearn and unlearn childhood prejudices, coping mechanisms, misconceived health practices and behavior patterns taught consciously or unconsciously by parental/authority figures, relatives, social media and television programming, and the environments we are raised in?

I've been through intense poverty situations, and I've also been among the most elite. I've seen the difference in the way people speak, think, and behave. As an observer, I began to collect the information within my mind, and noticed that one of the biggest barriers between people of color's success and others is the way we see ourselves when no one else is around for our ego to puff out. It's deeper than skin color, or just having someone look like us. It is the current systems that are in place, and the way we internalize these systems. Someone can look like us, and yet be subscribed to a self-loathing indoctrination.

Foster care is one of these systems that is, in many ways, continuing to carry out institutional racism. Whether that is done through the foster care to prison pipeline, high suicide rates, or not preparing young people to maintain employment, social capital, and housing stability.

Many of our families root issues may come from generations of behaviors that developed to allow our ancestors to cope with the true realities of white supremacy. There have been hundreds of years of destruction, unconscious programming to the point that we consciously are not able to recognize self-sabotage or self-hate. We accept it as normal and even fight for certain limiting beliefs, ideas, and self-destructive behaviors thus creating a veil around our eyes.

This veil disables the opportunity to realize true "self-actualization", as Abraham Maslow would call it. For generations, the veil can become layered to the point where it is now a thick wall, passing down the loss of our identity, culture, and ultimately, self-esteem. Many of us struggle to paint a clear picture of our history and culture to be proud of before slavery. And many of us still think that "Black history" began with the enslavement of our ancestors.

That is not true! Our history is rich and predates thousands of years before the colonization of our people! Whether you are Indigenous to the Americas or have ancestors originally from Africa, there is a whole other side to HIStory that is not taught in our schools. We must recognize, as humans, how pivotal this is. The history of our people must be understood and preserved. For far too long, our ancestor's side of the story has shut out or cut off. What about the side of the ones oppressed? How are we feeling about all of this? What damage has been done from keeping this side of the story out of sight and mind? What narratives are being passed down from one generation to the next? I bet the "triumphs" and successes may be illustrated differently when told from those were colonized.

A deer shot by a hunter provides a good story for the hunter. Perhaps, the hunter was in search of a deer stew to feed her family, and therefore, it was a good day. On the deer's family's side, the story could be quite different. The deer's family could have lost their father on a meaningful anniversary or immediate celebration.

BLACK HISTORY IS EVERY SINGLE DAY, THREE HUNDRED AND SIXTY-FIVE DAYS A YEAR.

Let us increase our celebration in February, but let it only be that-an increase! Not a substitute! Why should our search and celebration of history only be minimized to one month? I am a phenomenal woman of color every single day, and so are you! A phenomenal man, woman, or person of color that was birthed from pure greatness, beauty, and a warrior mentality. We are our ancestors each and every day. We must walk in this alignment every month, every week, every day, every hour, every minute, and every second that we proclaim to be alive and well.

It is our birthright... it is our duty! We are creating history with each and every moment. Now what history will you create? What history have you already created for yourself, your future generations, and "Melanated" people all around?

I'm not speaking to those that don't care about all our ancestors endured for us to be here. Or to those who disregard our ancestors' struggles as something they somehow deserved. I'm speaking to the ones who honor the literal blood, sweat, tears, and sacrifice to make it alive and one day for someone down the line to birth you. Think about that. Your lineage made it through all of that pain and anguish beyond what many of us could possibly understand to one day birth you. And that's just the tip of the iceberg. Your purpose on this planet is sacred.

So, let's stay focused! #BLACKHISTORY is 365 days a year. Not just one month of the year! Let's celebrate our history in February, but understand that the work continues for the months and lifetimes to come.

#IAMSUCCESS QUESTIONS:

◆   What comes to mind when you think of Black history?

_____

_____

_____

_____

◆   What do you think about when you think back to slavery?

_____

_____

_____

_____

◆   How is black and Indigenous history depicted in your school?

_____

_____

_____

_____

◆   What amazing things are you currently doing to support your community?

_____

_____

_____

_____

◆ What amazing things would you like to do to support your community?

_____

_____

_____

_____

◆ How can you begin to learn more about your ancestry?

_____

_____

_____

_____

I AM...

BY ÁNGELA QUIJADA-BANKS

I am a sister. I am a friend. I am a wife who loves all she touches with no end.
I am a woman of color who has the blood of the world etched in her mind coupled by the fire her ancestors endowed within her soul.
I am a granddaughter. I am a niece. I am the epitome of contradiction from what everyone believed my future would be.
Engulfed by the energy of the world in hopes of peace but still in the full vision of the ultimate reality that one must always be cautious...
one must always know that which you don't know.
I am a frequency. I am a warrior. I am the next legacy. I am a live masterpiece all by myself in all of my imperfection.

I am a Powerful multidimensional woman of color that is so tired of the mediocrity, stagnation and infiltration of our subconscious minds
and is deciding daily to answer the calling on my life.
No longer will I remain silent, turn a blind eye or close my ears to what I know and witness.
It's not an easy journey but, I'd be lying if I said it ever was...
Don't keep those ideas just in your head. Write them down, even if you get one while you're relaxing in bed.
You may be surprised how far you get, pushing play instead of Rewind.

Because living in the past can root you in stagnation.
Unless, you're saying kudos
to your past self on the path to soulful liberation.
Instead, look to the future and begin each thing you do with the end
in mind.
Because if you search for the greatness inside of you long enough,
you might be surprised at what you find...

CHAPTER EXERCISE

DIGITIZING MEMORIES AND ACCOMPLISHMENTS

Sometimes, due to back-to-back trauma, we forget who we are. I did. We are much more than cool titles, job positions, material possessions, and the accomplishments we acquire; however, that doesn't mean they don't matter. They just don't matter as much in comparison to our core values, the quality of relationships we keep, and our purpose in this life. Memories and accomplishments help us root in ourselves and build self-confidence.

Digitize your memories and accomplishments so if you have to move, you will have them with you. I left multiple items in the different foster homes I was in and unfortunately, I did not get them back.

Google photos is a free resource you can use to upload photos to the google photos drive. Another thing that you can do is Archive photos on Instagram or Facebook.

Honestly, the end of 2019 is really when I recognized I had a problem with completely forgetting who I was and the accomplishments I had. Why? Well, because I was used to being in survival mode all of the time. After recognizing this, I hopped on the phone to speak with my mentor Dr. Regina Williams. She suggested I create a Brag Board. I thought the concept was incredible! I had never thought about creating something to help me remember what I accomplished over the years. I didn't know what I would want to put on a poster board, but I would create something none the less because forgetting what I'd done in the past was an ongoing problem. After some thought and a few days passing, I made a decision to create an online portfolio to remind me of some of the most reputable accomplishments I fortunately got photographed.

(www.originalsoulflower.com under "who is she")

You do not have to create an entire website like I did, but you may want to create something that helps remind you of the amazing accomplishments you have completed thus far and in the future.

It could be a poster board, as she suggested, or it can be a private Facebook album where you document your fun, loving memories and celebrations that perhaps only you want to see. Maybe it is a private Instagram account where you document your weight loss journey.

I send photos and videos to myself all the time, and the portfolio keeps getting bigger!

Another idea is to create a hidden google photos album and only add people to it that you know will encourage a great business or college venture along the way!

But take awareness of yourself and your current ability to assess your accomplishments while documenting and savoring beautiful moments of the process.

Speaking of which, excuse me while I go revamp my online portfolio.

| CHAPTER THREE

THE MINDSET TO SUCCESS

"Stop counting your days and start making your days count."

- MUHAMMAD ALI

"All success starts with one. One step. One client. One order. One sale. While dreams of greatness are great, we must remember to appreciate the joy of the start."

-UNKNOWN

e have to start being active participants in our livelihood and well-being. If we say we want to be successful, we must define for ourselves what that means and how we can begin to mirror what we say we want.

When I was a Junior at William G. Enloe High school, I had very little hope. At this point in my life, I felt so tired of fighting. Fighting for my life, but most of all fighting my own toxic internal mental chatter that was programmed into my subconscious mind since I was a child. I constantly battled with panic attacks, thoughts of suicide, and black outs of memory. I often had involuntary reactions to these thoughts like laughter and crying. I carried a lot of pain with me. Sometimes I would feel it in different parts within my physical body, in the core of my spirit and lurking within the depths of my mind. Being in foster care did help me to see that my life could progress, because it was better than what my life was before. However, I just couldn't see my future past seventeen. I talked about this a little previously. This terrified me, feeding the pain I already harbored within. I thought that maybe it was because I was destined to die before I was 19 years old.

Yeah, that got dark real quick, but I'm just being honest. I was not okay. I would tell people, "I'm fine" or "Yeah, I'm good", but the truth was I didn't even know what it truly meant to feel good. I just had open gaps of pleasure.

I remember times where I'd try to find a release of the mental anguish. I remember trying to turn on the t.v., only to see the news of yet another Black face charged with some high level of crime, or worse, dead. On other days, I'd try to have a good day at school but the topic of our class discussion was, "What do we believe is the truth behind Black on Black crime?"

Thinking I might escape during lunch was a little far-fetched as my friends would prompt a response to questions like, "So what do you think about the whole Trayvon Martin situation?" I just couldn't get away from the reality of this world and my current circumstances. I began to feel trapped within this society, its issues, and my own pessimistic mind.

Considering the institutional racism in this world, systems like foster care can feel suffocating to our success.

We can question if it is even possible to succeed while with the background of trauma and being a person of color. And it is. However, we have to begin to speak up and do the work as well. We can no longer expect our supportive adults to be perfect or not make any mistakes. They can make mistakes. Whether they are a birth parent, foster/resource parent, guardian ad litem, therapist or social worker, they can make mistakes. All constituents within the foster care system are more than capable of lying or withholding information. This is because we are all human. So in order to ensure the safety and well-being of youth in foster care, we need more accountability systems in place. How do we start?

By learning, studying and implementing ways to understand our new reality. Foster care will not be your whole life. So, you must understand where you are now to better educate yourself on where you want to be and who you want to become. In chapter one and chapter two, we began diving into what it means to be you. And where you are in your foster care placement. In this chapter, we are diving deeper into some of the mindset shifts you will need in order to be on the right path toward your success and healing.

LESSON 7

YOU DO NOT HAVE TO DO IT ALONE

"I need to be strong and independent!" Sound familiar?

This is a lie. The truth is no one truly successful ever made it on their own. In fact, humans are not wired to be doing this alone. You will find this to be true in each autobiography and story of people who made it big. Oprah Winfrey, Nat Turner, Dr. Martin Luther King Jr., and even Malcolm X.

By the way, don't believe everything you read in school systems about people of color. Many times, I've found information to simply not be true... or to be a stretch of the truth... which is what? A lie. They are stories told in the perspective of those doing the oppressing of people of color. You know "HIS Story", better known as history. On the perspective of my Indigenous ancestors, Christopher Columbus did not discover the land they were already living on. Nor did the Spanish conquistador, Hernan Cortes, help my Indigenous, "Aztec" ancestors by colonizing their land and massacring millions of families and forcing them to learn and adopt Spanish as their own, relinquishing the culture and sacredness of our native tongue. Europeans did not save my African ancestors from living a "primitive" life, and most certainly did not afford them any opportunity by stripping away our tribal identity, names, native tongue, and other basic rights, including common human decency.

Guard your mind as you move about in this world, family. Be sure to educate yourself and analyze the sources of your information to be sure you are not perpetuating fallacies that will continue to feed generational colonization. Again, you do not need to do any of this alone. You do not have to be "strong" all by yourself and "independent". If anything, interdependence is truly adulting. It's operating in a sense of self efficacy and self-sufficiency without the subconscious idea that "you can't trust anyone" or "everyone is out to get you". In fact, this is the way we used to be. We, as a people, used to be in big communities that would care about one another. We fed and protected one another.

I learned not to adopt the westernized, modern idea to do everything alone the hard way. I'm hoping that with these words, if you find yourself in this trap that you will stop and reevaluate your next steps and begin to brainstorm what you need to do next.

Journal entry I wrote in July 2019 when in Seaside, Oregon:

I remember the last time I was here...

I remember thinking there was something wrong.

That maybe I wasn't doing it right...

Life, I wasn't doing it right.

I remember crying daily and being in this toxic relationship. I was asking for help, hoping to be heard when even my aunt, who I looked up to at the time... ignored me. She took my ex-boyfriend's side. She even bought him a car. Where was my car?

It felt like she didn't even care. The more I would ask her about what was going on or for some guidance, she would tell me that I need to figure it out on my own. Where did this shift come from? Why was she so cold?

She told me I needed to figure out stable housing on my own. But how could I when I never knew what that was? She told me I shouldn't look to anyone for help although, she helped my ex-boyfriend. She told me to do it alone.

But she was wrong...

I don't need to be alone. I don't need to figure it all out and accomplish everything alone.

I need to have more loving, caring and understanding people that are there to feed my flame and to nurture my soul. I need people who have full cups. People who are ready and willing to nourish every part of who I am as I do the same for them. Not to tell me that I'm not worthy of the success because I didn't hundred percent do it without anyone's help. And even when I do accomplish things without anyone's help, it's still completely disregarded.

What I didn't understand then was she was just another human being. She is capable of making mistakes just like anyone else...

There are people in this world who do not understand who they are or why they came into this life and that's okay. Many of us don't, but when is it not okay?

I think it starts to become an issue when the person is miserable with that reality and attempt to drag people down that lane of misery with them. It can become a problem when the impact of this person creates trauma for those that are around them and they have no regard to take a look at their actions. I refuse to be that type of person. A person who causes pain and confusion to others because I refuse to look at my own actions and refuse to heal.

I will not be that person. I am not that person.

It sickens me that I was in this extremely toxic relationship and she, among others told me to stay. She told me to continue on although she heard me calling for help. And she turns around and keeps him in her close circle. She wonders why I said what I said and removed myself from her, but with the messages I saw and the deep pain I felt... I knew removing myself was the best option. Ofcourse, she is only human...and as humans regardless of our label of "mom", "dad", "big sister" and the like...we can make mistakes.

The toxicity was still very apparent. I just don't understand why she told me to stay. Whenever I hear or see something similar to any of the extremely negative life experiences I endured in the past, I remember how I felt in that relationship. I do not let anyone I care about continue in it without knowing there will be consequences. I make sure they know that it is far from okay, that it is not normal. I let them know that they deserve better. They have choices.

So then why couldn't she give me that advice?

Maybe the cognitive dissonance?

Maybe she was going through her own motions in life?

I don't know.

But I do know that I am safe now, and no matter what anyone says about me or to me about it - I know the truth.

And I will hold my head high. I may cry tears of healing, but I will not waiver. I will walk in my truth and most importantly, I don't have to do it alone.

#IAMSUCCESS QUESTIONS:

• Have you ever felt alone?

_____

_____

_____

_____

• Do you believe that you do not need anyone?

_____

_____

_____

_____

• What is the importance of having healthy-minded people in your circle?

_____

_____

_____

_____

• Say, "I do not have to do life on my own. There are people who care about me. There are people who will support me. I am not alone." Choose one word to describe how saying the above statement makes you feel.

_____

_____

_____

◆ Write one word to describe how you feel right now.

| LESSON 8

EVERYTHING IS TEMPORARY!

Sometimes life is hard. And for quite a few of us, life can seem simply unbearable. It's important though, to not lose sight of the destination. And maybe that's a place to start...

What is your destination?

Who do YOU want to be in life?

Where is what you're currently doing taking you in the next 3,4,5 to ten years?

What do you want to ultimately do as a career?

What is the impact you want to make in this world?

Who are the people that are surrounding you and who has access to you?

You may not have all the answers right now, and that's okay, but you definitely need to get on that! Many people have trouble taking their life into their own hands. Sometimes it's hard to recognize that the reason for your future shortcomings may be, you. It is important to identify that pattern that self-sabotage can show up in and acknowledge that it's about that time to move forward.

Beating yourself up about what could've, shoulda, would've happened IF blahze blahze blah... isn't going to do much but plummet yourself into the mental space that will hinder you from moving forward. The more time spent wallowing in self-pity and blaming external factors, the more it will only inhibit you from reaching your true potential!

So, it's time to wake up, brush your teeth, get yourself ready and take on the day!

If you're truly serious and ready to understand that everything in this life is temporary, that it's YOU who dictates how your life turns out then take some time to write down the answers to the following #IAmSuccess questions at the end of this lesson. Answer them honestly and reflect on it. You've got to start somewhere and it's okay if the past wasn't picture perfect... but what are you going to do about it now? Waste your life away?

Perhaps a vision board will be of use... or a planner and a calendar. NO matter what you've gone through or are currently going through, remember that it is TEMPORARY!

Most things are! Yes, even good and joyful moments. It's up to you to change the reality of your current situation and fill your life up with more joyful moments. So, besides complaining and blaming... let me ask you... what can and are you actually going to do about it?

The things that you cannot change or alter then leave it alone. Someone once said "sometimes we win and sometimes we... learn." we give it our best shot, pick up the pieces and try again!

And if it isn't worth trying after doing your best then move on! Life isn't a race, it's a marathon with lots of twists, turns, trips, and bumps along the way. Train hard and be better than you were before. You are resilient, and the blood of warriors run through your veins. Find people that will hold you accountable and support you in your goals!

You can do this. Believe in yourself and your own ability to conquer any and everything life throws at you. The power is in your hands.

When it starts getting really hard... even if that's right now-it's time to ask yourself WHAT can I do RIGHT NOW to make my circumstances different? And above all, know and recognize that it's all temporary.

When self-sabotage comes up and in moments when you feel yourself being small in comparison to others and you question yourself with "Am I" this or Am I that?

Think about the question as it pops up in your head and affirm to yourself with I Am. Is the answer to the question, yes? If so, then say I AM, then complete it with affirming to yourself of who you are and what you embody.

Ex. Am I really smart enough to get through highschool?

Think about it and look at your track record and what you have overcome despite these obstacles. Would most people who have lived the life that you have been able to pick themselves back up and keep moving forward? Well, no. And most people don't. They'll give you every reason in the book as to why they couldn't accomplish what they set out to do.

Answer: YES; because despite everything that has happened in my life, I am still here. I still show up to school in the best way that I can. I acknowledge that graduating high school is important to my success. This is a milestone that needs to be completed. I didn't come this far to just quit. If I need a tutor, then I'll get a tutor. It doesn't make me less smart. In fact, seeking help to achieve my goals makes me even smarter because I've acknowledged that I just do not know a certain subject well enough (yet). Every skill can be learned and grown into an expertise. I can start today and do 10x as better than what even I was expecting!

What have you been through in your life that was hard? How did you overcome it? Did you have a time when things weren't so hard? If so, what was it like and what did you dream to be or do?

Think about that and cultivate answers to your own self-doubt. That way the next time that negative voice comes up, you can think back to this moment and remember your answers and show that negative voice the door.

#IAMSUCCESS QUESTIONS:

◆ Who are you today, and who will you be?

_____

_____

_____

_____

◆ What did you learn from the negative situations that happened to you?

_____

_____

_____

_____

◆ What can you do to change your current life outcomes?

_____

_____

_____

_____

LESSON 9

YOU CAN DEFINE WHAT SUCCESS IS FOR YOURSELF

"Start getting into a mindset where you expect something unexpected to happen. Like a sudden shift. An out of the blue miracle. A possibility of an instant breakthrough. Let yourself loosen up about how things will happen. Trust more. Believe more. Be open to receiving."

-IDIL AHMED

"What does it mean to succeed? Is it easily labeled by the cliché of going to college followed by an excursion of unlimited educational milestones to a doctoral degree? Is it the white picket fence, lavish outings, and marriage with 2.5 children? Is that truly the goal? Well, for some, but for me, it's not exactly in that order. My life has been a sum of one of a lifetime experiences, travel, trauma, healing, intense love, and many many lessons. Some say I have reached success already, but for me there is always another rock to discover, another idea to be birthed, another feeling to be understood and another breath to be meditated upon. Life is a journey, not a destination, and there is never a true end with success, if you set your mind on it."

- ÁNGELA QUIJADA-BANKS

"Success occurs when preparation meets opportunity"

-ZIG ZIGLAR

"Do not follow where a path may lead. Go instead where there is no path and leave a trail"

-RALPH EMERSON

This quote reminds me of a time I used to allow people to put me in a box by saying to me, "Oh ! You wanna be an entrepreneur, but you're studying political science and you wanna write a book?" "Oh, you had an art gallery and you're a poet, and now you have a podcast? You have to pick one! You cannot just have all these different things going on! You're confusing people, and you're going to lose momentum and end up doing nothing."

So, for a while I bottled up most of my dreams and aspirations and put them on hold. I did only what made sense to others. I neglected the fact that I knew my path and my purpose. I attempted to make a clear Point A to Point B trail for others to follow... and, well, I ended up depressed and suffering with severe anxiety while in my first years of college. Literally days would pass where it was hard for me to even attempt to wake up and get out of bed. Eventually, I had the realization that it's my life and throughout this journey within my story... it's never been a linear path, so why was I trying to cramp my passion and purpose into others expectations?

From having mentally ill parents, coping with a past of extreme abuse, poverty, homelessness, and abandonment as a child and well into my teenage years... I never had a moment where I just was. A time where I could just be. It was always moments filled with some form of anxiety, lots of pain, anger, and even feeling clouded about what I was even doing in my life. I never truly felt like myself. What did that even mean? To feel like myself...

Less than 4% of youth that experience foster care graduate college.

Less
Than
Four
Percent

And throughout my journey, I started to learn why. I was a first generation college student with a flaky support system, and no one in my family knew what college was like and somehow thought I'd made it already. It seemed as though they fantasized about me having all this money, even though college is like debt central.

I was so overwhelmed. Not being able to stay in one place due to the way foster care is set up and not knowing basic financial literacy skills to help me maintain, save, and invest my income. At 18, I had issues with personal boundaries so I was paying bills for family members that barely showed an interest in my well-being. I paid for my colleagues' food, and sometimes their bills, too. They would never show up for my awarding ceremonies, scholars recognitions, anything! They barely could even like my posts on Facebook. And yet, here I was, stressing about them and sending them money. Lawwwddd I was way too giving. I rarely looked for anything in return. I didn't even get a thank you. And as the money ran low, so did their presence in my life.

As the years went on and I began to challenge my own narrative, I realized that many of my "beliefs" about myself and my own abilities came from other people and their narratives of how life panned out for them. From relationship advice, financial advice, health advice, and even career and lifestyle advice. It was all through the lenses of their own story, pain, mistakes, and possible loss of hope within their dreams and aspirations. That's anyone's way of educating, through their own experience, but it's like they never learned from those lessons and kept giving the bad side of the advice.

I feel like throughout life, in certain situations, we are given chances to make a different decision then the one we made previously. Every now and then, this lesson comes back around with different people and experiences, and we are given choices. Will you repeat your mistake? Or will you apply what you learned from the first or second time? Are you able to receive it in love with the understanding in the power of perspective?

There was a post on Facebook that I shared the other day. It said, *"Heal, so you can hear what's being said without the filter of your wound."*

I think it is so profound because sometimes when people are speaking to us we take it so personal and internalize their own perspective as them talking down to us. We miss the message, and our wounds are triggered.

I've found that most times, it has nothing to do with us specifically. Everyone has their own filters of what brings them joy, fulfillment and their version of success. A lot of these filters come from a young age and as we grow older, we add more. We are asked questions like, "What do you wanna be when you grow up?"

No one truly knows who they'll be for the rest of their life in terms of career path, relationship status, or spiritual dynamic at five or six. There are way too many variables!

At 6, I swore up and down that I wanted to be a MAD SCIENTIST until a doctor's visit. I remember hopping on a table as the doctor put on his gloves. He began checking my reflexes and asked me what I wanted to be when I grew up.

Ecstatically, I looked at him and said, "I wanna be a mad scientist! I'm going to help find the cure to cancer and bring world peace!"

He chuckled then looked at me and said, "that's not a realistic profession." That stung. And as you see, I still remember that he said that.

After that doctor's visit, I switched to wanting to be a forensic psychologist because I thought that's the next best thing. I watched a lot of Crime Scene Investigation (CSI) shows with my grandmother, so I thought it was pretty close to being a mad scientist. And, it was a *real* profession. Within my first few years of college, I was a double major in biology and psychology with a concentration in legislation.

It worked out okay until I realized that C.S.I. is just a t.v. show, and what that profession would really require. Shout out to forensic psychologists, by the way. I discovered that I would be around way more dead people than I'm comfortable with. After deep introspection, I finally admitted to myself that I didn't wanna be around any dead people, no morgues, no crime scenes, and definitely no 2.am lab nights. I knew I wanted a family someday and that it would be extremely important that I was present.

But did I still love science? Yes! And I study science all the time, and practice science pretty much every day.

As a kid, I had a microscope and slides, thick encyclopedias, and a journal with me at all times. And I would always annoy my family because I always had to know WHY something happened or someone did something. Accompanied with the "Why" questions, came the "How" questions?

Questions like, *How did I come to be in this world? How did earth get made?*

And that sense of curiosity has stuck with me. I think if we aren't careful, we can begin to lose our sense of curiosity as we grow older.

We change, we grow, and we evolve into better versions of ourselves. Well, ideally, anyway. The power of perspective comes with introspection as I stated previously. And uncovering questions to who will I be in terms of my core values, core character, and what impact do I want to make on the world? What community do I want to serve, and why?

It is important not to focus so much on *for the rest of my life...* part but just starting with *in this season* instead.

THE 7 P'S OF SUCCESS:

1. Personality

Your personality will either open doors for you, or close them tightly shut. A personality that is generally optimistic will prove to be most fruitful for your own success. And no, I am not referring to the false sense of positivity that mainstream media promotes. In order to become more optimistic, you have to go through a paradigm shift as well as self-reflect on what needs to change in order for you to align yourself to that way of thinking. By now, from chapter two, you would have discovered the sixteen personalities and which one you are. Revisit your strengths and weaknesses. And maybe add some that you have learned about yourself. Then brainstorm ways to sharpen your skills and turn those weaknesses into strengths.

2. Protection

Our mind, body, and spirit must be protected. There is so much that goes on in this world and we must be mindful of what we allow our mind, body, and spirits to consume. What we feed ourselves matters.

What you focus on your mind will magnify.

And what you magnify will continue to show up time and time again.

Have you ever noticed a certain color car and told someone how cool that car and the color of it was? Then you noticed for days on end, you would see that same color or type of car over and over again? That's how powerful your mind is. It's kind of like hashtags on social media. The more you like the items that are under a certain hashtag, the more those pictures or posts will show up with it. Your mind places a tag on what you focus on and begins to magnify your exposure to it.

Protect your mind by limiting it's exposure to intense horrific events or loud and vulgar language. That doesn't mean you have to tune everything out and remove it completely out of your life, but make sure you are planting in your mind ideas, thoughts, movies, songs, shows, and social media posts that will be fruitful over time.

No one wants weeds on their brain.

3. Purpose

Knowing your purpose helps you to prioritize the tasks and material possessions that will bring you the most fulfillment in your life.

Productivity isn't all it's cracked up to be if it isn't aligned to your purpose. You're just being "busy" with several meaningless tasks that are taking up time, space and energy. You end up burning out and getting tired. Your low energy takes you to lower thoughts of consciousness and may even, over time take you into a spiral of depression.

People always ask me, why I stay so busy juggling five things at once.

This was one of my responses to that, "I'm living in my divine purpose... And in this season I am called to host a podcast, write a book, and develop my purpose coaching program. If I am disobedient to this calling, my life will become a wreck. It will be like I'm swimming upstream. I've tried that way already. It doesn't work for me. I like being joyful. I like feeling excited about every day. So, it may seem like just busyness to you, but I'm fulfilled! And no one has to understand my purpose but me. Are you living in your purpose?"

A lot of times, people would say, no. Others would say, what is a *divine purpose*?

A *divine purpose* is the mission you were called to fulfill in this lifetime. It was predestined to your birth and most times, we have forgotten that it even exists. You can have a big overarching purpose that overwhelms you until you realize you have to level up in order to uncover and fulfill it.

4. Perseverance

My dad always tells me, "No matter what, you've got to strut."

Which means, no matter what the situation is to keep going. If you have to crawl, then crawl until you can walk again.

If you can walk then walk until you can run.

And if you run, then run until you can jump.

And once you're jumping, smile. Smile hard. Smile until you feel goofy and laugh then look back at how far you've come.

Then look at how far you've got to go to start flying. Take that first step. Who cares if Jeanette is flying her plane already. Go at your own pace and maybe you start out with a paper airplane and in a few years, you're the pilot of your own jet. Maybe you're even hiring a team to fly you out in your own space ship? Who says the sky's the limit?

5. Persistence

Staying steadfast in something that you truly would like to achieve is essential to your success. However, something I've learned throughout the years is that you are able to pivot. Just because people preach to have a 9 to 5 for the next 40+ years of your life, to be married and have

2.5 kids by thirty five years old; doesn't mean you have to... nor does it mean it has to be in that order.

We all have different lives with different challenges and a different purpose. Go at your own pace, but do not just quit.

Learn to pause and rest without completely giving up.

6. Patience

People say that patience is a virtue.

And I'd agree. Over the years, I've had to learn patience and I think every year, I also learn that I need more of it. The irony about this success trait is that it requires patience to learn patience.

7. Preparation

Notice that nothing was said about perfection. Dan Peña, says Perfection equals paralysis. So we cannot focus too much on being perfect although, I've recognized that for many of us, this ends up being the case. We must release the need to have everything perfect before we begin. We must become friends with the process and struggle of becoming. We do not have to know everything. We do not have to only have perfect work for something to be of notable quality. We can put the cape down and just be, sometimes. We can create our own ideas of success and still actively achieve greatness.

#IAMSUCCESS QUESTIONS:

• Which of the 7 P's of success stood out to you the most? Why?

_____

_____

_____

_____

• What type of shows/music/movies or social media posts do you feed your mind with?

_____

_____

_____

_____

• On a scale of 1-5 (5 being the most patient), how patient are you?

_____

_____

• Do you usually give up when things get tough? Why or why not?

_____

_____

_____

• How do you define success?

_____

_____

_____

LESSON 10

Check Yo' Self Before You Wreck Yourself

"The Lack of Money is the root of all evil"

-Robert Kiyosaki, Rich Dad Poor Dad

I finished Rich Dad, Poor Dad by Robert Kiyosaki in January of 2020. This quote helped me see something I had been told for a long time in a different light. And it's changed my viewpoint forever.

Growing up, I was told that " Money is the root of all evil". If that's so, why would I want to be associated with it? I mean, if I have any ties with this so-called "root of all evil", then wouldn't it make me "evil" too?

And it's saying money is the "root of ALL evil", so I'm really getting myself into deep trouble trying to follow this "money" thing. Right?

I've thought about this a lot throughout life and I didn't realize how many biases I had formed and how I exercised these biases against money into adulthood... until I read and began to understand the difference in the slight wording of " money is the root of all evil " to "the LACK OF MONEY is the root to all evil". You see? Prior to reading that statement there was a different internal conversation about money.

One internal conversation is the entire concept and association to money is evil. The other is that the "lack of money" is evil or not good. Evil defined by dictionary.com is to be "profoundly immoral or wicked."

To be without money means that I will not be able to contribute to the solutions to the problems I that I believe need support. I would not be able to support the people I love or invest in my own well-being and success. I will not be able to support myself. I will cause others pain and agony by worrying about me. Lacking money also limits my exposure to events, people and material possessions that could help me move forward in life.

I can agree with the lack of money not being a good thing as it will also wreak havoc on my self-esteem. Being able to maintain financial stability is a basic need that must be met. It builds confidence in your own ability to take care and provide for yourself and in time, others. The statement, claiming that money itself is evil, makes me feel guilty or shameful for wanting a life of financial stability and freedom. However, knowing that it is the "lack of money", and not just money in general, helps me feel empowered and ready to step into my greatness because to be without money would mean it was wrong.

Instantly the paradigm shifts! The lack of money truly is the root of all evil. I mean think about all the things people feel like they have to do to obtain it:

-Steal

-Lie

-Murder

And maybe unbeknownst to them they begin to:

-Envy

-Judge others

-Have A Scarcity Mentality

-Harm Others or themselves

-Put others and themselves down

-Develop a mental illness

So we begin to create this confusing conversation within ourselves-"I don't want anything to do with money, BUT I do need it to survive and maintain a good life." Well, you do get what you want in life if you position yourself to achieve it.

Which means you have to sow a seed. And a lot of times that means, educating yourself first! The crazy thing about it is if you have already subscribed to the belief system that "Money is the root to all evil" then yet again... why would you want to study that evil? So we end up self-sabotaging our minds and behavior before we even have a good running chance.

It's horrible! When instead, the truth is-we can build all that we desire and we need money to do so. We have to confront those ideas and sayings that may have been told to us in "good faith". Unbeknownst to our loved ones, these were lies told to them to keep them in a certain state of thinking and out of the journey to wealth.

Another common one is that the love of money is the root of all evil. The truth is if your core value system is jacked up, it will reflect every area of your life, not just the infatuation with money.

I've closed that chapter of belief that I don't need money or I don't want money because the truth is... the real truth is, that we need and most of us want what money can provide, therefore, we want money. To ignore that fact would be to do a disservice to ourselves and create yet another breeding ground for self-sabotage. How many more generations will have to endure poverty before we wake up and start recognizing that our time to create wealth is now?

We are our own creators, what we think and say will literally manifest. We can't keep wasting our breath on generational curses. It's time to change the narrative!

Does my mental attitude towards money follow what I say I would want?

#IAMSUCCESS QUESTIONS:

Two Different Mindsets:

1. Abundance

- I can earn all the money I want
- Maybe I don't know how but I will find a way
- How can I afford that?
- There's a lot of possibilities out there
- All I have to do is learn and I will apply the rest
- I'm going to start reading financial literacy books or watching financial education videos on YouTube

2. Scarcity

- Broke as hell, help me
- I wish I could afford that
- I am not going to make it
- There's no hope for me
- This is just the cards I was dealt
- I don't know how to start so I guess it's not for me

- Which one sounds more like you? Number 1 or Number 2?

_____

_____

- Has anyone ever told you that money was the root of all evil?

_____

_____

_____

◆ What is the first step you will take to ensure you begin learning financial literacy?

_____

_____

_____

_____

◆ Why is becoming financially literate so important?

_____

_____

_____

_____

◆ What would you do if you made the money you desired?

_____

_____

_____

_____

LESSON II

EMOTIONS ARE ENERGY IN MOTION.

"Don't just listen, feel it."

- ÁNGELA QUIJADA-BANKS

There are so many ways to express your emotions. One of my favorite ways is to dance. Even if it's not the latest or coolest dance to everyone else, it's not about that for me. It's about moving my body because I feel like it and it makes me smile. Everyone has their choice of music, and that's beautiful. I think being able to express yourself has a lot to do with the way you view yourself in the world and standing up for what you believe in. It is also, putting a belief down if it no longer serves us or can limit our potential. I think if you feel like you want to dance then dance! The way you show your love for yourself around others is another way to boost your self-confidence. Not just alone, behind closed doors.

As a child, I learned that being yourself sometimes will cost you "brownie points" or others approval of your words or actions. So, I had to let that shhhh-t go! I remember being at a speaking event in 2017, and a song came on that I really loved... it had all the right beats and vocals.

Oh, I wanted to jump up and down right then and there... but everyone was staring and thoughts flooded my brain. *What if they don't see me as professional? What if I look stupid?*

I had to make a decision. I turned the music up and started singing and dancing.

Soon, my colleagues joined me, and a minute in... I guess once everyone recognized we were fully committed... more joined us and half the room was filled with laughter and excitement as we sung our hearts out to the song. We began twirling each other and danced for the remainder of the song. After it was over, I turned the music back low and we went back to our meeting.

I learned that the only one holding me back is me, time and time again. I learned that so many people probably were self-analyzing like I was, and that I could completely change the atmosphere in the room! I chose to love myself out loud! I chose to not only listen to the music and myself but truly feel it. . . To play full out! I mean, what's the worst that could happen, right?

So tell me, are you taking control of your internal conversation, or is it the one controlling you ?

Are you feeling and thriving? Or are you just listening to the music and ignoring your call for the next step?

THIS IS THE ULTIMATE FORMULA... AND PLEASE UNDERSTAND IT.

Our thoughts control our feelings &
Our feelings control our actions.
And we control our thoughts.
You always have a choice & you are always in control of you.
Now, it's up to you to feed your mind the right thoughts. Thoughts
of love.
Thoughts of compassion. Thoughts of joy Thoughts of wealth.
Thoughts of healing.

Thoughts of incredible success.

Thoughts of family and beautiful memories.

It may be difficult at first but you must learn how to train your mind.

You have the key. You can do this and only you can make that decision.

So, why not make it now?

#IAMSUCCESS QUESTIONS:

♦ What is the true definition of EMOTION?

_____

_____

_____

♦ Which emotion comes up for you when someone or something upsets you?

_____

_____

_____

♦ Why is it important for you to cultivate this energy in motion?

_____

_____

_____

♦ How will you use that energy into something constructive moving forward?

_____

_____

_____

♦ What are some ways you can share this energy in motion with the people you love and care about?

_____

_____

_____

◆ What is your favorite genre of music? Why?

_____

_____

◆ How often do you listen to music?

_____

_____

_____

◆ Name a time that you felt called to speak up and you didn't.

_____

_____

_____

◆ Name a time you said something and you wish you didn't. Why? What happened?

_____

_____

_____

◆ Think back to the first time you danced. How did you feel?

_____

_____

_____

◆ What can you do today to connect with your emotions in a healthy way?

_____

_____

_____

| LESSON 12

DREAM BIG... NO. BIGGER!

"Don't be afraid to fail big, to dream big, but remember
dreams without goals are just dreams. And they ultimately fuel
disappointment... I try to give myself a goal every day."

-DENZEL WASHINGTON

"Dream big! Aim high! Dream big! Aim High!", we yelled as we made our way to the stage at the Oregon Teen National Conference at Camp Arrawana at the dead of night. The little crowd of people yelled and clapped awaiting my team of four's performance. We had L, T, C, and me! I felt my heart beating out of my chest as we made our way in our football huddle to the center of the stage. As the clapping began to cease, it was my turn to kick us off with the negative statistics for young people in foster care. I stepped forward to then proclaim my resilience despite those statistics. Then L went next and the crowd's energy made us all beam. Before long, it was C's turn and, well, she forgot her lines. She froze. I felt my chest tighten. Oh no! As T tried to go next, I sensed the energy had been shifted. T started off then forgot her lines. We all looked at each other and instantly knew what I had to do. I took a step forward and let the crowd know we were going to have to come back at the end of the camp to show them our performance and to teach them the Resilience step. They clapped and we rushed off the stage. It was humiliating.

For the remainder of the night, that's all we could think about. It's all we laughed and joked about. We came off the stage and made sure to separate ourselves from the crowd. We went all the way to the back, toward the trees on the darker side of camp. I felt the weight of being the camp leaders, some of the only people of color and the only ones to completely bomb our performance on my shoulders. My team shared they felt the same way. I knew the only way to relieve us all of this feeling was to go back, see where we went wrong, and practice, practice, practice!

So, that's what we did. For the remaining days we had, we used to be clear on our performance and rehearsed. We used every open moment and our down time between leading campers, we would go back to our cabin and practice. One of the reasons we failed the first time was because we kept switching ideas. We knew we wanted to create a step, have a skit and dance, but the order was all over the place. And that night, we only had 30 mins to figure it out and practice. Honestly, twenty of those minutes were spent going back and forth on ideas. We had little time to gain traction in one then we tried to wing it. We failed, but that just meant we needed to revisit our plan and make adjustments.

Before we knew it, the night before the last day of camp arrived. Here we were, rehearsing and perfecting even the slightest of hang ups all the way into the beginning of the next day. I went to bed that night with two split types of feelings. On one hand, I felt confident and excited to show everyone what we had been working on. On the other hand, I was nervous, sleepy, and worried that we would completely tank it again and feel even worse than before. What if we fail twice?

Alas, the day had come. I decided to keep those conflicting feelings to myself and hope for the best. Afterall, I believed in my team, and most importantly, I believed in myself. If I hadn't, I would not have told the crowd that we would be back. We went through the day, giving each other encouragement as we passed each other transitioning between different workshops we were leading. The last event of the day approached and I reminded the camp staff of our plans and when we would like to go up. They agreed and we sat over to the left. After our groups went through our own performances, the four of us got together a couple of minutes before we were supposed to go on. The lights dimmed and the music cut. It was our time to shine.

We got into our huddle and with all our might, yelled, " Dream! Big! Aim! High! Dream! Big! Aim High! Dream Big! Aim High!" as we made our way to the center of this new stage inside the building with the staff, campers, and other camp counselors. I felt the fear that we would fail come up, and in the moment decided it didn't matter. I focused on what needed to be done at that moment. I encouraged my team and gave cues just as we rehearsed. And this time we had a standing ovation.

At the end, we decided to free style our Resilience step and taught each person who was able to move how to do the resilience step. We explained how powerful it is to get back up, even when you feel like it will be scary. As people were practicing, I took a deep breath and scanned the room to discover over sixty people doing the resilience step that we created. Wow. This is how important it was for us to pick ourselves back up and try again. For the remainder of the camp, I would see young campers doing the resilience step alone or with their groups.

When we bombed it the first time, we had choices. And not coming back to complete the performance, I believe would have been the easier route. I could always say it was just not a good day or blame it on one person when telling the story to others. Or I could go the route that wasn't comfortable and push myself to do something I had never done but yielded the highest return on my investment of time, energy and resources. I say, the impact was worth it. And I'd do it all over again.

CHAPTER EXERCISE

HOW TO START AND FINISH THE NO NEGATIVE SELF-TALK 72 HOUR CHALLENGE.

For three days (72) hours, you will refrain from talking negatively about yourself and others.

You will unfollow/ unfriend/ block any pages on social media that do not contribute to the person you are becoming. You will not make excuses for why you need any form of toxicity.

You will write in your journal or say out loud, something or someone that you love whenever a negative thought comes up. You will focus on harnessing and creating new happier moments.

To help you stay focused, write down affirmations or positive, uplifting quotes from people you respect and admire. Put them all over your space. Put them on your laptop screen. Make some of them your phone screen saver. So that way, when your mind starts drifting you can find encouragement in as many spaces as you can.

Go back through your rising routine and be sure when you are waking up that you are taking control of your day. Declare that you will not allow that negative voice to win.

One thing that helped me when I was starting out was giving this negative voice an image... an image that made me laugh.

For instance, when that negative voice with limiting beliefs would come up I'd envision it being a kissy face emoji. The voice isn't so scary as a kissy face emoji. Then I gave it a different voice. A squeaker voice. And now it's a kissy face emoji with a squeaker voice. How hilarious!

After envisioning this in my mind, I would move this hilarious image to be right in front of me. I'd laugh at it as I lower the voice into a whisper. Then I would minimize the gigantic kissy face emoji to fit in the palm of my hand. I really would have fun with it. I threw it on the floor and stomped on it. No more negative voices.

If you recognize your negative self-talk is coming up more and more, that's okay. It's all a part of the process! You just have to stick with it. Maybe start off with a 24 hour challenge and then slowly move up to a 72 hour, a 7 day, a 14 day, a 21 day until this becomes second nature for you! Remember, this is not about who gets it done faster or the best. It's about your own individual progress in taking control of your mind and your own internal conversations. You got this!

For my high achievers, here is a Streak tracker for a no negative self-talk for 21-28 days challenge! Be sure to establish what you will be doing for this 21 day challenge, why it is important that you do it and the reward you will receive once you complete it!

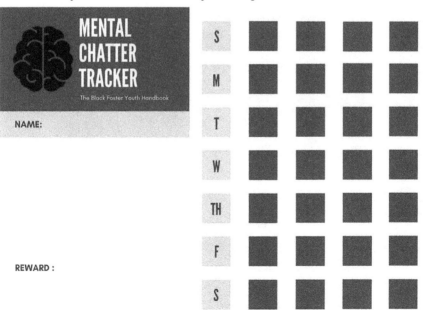

MENTAL CHATTER TRACKER
The Black Foster Youth Handbook

NAME:

REWARD :

S M T W TH F S

Congratulations!

You have just completed Phase 1 of the Black Foster Youth Handbook.

How do you feel?

Before you rush to move forward, take some time to pause.

Reflect and record your thoughts and what you've learned in your notebook/journal.

Take a day to think through what you have been reading about and doing in your every day life thus far.

And celebrate!

How will you celebrate this incredible milestone?

You've been doing the work!

You've been showing up and taking steps (even if they seem small) to heal and process where you are to envision where you are going!

Congratulations on completing Phase one: root.

Let's Move Forward.

"You don't have to be great to get started...but you do have to get started to be great!" - Les Brown

Phase 2
Envision

| CHAPTER FOUR

EVOLVING DEFINITIONS

"Sit with women who are winning, the conversation is different."

- UNKNOWN

"You only are free when you realize you belong no place- you belong every place- no place at all. The price is high. The reward is great... I belong to myself."

-UNKNOWN

"Identity is something that you are constantly earning... a process that you must be active in."

-MAYA ANGELOU

In order to move forward with our lives and open ourselves up to a world of infinite possibility, sometimes we have to take a look at our own narratives and redefine for ourselves what the new pieces to the new puzzle really mean. Will they even fit now? I mean how useful can old puzzle pieces to a new puzzle be?

Maybe it's time to self-reflect before just pushing on once more. Maybe it's time to pause and visit the big picture. Have you made time to create the big picture?

Have you married an idea that no longer serves you?

Unfortunately, for a long time, I was crippled by the "WHY ME" limiting belief.

Les Brown Says, "Why not you? Who would you suggest?"

And even if you do have a suggestion to that question, lol don't answer that... it's rhetorical.

It's important to recognize that we go through these situations not only because we were designed to handle them but also, to go back into these communities and create a solution for those problems, those hardships ... the barriers that made whatever it is so difficult to achieve and make sure that those coming after us have at the very least, a simpler way of achieving or getting through those systems and setbacks.

So, now is the time for you to redefine what success looks like to you... and not by society's standards. Maybe you don't fit into that.

It's okay to change and evolve. You may think life is one way and years down the road you discover it is something completely different. You're human. You are here to learn and level up.

This is just a chapter in your book. And you are the author of your own book of life .

Stop giving your pen away to other people.

Whose bright idea was it to make us choose so early? You do not have to stick to something you said when you were five if you realize it's actually not what you want anymore. The world will not end if you change your mind. You've grown and evolved. You don't have to stay in that relationship with the idea of who you were.

Don't marry that version of yourself, at least take it on a date first.. Get to know it, get to know the new you. The version of you that is here now with what you've accomplished and what you've endured this far. And don't stifle your dream. Dream big. Aim high for yourself and create a plan.

Not because you want to limit yourself, but to liberate yourself in alignment to your purpose. The plan can shift once crafted and it's better to have an outline for yourself designed by yourself than to create a space of scarcity and urgency... a state of emergency because you didn't want to honestly self-reflect, level up your definitions, and do a little planning toward your mission in life. Think about the impact you could make toward alleviating the issues that rise up in the world.

Many of us are going around measuring others and ourselves through the lenses of other people's and society's version of success. And overall, what a successful person is and does.... But behind all of those accomplishments, features in newspapers, blogs, labels, or even degrees... it's important to get back to who you are as a person and to build on a plan you are rooted in.

During this chapter, we are looking at the five lessons I learned and how I evolved definitions to support the new life I am living. At the end of each lesson, you will have a chance to check your own definitions and craft new ones, if that's what you feel called to do.

LESSON 13

HOME IS NOT JUST A FIXED DESTINATION

Ah. What a life. To feel safe, secure and stable would seem to be a luxury in most confinements within the poverty-stricken society and those engulfed within the foster care system.

A basic necessity you say? Well, I didn't feel "at home" often at all.

In fact, the phrase "make yourself at home" gestures to me a more unpleasant feeling than most common phrases. Maybe because it is so cliché and the majority of the people who uttered those words to me did not genuinely mean it.

Nevertheless, I have redefined home for myself as no longer a material object, but perhaps a metaphysical one. Home is a feeling - a vibe. I've come to understand that it is not a place but rather home can be found within a person... within people.

For a long time, I would define home as a nice house that encompassed my family. In my case, with years of bouncing from one house to the next, even before foster care, I realized that my definition of home had to change. Along with many other definitions to evolve into the life I desired.

Home gives me several different mental images, now. A sip of warm tea. A nice comfy couch. Being able to read a multitude of amazing books to support my personal development. And a space full of love from the people around me and most importantly by the soul that resides within this body.

I thank the love of my life, Michael, for truly being a piece of home to me. Home is not a building. Home is when you know that you feel genuine happiness, a familiarity and undeniable immense love.

Home is a spark that you can't really explain within the pit of your soul that beams brighter and brighter within you and you know that everything-no matter what happens outside of you will turn out okay.

Home is a state of mind and a feeling that you have within you and can be found around the people you love and that love you.

#IAMSUCCESS QUESTIONS:

◆ What comes to mind when you think of the word, "home"?

_____

_____

_____

◆ How do you define a home?

_____

_____

_____

◆ What could you or your supportive adult do now, to make you feel more at home?

_____

_____

_____

◆ How would you like to redefine home for yourself?

_____

_____

_____

◆ Home is_____ (fill in the blank)

┃LESSON 14

NOT EVERYONE IS YOUR ENEMY

"Sometimes the hardest decision is who to cut off vs who to be patient with."

- UNKNOWN

"Communication and understanding are pivotal because you don't have to agree with what I'm saying, but I do need you to comprehend it. I need to feel heard and validated. We don't necessarily need to be on the same sentence or to finish each other's sentences, but let's be on the same page, the same chapter and in the same book. And finish the ending together."

- ÁNGELA QUIJADA-BANKS

"Stop reconnecting with toxic people from your past because you're lonely. Focus on getting better and attracting better."

- UNKNOWN

Yes, I'm talking to you. Stop reconnecting with people who consistently show you their negative intentions. Leave them where they are at. Don't you dare ruin your growth. Don't you dare taint your peace. What you feel is temporary... allow it to be felt, and then let it go. Continue to heal and prosper.

Although you may not have had the best experiences in the past, with adults or peers, that doesn't mean that it's everyone. You have not met everyone in the world to now determine that everyone is bad and out to get you.

I used to think that everyone was just trying to get one over on me or that they didn't have my best interest at heart. However, as time went on, I learned that there are billions of people in the world... and I cannot base the entire human race upon a few hundred or thousands of people who had negative intentions I met throughout my life experience. They are not the reflection of the entire human race.

To this day, I still do come across people that are not in my best interest, but I have a tool that has taken years to trust, discernment. I wouldn't say that I've mastered this, because sometimes people can pretend to be something they are not. I've been strung along to believe that someone genuinely wanted to see me succeed, only to find out that once my success began to intimidate them, they'd leave me high and dry. Other times, they'd be on the sidelines copying and pasting my every move.

In this world, there are people that want to see you, help you, and celebrate your success for no other reason than to be of service. It's important you know these people really do exist, and are within your reach.

HERE ARE SOME DEFINING CHARACTERISTICS OF PEOPLE THAT DO WANT YOUR BEST INTEREST:

1. They don't get easily distracted when you are talking to them. They aren't constantly making up reasons why they have to interrupt you when you speak.
2. They won't blame others for everything that goes wrong. They may deal with something difficult, but will eventually recognize their part in the situation and choose to take responsibility and change.

3. When you are talking to them, they aren't always checking their emails or mobile devices and halfway listening. They aren't checking for social media notifications every 5 minutes.

4. They make sure they are present in the moment with you. When you are talking about something, they are actively listening and going through the motions of the topics with you.

5. They don't act differently when you begin to say how excited you are about something. They show genuine interest in what you have to say and express how proud of you they are. They share your accomplishments and support in any way that they can, even if it's a share on social media.

6. They advise you not to waste any energy or time with people who are not adding value to your life in any way. (Value meaning emotionally, physically, spiritually, or financially. Relationships are not just for one person to be contributing and the other just takes.) Every relationship must be reciprocal: A continuous give and take exchange... not just one-sided give, give, give, or take, take, take.

7. They are not always talking about a problem or in a problem. Every time you talk with them, they should not have a whole bucket load of issues that they are not proactive about solving. Some issues take longer than others to resolve; however, they should not always have a horrible, dire situation going on every single time you all interact.

8. They learn from their mistakes and are willing to tell you how to not make the same ones. They are not stuck in a loop of the same bad decisions.

9. They do not talk behind other people's back. Venting and gossiping are two different things. Venting is when you are releasing

emotions, energies, and thoughts with the intention of resolving an issue. Gossiping is senseless (poop) talk. When you participate in gossiping, you are losing time that you could be organizing a business plan, spending time healing, or hanging out with family and friends.

Gossiping is an energy killer. If you are a known gossiper, make it a goal that you will cut it down to 2 mins then stop. Once you've mastered that, begin to brainstorm how you will remove this out of your life. Gossiping does not have a place on the roadmap to purpose, fulfillment, or success. Release the need to do it and replace it with something more fruitful.

10. They are not people pleasers. They will not agree to something that they do not want to do. They will be honest with you and tell you that they are not interested if they are not. They will tell you when you are wrong and support you in making the best moral and logical decisions.

11. They do not allow fear to consume them. They will leap into opportunities that will be for their own best interest. They will share opportunities with you that they believe are in your own best interest as well. They will be very generous in nature with how they view the world and their life. They will support you and celebrate with you throughout your journey in life.

#IAMSUCCESS QUESTIONS:

♦   Have you ever had someone mistreat you?

_____

_____

_____

♦   What is your definition of trust?

_____

_____

_____

♦   How do you show others that you trust them?

_____

_____

_____

♦   How can you tell if someone is trustworthy?

_____

_____

_____

♦   Do you gossip with others?

_____

_____

_____

◆ What is one thing you can do to replace gossiping?

_____

_____

_____

LESSON 15

SETTING BOUNDARIES IS AN ACT OF SELF-LOVE

"Daring to set boundaries is about having the courage to love ourselves even when we risk disappointing others."

\- BRENÉ BROWN

"Life will never stop pushing you, so you must know when and how to push back."

\- ROBERT KIYOSAKI, RICH DAD, POOR DAD

I've learned the significance of setting boundaries the hard way. Although, you may want to see the best in everyone, everyone may not want to see the best in you. Believe people when they show you who they are.

Loving yourself is not only how you choose to treat yourself, but also how you allow others to speak to you and treat you.

Don't sell yourself short by allowing others to use and abuse their access to you.

You deserve better, and as a matter of fact, you deserve the best!

Don't play ya self! We aren't accepting verbal apologies alone this year and moving forward. Only a sincere apology, recognized impact and changed behavior.

I'm not sure when I'll fully master this skill of knowing just when is the "right time" and exactly how to maneuver a given situation, but I do know that I'm improving over time.

From the past two decades of my life experience, I would say I've done pretty well considering the unfortunate circumstances of life that felt completely unbearable.

After experiencing back to back heartbreak whether it was romantic, platonic, and familial... that shit HURT, but I somehow picked up the pieces each time. I eventually figured out what to do with it. Ugh! It was not easy, but I did it.

I remember having a really close friend, Cristina P. whom I thought would be my friend forever. I was about 8 years old. My parents decided it was time to move from the beautiful sunny state of California to... Augusta, Georgia.

I was devastated! This was my 3rd move, and I was only in 2nd grade! I thought for sure I'd be with these kids forever and began rooting friendships. But no matter how much I begged and pleaded, it was time to go.

I stayed in contact even after the move, and a couple of years later moved back to Cali. Turns out, I moved into the same district and elementary as this old friend. I was excited to reconnect! We became inseparable!

By the end of 6th grade, I moved away again. Eventually, I was living in North Carolina, went on to skip the 8th grade, due to academic achievement. At the end of ninth grade, I had a lil "boyfriend". My first actual boyfriend, we'll call him X, that I had known since middle school. Due to a tragic series of events that I will not share here, we broke up.

My "friend" from all these years back in Cali found him on social media and began flirting with him. Some months passed, and I saw an updated relationship status reading, "X is in a relationship with... Cristina P." I couldn't believe my eyes! I quickly clicked the profile picture... What?! How?! She's all the way in California. I was in utter disbelief. It was getting late, and I decided that I would call her the next day.

Ring ring! ... no answer... I left a voicemail. I needed answers! What the hell was going on? Unfortunately, all I got back were some subliminal tweets, and the two of them making fb posts about me and adding ruthless comments under all my pictures. I was so hurt. How could this have happened? And why? Was this for real?

Unfortunately, I never fully got the answer to these questions. Over the years, through sheer pain, understanding, and forgiveness, I've learned how to deal with situations similar to or worse than this.

Life always gives us lessons, especially in the midst of suffering, but sometimes we aren't trained to see those lessons. We don't know when and how to deal with the pain of those lessons... what we don't realize is that's exactly why it's YOU that's experiencing it.

Other takeaways from unfortunate situations:

I do not take the way someone is as somehow an issue against me unless there are actions and words explicitly toward me.

I see people as just people. They can make mistakes, and maybe even have a hard time accepting that they make mistakes. I used to be that way.

I have come to learn my role in each situation. I push myself to understand what happened and how I can prevent it from happening again. What do I need to learn?

I come from a place of understanding, but also mindfulness of my own self-love.

I ask myself if the relationship with this person, during a verbal disagreement is worth putting in more effort.

Is this person mentally mature enough to comprehend communicating efficiently? Do they know how? Are they open to learn, or open to seeing their own faults? I am always open to constructive, loving correction and have learned that almost every situation can be worked about by communication if all parties are cooperative and want to find a solution.

It also depends on timing, dedication, the goals of everyone involved, and if everyone sees the bigger picture despite the initial dispute. It is important to look at all the factors and come from a place of understanding. The questions that should come to mind are, "Although they acted this way-is there any way that I can support them in becoming a better version of themselves? Is there something that I could have done to prevent this? If not, what can we do now to move forward?" These are all important things to consider because no one is perfect, and sometimes we all just need that extra hand in life. Or even that extra listening ear to think about what needs to be done and the most efficient way to accomplish it.

We don't have to write someone off as being " toxic" and block them all of the time.

Maybe we just need more space between us and them. Space provides an opportunity to allow them to grow and understand who they are. Maybe one day they'll come around, and maybe they won't. Either way, if you are in a *toxic* friendship or connection with someone, take space to assess the relationship. What are the pros and cons? Is it worth taking space for a while and seeing what happens?

There are many ways to set boundaries so I invite you to learn how you can begin to firmly set some up for yourself, your well-being and success.

#IAMSUCCESS QUESTIONS:

+ Why is it important to have boundaries?

  _____

  _____

  _____

+ Does everyone in your inner circle honor what you think and say?

  _____

  _____

  _____

+ How do they show that they honor you?

  _____

  _____

  _____

+ Do you feel like may be walking on egg shells with certain people?

  _____

  _____

  _____

LESSON 16

BLOOD ISN'T ALWAYS THICKER THAN WATER.

"I am only here to make sure you have the basics covered." My social worker said to me in my new foster home as she looked around my 'new room'. I looked at her, not sure how to respond, and decided to say nothing. "And another thing... this is supposed to be a more permanent placement, so I hope you're not conspiring about anything..." she added.

The rest of this conversation had the same undertone that the first sentence did. It was the middle of July of 2015 and I was in my first year of college, juggling online classes and a summer internship. I was mentally exhausted and not really trying to open up to this new family, but I promised myself that I'd try my best. I didn't know anything about how to truly advocate for myself, and I certainly did not feel like I had a team of people to support me with what I needed and wanted.

My social worker at the time was an older white woman who said many out of line things to me. When I did speak out about it, I was told to recognize all the things she had gone out of her way to do for me. To be more grateful for all the good gestures she had committed. As if that was supposed to shut me up and stop me from bringing up the things that bothered me. It didn't. The more emotional and vocal I was, the less they listened, it seemed.

Foster Club has a great workshop called Youth Adult Partnerships. I attended it during their summer All Star internship in 2017. It encouraged me to change my perspective on how to approach professionals within my case, and I began sharing ideas with social workers in a speech at North Carolina State University on how we can begin to recognize the value within each role.

It's hard to see an upside when you are in the foster care system. We begin to think, "I was taken from my parents and I'm with strangers, and now what? What am I supposed to be happy about?"

Add on the aspect of being a youth of color, and things just begin to sky rocket. With the reality of other people's perception of you, it can feel like there is no point in trying to be "good" or "successful". (more on that later)

I think it's imperative to know how we can begin to see the value of the adults in our circle. It's definitely complex, but imperative in our success through foster care. We need to see how much simpler life can be when we work together with the supportive adults toward clear goals. Foster/resource parents, guardians, social workers, and other constituents have a wealth of knowledge and wisdom about life, love, and how you can begin to prepare for a bright future. They may even have an expertise about specific aspects in a career field or personal venture that you may be interested in. By writing off all adults in our circle, we are missing out on learning helpful life advice. Not only that, but we are also missing out on learning about some truly incredible human beings, and finding long term additions to our family.

Some of the best relationships, if we open ourselves up to engage in them, can be the most beautiful and healing. I know it can be hard to understand what our new reality is, and the people that make up this new reality, but it's important to know that these people are literally paid to support you.

Don't think of it as, "Oh you're being paid to do this, so it's not as genuine." Although that can be the case for some, let's not assume that is the case for you. We do not question teachers if they teach genuinely, and they are paid for teaching. We do not automatically assume sports instructors, therapists, or professors at colleges are just doing something for the money.

If you are curious why your guardian, foster parent/resource parent, or social worker chose this opportunity to support young people in foster care, then simply ask.

"What influenced your decision to become a foster/resource parent?"

Do not assume their response. Allow them to respond.

This may actually prove to be a valuable bonding experience. Yes, you may have been hurt by a caregiver in the past, but that doesn't mean that this new experience will turn out the same way.

They are being paid to look out for you and support your success.

So, why not allow them to do just that?

#IAMSUCCESS QUESTIONS:

◆   What can you do when you need extra support?

_____

_____

_____

◆   Who do you trust the most in your circle right now? Why?

_____

_____

_____

◆   What is the importance of your supportive adult(s) in your circle?

_____

_____

_____

◆   How can you begin to better get to know your supportive adult(s)?

_____

_____

_____

◆   Why is it important that you get to know them better?

_____

_____

_____

LESSON 17

RELATIONSHIPS ARE PIVOTAL TO YOUR SUCCESS

"People are not lazy. They simply have goals that do not inspire them."

- TONY ROBBINS

"It's the ones who are against you that believe in your power the most."

-SILKY MAFIA

WHY IS BUILDING SOCIAL CAPITAL SO IMPORTANT?

You need a team of people that think you're awesome.

When I was a teenager, apparently, I understood this very well. I created a fb group named "Team Angie", and another named, "Team awesomeness". I used the Facebook group to help me stay connected to people as I moved from one place to the next. I do believe it rooted me to a degree and helped me stay sane. These individuals did not know much about what was happening with my family but instead served as a place to check in or share funny memes. I knew that everyone in this Facebook group cared about my wellbeing and success.

Be proactive about your social life. Know what you enjoy doing and make it a priority to do it. Be in congruence to understand the aspect of what truly sets your soul on fire.

More ways you can tell you're in a healthy relationship:

1. Your communication is clear and open. Everyone is listening and feeling heard. Both parties are speaking honestly about the topic of choice. The body language and word choice are respectful and understanding.

2. You may have disagreements sometimes. Arguing is okay. That just means you and the other person have different views and opinions. The good news is that you aren't just letting it get bottled up and exploding with resentment. What matters is HOW you resolve the argument. You do not have to have a carbon copy of yourself in order to get along. People have different perspectives, what's most important is recognizing the other person's side and understanding what they convey. You do not have to agree, but you do have to understand. Above all, if feelings do get hurt-apologize. If you recognize that you were wrong or misspoke during the heat of the moment, apologize. Apologizing doesn't make you any less of a good person. In fact, admitting and showing empathy for the other person makes you an even better person. Check your ego, apologize, and change the behavior.

3. You keep relationship problems private. We all need a sense of privacy in order to feel safe. Unless you are in an unsafe environment, keep anything that you all get into a disagreement off of social media! Keep your relationship bumps between you two, your therapist, and close trusted family/friends.

4. The more that you get to know each other, the more susceptible you are to be annoyed with the other party. If you or your partner are not on good terms, take some time to reflect on your words and actions. If you recognize that the issue is harder to navigate

on your own, speak to a trusted adult about the scenario. Then go back to your partner and tell them what is on your mind. Listen to understand their side. There is no such thing as a "perfect" person. Everyone has flaws and makes mistakes. It's important not to hold grudges and instead apply the 3 A's.

Assess. Address. Alleviate.

Assess the severity of the situation or disagreement. Assess your feelings and thoughts around it.

Address the matter when you are in a calmer and more collected demeanor.

Alleviate the issue by apologizing, taking space from the other party, or utilizing overall removal with forgiveness of self.

5. Realistic expectations are essential in relationships. Again, no one is perfect. The key is commitment and open communication. Be honest about your expectations.

6. You can have space, separate friendships, and interests in each romantic relationship. This is healthy. Take time to focus on you. Spending time to reflect on life, your future, and appreciating the small things can be beneficial in the long run.

7. Taking time away will not mean your phone is being blown up after the first 30 mins.

   My ex-boyfriend, (D.F. standing for Definitely Not) would call me nonstop when I was away on business trips. He would claim that he trusted me, but when we broke up he finally admitted the contrary. If you are someone that is blowing up your partner/ friend when they are not constantly messaging or with you to see if they are betraying you in some way, you may have a problem with trust or codependency. You must first trust yourself before you are able to trust anyone else.

8. It's important to be able to confide in one another. Making time to spend together is essential to any relationship. Prioritize the relationships that matter to you.

9. Considering your partner's thoughts on a decision you have to make will strengthen your relationships. Whether or not your partner agrees with that decision is their opinion. Ultimately, the choice is yours. However, it is important to note that when you are in a relationship, depending on what you all establish as your agreements, it may serve you better to find middle ground.

10. Creating and maintaining intimacy (I will dive deeper into this in a further lesson)

11. The person you are around makes you better and you make them better. From foster parent to platonic friend to romantic partner. Another way that you can tell that you are in a healthy relationship is if you are improving each other in some way. Whether that is eating healthier, laughing more, being able to have an emotional release, learning new things, or celebrating each other's successes.

Healthy relationships are a two way street. Be reciprocal in all of them.

#FOSTERINGSUCCESS TIP:

As a supportive adult, it is imperative to maintain stability in your young person's life. Otherwise, the instability of housing, supportive people, food and other factors can create an inconsistency within the success of young people.

Please take the time to begin to take note of at least 2-3 other supportive adults that already are or may consider being a foster/ resource parent in your circle. Make a list and be sure that other constituents on your team such as your social worker become aware of who is on this list. Discuss the possibility of having options and who you think would be a great fit in supporting this young person as well. Make sure to prioritize the safety and well-being of your young person by having open dialogue and allowing input from your young person.

Then perhaps, schedule a meeting in which the whole team and possible new foster/resource parents meet with this young person. It is imperative to have young people know who they could be living with if you decide you are not in the best health or position to continue on in your dominant role in their life. I do agree that you must focus on what will be best for you but do not forget about the safety and wellbeing of the young person. When the tides of life become high, everyone needs someone to care for us when we are down, celebrate with us when we are up and love us in all of the in-between. That doesn't change just because it's foster care. It may not just take you by yourself to help support this young person. You will have hard and challenging days. I do not think it is in the best interest of anyone involved to cut ties and ignore the issues.

Myself and others share stories of having to pick up and move our entire lives in black trash bags as if we, too are just as easily disposable and replaceable. Please be mindful and remember, we are human beings just like you. We have been through a lot and at the core, we all want to be loved, cared for and celebrated.

Whether you were able to have a lot of support or not during your childhood is not how you should lead your life today. And it certainly is not conducive to the support of your young person. Consider therapy alone and in congruence with your young person to iron out these ideologies, maintain support, and heal.

**If you notice that you are feeling more frustrated by the thought of having to do so much for someone you barely know and feel like it isn't fair that you didn't have this level of support or resources growing up and you made it just fine without it... then... you may want to seek therapy. This is not a healthy mindset to have around a young person that is looking to you for support.

CHAPTER EXERCISE

SKETCH YOUR MESS

You will need:

- 2-4 sheets of paper
- Something to sketch with
- colored pens/crayons/ markers to add details
- Minimum of 30 minutes of spare time
- You may do this alone, with other young people or with a supportive adult

Set a timer for 10 minutes. First sketch the person that you have known yourself to be. The sketch does not have to be perfect. You do not have to be extremely artistic to complete this exercise. Be detailed in your perception of yourself. Add descriptions to your sketch to label your hair, your lips, your body, your clothing and your personality. Now, sketch two people that are always around you. How do they look? How do you perceive their personalities to be? Make sure to use captions and descriptive words to bring clarity to your sketch. Take your time and use all of the time allotted to be detailed in your sketch. After the timer has run out, take a step back and look at your sketch.

Now, set your timer for another 10 minutes. This time, on a separate piece of paper draw yourself with the physical and personality characteristics you wish to embody. Maybe you are smiling in this picture and your hair is done up a certain way. Maybe you are holding a book, like this one ;) to resemble that you would like to be a reader. Maybe you sketch yourself outside, meditating because that is something you want to begin adopting into your habits. Wonderful, now that you have sketched your ideal self- it is time to sketch who an ideal supportive adult would look and act like. Take a moment to think this through. Do not rush the process. Think of the physical and personality characteristics you would want two supportive adults to embody. What do they look like? How would they act toward you? What is it feel like to be around them. (Btw: "I don't know" is not an acceptable answer.)

CHAPTER FIVE

BUILDING YOUR SUCCESS TEAM

"The road to the bag is definitely tied to your team and the company that you keep. If you are surrounding yourself with different energies that aren't on the same wavelength as you. If they aren't praying for you, inspiring you, supporting you or showing you a better way...
REMOVE THEM IMMEDIATELY..."

-SEAN COMBS

"Associate yourself with good people of good quality, for it is better to be alone than in bad company."

-BOOKER T. WASHINGTON

"Are they feeding your flame or are they pissing on it ?"

- WILL SMITH

"She slept with him too, girl!" I heard someone say as I walked past her in the cafeteria at North Carolina Central University.

During my freshman year of college, I had all male friends. I didn't think much of it until others started rumors that I was sleeping with them! I cannot stand the fact that if people see a male and a female walking, laughing, or showing any interest in what the other is saying or doing then that is translated in meaning that there is some form of sexual relation. Ugh. It's so frustrating!

I think the most frustrating part is that I didn't think this would be an issue as an adult. I thought I wouldn't have to deal with it after I got to a certain age. I had a rough time when I attended West High School in Knoxville, TN, but I thought all the petty and childish games from others were behind me. I mean, this was college! We were all adults and we didn't have time for any unnecessary BS... or so I thought.

Just because I didn't have any time for shenanigans didn't mean other people weren't going to prioritize time to do so.

I wasn't a tomboy but I was a girl that had a lot of male friends. It wasn't because I was a massive sexual fiend or because I wanted all their attention. I actually never had sex before. It wasn't because I didn't want female friends, I just didn't have many positive interactions with women, including my mom. I didn't know it at the time, but not having a positive relationship with my mom affected me in so many ways, and this was just one of them.

I actually really craved feminine community and guidance. My grandmother lived in Washington state and my sister was inaccessible. So, in my second semester of my freshman year I vowed that I would really try to make female friends.

It was now the spring of 2015 and I had been living with my Aspiring Eagles Academy family in Rush hall for over a year now. We had all come on campus for a summer bridge program and signed a contract to live in Rush dormitory for a year. I actually hated it. My high school boyfriend, (we'll call him Frank) had applied to the same school as me. As we both struggled to balance our mental stability and make our relationship work, our level of toxicity skyrocketed and our entire cohort saw the craziness we both endured.

I had moments where I'd disappear from my consciousness for minutes at a time, paralyzed by the thoughts of my past racing in my mind. Other times, you could find me chasing Frank in the middle of the night outside convincing him of all the reason why it was important for him not to end his life. Sometimes, after he was done having an episode, I would be fighting my insomnia, trying to fall asleep and wake up to him having a rubber bracelet firmly pushed over his head and around his throat, choking him. In these moments, I'd calmly turn toward him and gently remove the bracelet, tell him I loved him and to stop doing that.

It became normal. Toxic love was my normal.

I knew something was wrong, but I didn't know who to turn to. We tried couples counseling, on campus but to no avail. Who could I talk to that wouldn't judge me or make me feel stupid? Who could I turn to that would listen to what I had to say and give me some sound advice? What if I was ready to leave him, but I just didn't know how?

One time, I was alone in my room. My roommate was gone and my neighbor across the dorm hallway (we'll call her S.T.) came in and started asking me how I was doing. I thought to myself, *well horrible... my sister's locked away in a behavioral facility in another state, I can't get in contact with my brothers, my parents have seemed to ghost me, I'm still in foster care, I'm in a crazy relationship that all of you mock me for being in and I have a horrible gas problem!*

Of course, that is not what I said. Instead I opened with, "I'm just focused on this English class. How about you?"

She laughed and told me she actually was thinking that we should room together and have our roommates switch with us. I actually liked the idea because she was the only person who spoke Spanish in our cohort and I thought we could bond since my mom is "Mexican" and she was Panamanian.

At the end of our chat, we agreed to let our roommates' know about "the switch", as we called it. A week went by and our schedules were so crazy that I didn't see S.T. again. One night, a few of us gathered in the hallway outside my door. We came on to the topic of languages. S.T. ended up coming out of her room and joining the conversation. " Do you even speak Spanish?" she laughingly interjected.

I laughed back, " Yeah, a little. My mom's Mexican, but she didn't really teach me." I absolutely hated talking about this. And, I actually didn't find it funny at all. Why was she asking me this in front of all of these people, anyway? What was her motive?

"Oh, because I saw your mom the other time she came to visit and she didn't look Mexican. Come to think of it, you don't really look Mexican." Everyone in the hallway grew quiet. The air in the hallway felt staler than usual. She was referring to my foster mom that came to drop some groceries off for me. Of course, she didn't know that. And I would never tell her. "Okay, what am I saying then?" She began to speak Spanish, then waited for me to translate it into English, while folding her arms.

It's important to note that S.T. was very connected to all the other women in our cohort and dorm. In fact, every female except for me. It felt like at times she made sure to exclude me to be known as the only Spanish-speaking and so-called "Hispanic" person in our cohort. When she came to my room earlier to ask to be roommates, I put my feelings about this aside and thought that maybe I was just overthinking it and self-sabotaging.

However, in this situation, I was right. And as she continued to say various words and phrases quickly in Spanish, knowing I was unclear of what she fully said in front of everyone I learned that my gut feeling was right and this was not a healthy friendship.

To this day, she still talks to people about me. I've been told that she tells people that I am not truly half Mexican, that I lied about who I was and my origin. What she didn't know was how badly I wanted to be fluent in Spanish. What she didn't know was how many times I would beg my mom to teach me, attempt to take online courses and plead with my foster parents to let me practice in their home. My foster parents didn't agree with allowing me to speak Spanish because they couldn't understand what I was saying. They assumed I would be talking about them negatively. When in fact, I'd say something about the food or something completely random.

It's sad, because the truth is she didn't even try to get to know who I was. On the other hand, I'm grateful for this experience. From the looks of it, if I had shared even 1/1000th of my story with her, then it could have left a scar even deeper than the one that I've had to heal over the years.

Have you ever associated yourself with BAD company?

It took a million times of heartache, pain, lost money, time, and resources for me to finally understand the importance of heeding my own intuition and setting ample boundaries to people that have shown me exactly who they are.

I do think that there needs to be balance because I do not believe you should just go around blocking people. That's what I used to do before I learned better ways to handle difficult conversations and situations with poise.

As soon as anyone showed any signs of *toxicity*, it would be more than enough reason to block them.

Ironically, I would become confused when others would block me and tell me I was the one being *toxic*. Was I being toxic? No! I couldn't be. I didn't have a toxic bone in my body. *It just isn't possible*, I'd reassure myself.

Over time, I began to #SelfReflect on my past interactions, behaviors, and thought patterns around relationships. After being honest with myself, I began to do the internal work to address some hard truths that came up.

Here are some of the lessons I've learned about building your success team.

⎸LESSON 18

YOU MUST BE A GOOD FRIEND
TO HAVE A GOOD FRIEND

"Don't roll up on me unless you're leading with love"

-JENIFER LEWIS

"Invest in people who invest in you. Make to keep a look out for consistency, transparency, reciprocity, and honest communication in every relationship to nurture your higher vibrational frequency."

- ÁNGELA QUIJADA-BANKS

They say that you are the sum of the 5 people you hang around the most. So who do you hang around? What are their goals and aspirations? What do they say about you when you are not there? Do you trust them? What is the company you keep? And are you positive that they are supporting you as a human being now? Will they in the future?

Whether it's a love holiday like Valentine's day or not, there is no need to put pressure on whether or not you give material gifts/ possessions to your significant other.

Don't put pressure on whether or not you have a romantic relationship either.

There doesn't even have to be a holiday for you to do this, but...

Celebrate by yourself
- jamming out to your favorite songs
- pedicure

- self-care day with masks and warm baths
- chanting affirmations
- creating a vision board
- creating a collage of photos of you from last year at this time to now!

Celebrate someone you love with:
- a phone call
- FaceTime
- hanging out
- eating a home cooked meal together
- go out to the park and talk about how far you've come in your friendship/ things you've overcome

Show love to a stranger
- volunteer for a homeless shelter
- compliment someone you see randomly
- gift a homeless person a care package

Remember: It doesn't have to be EXPENSIVE to show love.

#IAMSUCCESS QUESTIONS:

♦ Are you a good friend? How do you know?
What is the evidence to support that you are a good friend?

_____

_____

_____

♦ How Can you be a better friend to others?

_____

_____

_____

♦ Do you have good friends in your circle?

_____

_____

_____

♦ What is one way that you like to show love to others?

_____

_____

_____

♦ How would you like your friend to show love to you?

_____

_____

_____

LESSON 19
REAL LOVE IS NOT HARD TO IDENTIFY.

"Love is... Being Seen, Felt, and Heard."

-THE BLACK GIRL BRAVADO PODCAST

"We must stop glorifying toxicity in relationships. Can we stop romanticizing BS standards like, "Oh she needs to put up with him because he's still growing" or "He needs to learn how to 'handle her attitude'"... like no one needs to be putting up with all these childish mindsets. Get some therapy, meditate, spend some time alone, drink more water, and work on your character flaws. No one's perfect, but that doesn't mean be the complete opposite. Let's bring back real love, because this toxic fake romance isn't conducive to anyone's health and longevity. I'm seeing too many prolonged toxic relationships. People just settle because their family told them to, or that's the only version of a relationship they see."

- ÁNGELA QUIJADA-BANKS

No relationship will ever be perfect, well unless you take a hard look on what you deem to be perfect in the first place. How have you defined a *perfect* relationship? How do you act when it does not happen that particular way? Before determining what love was, I had to learn what love was not.

Honestly, I had a really twisted version of what love meant to me as I grew into adulthood. I didn't realize it until well into 2018 when finally, I took a hard and well-overdue look at my ego.

Did this translate in my relationships?

Hell yes! Unfortunately, I was sabotaging my friendships, familial, and romantic relationships by projecting my childhood survival behaviors before anyone ever did anything to invoke them. I'd react severely to almost everything people did. I took almost everything personal. If someone was busy when I would text, I'd take it personal. If someone was having a bad day, I'd somehow take it personal and begin to isolate myself to avoid "being a bother".

Of course, at the time I didn't know that was one of the reasons I'd always isolate myself for months at a time, but as I've dug deeper, I've found this and others to be the case.

The truth is we deserve to be seen, felt, and heard... by everyone we consider family, friends, our spouse, or just a significant other. Many of us mislabel the people in our circles with an expectation that they just cannot fulfill.

You shouldn't take this personally as it has absolutely nothing to do with you, but just the nature of the way that person/people view the world and how they've learned to love. What does that mean for you?

You get to choose whether or not you will accept this person's way of showing love or lack of. You have the responsibility of giving someone the privilege of being in your inner circle or being someone of arm's length. You determine the criteria for others to have access to you with clear guidelines, boundaries and expectations for yourself and everyone you come in contact with.

So I ask you, are you being seen, heard, and felt in your current relationships?

#IAmSuccess Questions:

+ What does a "toxic relationship" look like?

_____

_____

_____

_____

+ How many toxic relationships can you count in your life right now?

_____

_____

_____

_____

+ How many toxic relationships are you in?

_____

_____

_____

_____

+ What does a "healthy relationship" look like?

_____

_____

_____

_____

◆ How many healthy relationships can you create?

_____

_____

_____

_____

◆ How can you learn more about how to create and maintain more healthy relationships?

_____

_____

_____

_____

⌶ LESSON 20

MARRIAGE IS STILL AN OPTION

"The idea of soulmates has people thinking that once they find "the one", everything is smooth sailing from there.
No. You still have to communicate, face past demons, set boundaries together, build and sustain trust, and weather storms that come to tear you two apart."

- DERRICK JAXN

Sometimes, I step back and think... "Wow! I'm really a whole #wife!"

After some relationships that went south, I had vowed that I would no longer seek "romance". I just wasn't interested anymore. I began to imagine myself as an elderly woman. I remember telling myself, *No, I wouldn't be ill and frail... I'd be strong, fearless, and armed! I'd know several self-defense techniques that I'd study and focus in on while youthful. I'd be wise. People always compliment me on being wise beyond my age. I'd drink my tea, burn my incense, cook delicious plant-based food, and smile hard every time someone asked me about my life because I would have built an empire.* I remember seeing myself with like 4 cats in a huge home.

I remember just feeling at peace with the reality that maybe "my person" would never find me or that they just simply didn't exist for me in this life. I remember jokingly telling friends, "It's a crazy world out here and even crazier that out of 7 BILLION people on this earth... I'm still single." It's funny to me now, because I mean I wasn't even past 23 with a mindset of complete loss in "romantic relationships" as if I had met 7 billion people to even decipher that.

Soon after that time, I began having conversations with a guy named Michael. It was just casual and friendly conversation. I'd never known him before and he was 3,000 miles away from me. He wasn't anyone I considered romantically since the distance was so much. At that time, I had a male friend who was in a long-distance relationship and that individual constantly cheated on their partner. That wasn't reassuring about the whole long distance romance idea. Plus, I had my own stories of people cheating on me. I really didn't like that feeling. I pondered on that pain, that heart break, and said, "Nah, I think I'll sit this out." So, alas, Michael was automatically in the friend zone.

Little did I know that less than 1 year later, I'd fly out to Japan to attend the Marine corps ball with him. Or that he would propose for my birthday and confess his love to me each and every day. Little did I know that he would not be just a friend, but my very best friend and my husband someday.

I can still be that old woman that I envisioned, but I don't have to be in that big ole house alone. The journey doesn't have to be by myself, because not only do I get to have my 4 cats... but the best of both worlds since "my person" had found me.

"What does a healthy relationship look like?"

-Me at 17 in search of an answer but unfortunately enrolling myself in yet another toxic relationship.

This question led me to many discoveries in the quest to understand how to achieve a loving, romantic healthy relationship.

What I learned throughout the years since then is that I had to first take a look at the relationship I had with myself. Instantly, I found the roadblock. It was the way I viewed myself and the subconscious thought of what I believed I deserved. After years of mistreatment from many platonic and romantic relationships, it was time for me to take notes of the common denominator. Was it me? What was I missing?

For me, my answer was BOUNDARIES. I didn't know that it was OKAY to say "NO". I didn't know that I had permission to NOT be nice in times that I needed to be protected.

I found many ideas that had been passed down to me as well as supported by mainstream society that were literally suffocating me from the inside out. No wonder I wasn't finding any luck with having a healthy and loving relationship. I never truly seen it in person before... and I certainly didn't have a healthy, loving relationship with myself.

Within 8 months of me putting my thoughts and desires in motion, not only did I have a healthy, loving, and incredible romantic relationship, but I got married!

#IAMSUCCESS QUESTIONS:

- What have I learned from people in my circle?

_____

_____

_____

- What do I value most from myself and others?

_____

_____

_____

- Who are 3 people I trust and admire? Why?

_____

_____

_____

- What have I learned from past interactions the hard way? What were the lessons?

_____

_____

_____

- How can I be sure that I am not repeating the same mistakes in my relationships?

_____

_____

_____

LESSON 21

INTIMACY IS NOT JUST SEX

"Most adult children of toxic parents grow up feeling tremendous confusion about what love means and how it's supposed to feel. Their parents did extremely unloving things to them in the Name of Love. They can't understand love is not something chaotic, dramatic, confusing, and often painful-something they had to give up their own dreams and desires for. Obviously, that's not what love is all about. Loving Behavior doesn't grind you down, keep you off balance, or create feelings of self-hatred. When someone is being loving to you, you feel accepted, cared for, valued, and respected."

- SUSAN FORWARD

"Intimacy is a divine connection and it doesn't require a sexual connotation at all. Just have to get your souls talking"

- ÁNGELA QUIJADA-BANKS

There are many ways we alchemize pain, both positively and negatively. When we have experienced strong levels of trauma, it is difficult for us to recognize the different avenues of pleasure that we indulge in order to cope with how we truly feel about different aspects of our lives. These different avenues can often give us a heightened sense of temporary fulfillment. Whether it is the past, present, or future when we are not satisfied with something, we believe that we do not have choices and the only way to have some relief is to engage in some type of behavior to distract or dilute the feeling of that reality.

Intimacy is not just sex. And sex is not just intimacy. Sex is a (s)acred (e)nergy e(x)change. It is much more than just a casual interaction. Or a metaphorical "bird and the bees" mental image. Sex is a sacred interchanging of you and another person's soul. Mainstream Society has created this idea that sex should be done with anyone and everyone as long as you both want to. But from a different perspective, what dictates a want?

Is your desire for a sexual connection coming from a healthy place, or an unhealed place?

Joy, true healthy love, and a healthy lasting connection may seem like foreign concepts that are impossible to achieve, but that is far from the truth. As you continue to grow and heal as a person you will begin to be mindful of the decisions concerning who can partake in different levels of intimacy with you.

Before you partake in any level of intimacy with others, be sure you are first establishing intimacy levels with yourself. As stated previously, intimacy is not just sex. Intimacy is having a loving conversation with another human being. Intimacy is comfortable silence, and yet you both feel what doesn't have to be said. Intimacy is falling asleep on the phone with someone else and listening to their breathing pattern as it brings you comfort or soothes you to sleep.

When I was in elementary school, I made a habit of waking up and drinking a cup or two of coffee and maybe even having iced coffee when leaving school. I did this nonstop because it tasted really good and it became my ritual. It gave me a sense of pleasure as I smelled the strong coffee bean aroma and felt the cold, rich substance touches my tongue and go down my throat. It was a very pleasurable experience. So, naturally I wanted more of it.

I drank the coffee for many reasons. I felt cool doing it, it tasted really good, I enjoyed the aesthetics, but amongst them all, it gave me a sense of pleasure. Then it went away, and I had to wait until the next time I had a coffee in whatever form to feel that sense of pleasure again.

Honestly, I would not have stopped. Except one day, I became very sick. I was hot and then I was cold. As I was coming back from school, I didn't feel well. I laid on the couch and felt exhausted. I was sweating profusely. Either I had consumed far too much in a short amount of time or all the other days had finally caught up with me. I'm not really sure, I just know I was hurting and it didn't feel good at all. And then there's the factor that I was only ten years old and I shouldn't have been drinking coffee like that anyway.

To help you learn more about the way you might want to establish different forms of intimacy, I'd recommend finding out what your love language is. You can do this by reading The Five Love Languages by Gary Chapman or doing some research online and with other books.

#IAMSUCCESS QUESTIONS:

◆ How do YOU define love?

_____

_____

_____

◆ How do you express love?

_____

_____

_____

◆ What do you know about sex (other than you or your partner needs to wear a condom)?

_____

_____

_____

◆ What are ways that you can be intimate with someone without sex?

_____

_____

_____

◆ What boundaries do you have for yourself when it comes to sex?

_____

_____

_____

- What does having sex mean to you? Have you ever thought to give it a meaning?

  _____

  _____

  _____

- Why is it important to have clear expectations of intimacy?

  _____

  _____

  _____

- What are your clear expectations when it comes to romantic relationships and sex?

  _____

  _____

  _____

| LESSON 22

HEALTHY RELATIONSHIPS ARE RECIPROCAL

5 WAYS TO KEEP A HEALTHY AND STRONG RELATIONSHIP WITH ANYONE:

1. Communication:

The Good, Bad, and the Ugly. There must constantly be one listener and one speaker throughout each conversation or dispute. Nothing will be communicated if none are listening and both are speaking. Listen to understand not just to respond. If something bothers you, take some time to think it through then arrange a time to talk it through with your partner/friend/foster/resource parent or social worker. Don't keep it in!

2. Build trust:

It can be difficult to understand what trust really even means. Foster youth especially may struggle with trust, many of us struggle to trust even ourselves. This aspect can negatively impact relationships if we are not cognizant of it. We can end up creating a long list of what has happened in the past and bring it over to our new friendships, romantic relationships, and possible career/business opportunities. If your partner hasn't given you a reason to distrust them, then don't treat them as if they have. Constantly celebrate your partner for their trustworthiness. Have a look at your own actions and make sure you are showing actions of trustworthiness as well. Reciprocate that energy. Don't be shady!

3. Be Honest:

If you fear how your partner will react from you being truthful, that should be a red flag of toxicity. You should be able to speak to your partner about whatever comes to mind, if that's the type of relationship you desire. Whenever you are thinking about something, allow yourself to process the information. If it is trauma, allow yourself time to understand what is coming to your mind and what caused it to come up. Was it the way someone touched your hand, or a certain smell? Although, your friends and partners are here for you-that doesn't mean dump every single trauma onto them. Agree on code words that will help them know when you are about to share something that could be heavy.

We must also be mindful of how that information could impact them and what is the end result you'd like to unpack. Perhaps, this friend or partner is not the best person to share (that) particular information with, but you have another family member that might be better suited to handle it. Or maybe therapy is a better option, to get a completely unbiased ear (since they were not there) to listen to what you need to get off your chest. Maybe that's all you need. Either way, don't keep it to yourself.

Share your concerns if the thoughts are too heavy with your foster parent/social worker so that they can get you the support you need and deserve. You deserve peace of mind. You deserve a life without continuous pain and suffering. You do not have to keep it all in and figure it out by yourself. Be honest with yourself, your people in your circle and share what's going on with those you trust. It's important to be able to have people you can call about whatever, whenever, but not however. Mind your tones. Assess your energy.

If you are being honest with yourself and find that you are feeling off, then ask yourself why that may be. If it's difficult for you to pinpoint what's going on then apply some of the lessons you have already and will find in this book. What is the end result that you would like to happen to help you feel centered in self and continue with your peace of mind? Do not be rude to others because you are having a bad day. If you find that you are, apologize and correct it. Honesty takes courage, but it also takes accountability. Be accountable through your trauma. Own what you are working on, no matter how difficult it may be. Be honest.

4. Own your individuality:

I've noticed that a lot of people think that they have to assimilate to all of what their partners or friends like in order to be friends/in a romantic relationship with them. Not true. You do not have to be a carbon copy of another human being in order to create a bond with them. I've come across people that love heavy metal music and doing deep cleaning in their free time. Neither of those are my cup of tea. However, I am able maintain friendships with them because I do not expect them to conform to what I enjoy doing. On the other hand, I've had people who said they loved drinking soda or eating ribs but as soon as they heard that I am plant-based and am not a fan of soda-started completely changing their lives to mirror mine. For months, they began to assimilate to everything I posted about on social media and anything I said I thought was cool, they came back with me too! From quantum physics to Thai food after previously sharing they did not know what that concept was or that they hated it.

Now, I'm all for growth and changing your mind for people to completely revolutionize their life to experience more excitement, joy, and purpose. I do think there is a fine line to consider with motive. Are you doing this so you can relate to this person, to uncover a sense of intimacy that you crave, to be liked? Or are you genuinely interested in a certain subject or experience for yourself and it aligns with your own core values and path in life? If you say you value, a good beef burger but when meeting someone who you know doesn't like beef burgers, you refrain from eating beef and tell that person you just can't stand the sight of it... well, that's an inconsistency. You are not being authentic in your individuality.

Don't change yourself in spite of wanting to be liked or connect with that person. It wreaks havoc on your self-esteem.

When I was in foster care, I'd try to change myself due to which foster home I was in. I'd try my best to do all of the things my foster parent(s) would suggest I should do, even if it went against what I believed in. I struggled with speaking up for myself, in order to people please and because I did not want to move again. I just wanted to feel stable. I wanted to be liked, loved, even. I wanted these foster parents to ask me to stay with them forever. I wanted a family. So, I tried to keep quiet, do what I was told, and not do or say anything that could jeopardize my ability to live in this home.

Sometimes that meant going to church three times a week, even though I knew I wasn't religious. Or when asked how I felt about being in the home, not speaking up about how I did not feel safe. All I could think about was, *Well, what if it's worse somewhere else? What if I speak up and they don't believe me? What if nothing happens?*

I realize now, that I needed to just be honest with myself and others in order to actually have something change. And I was right, I could have spoken up and nothing could have changed. But that was only option one out of a series of other ways I could have my situation changes and elevated. So, if something didn't get better after speaking my piece with one person, there were so many more to talk to about it and other actions to take.

Own your individuality! Whether you are navigating your LGBTQ+ identity, a comedian on the low, feeling introverted, super extroverted, or processing trauma. Be willing to grow through the process. Be honest about who you are in this current moment. Express yourself and speak up! Don't change yourself to fit into other people's boxes. Assess your motivation for changing who you are, and see how it will benefit you.

5. Show Respect:

Do not call others out of their name. And especially, not those you say you love and care about. Do not degrade or undermine another person's feelings or experiences. If someone has gone through something that they are expressing was hard for them, don't compare your experience to theirs. And vice versa, do not allow others to do it to you. Be mindful not to dismiss another persons' dreams and aspirations. Invalidating others is a form of disrespect.

Respect yourself and respect others by reciprocating the amount of effort and gratitude for each other in the relationship.

If this is a romantic relationship, it can look like:

Your partner always complimenting you and giving you a ride home from school.

You then will accept the compliment by saying, "Thank you." (not, "Oh stop... no I'm really not.")

Then you will also give compliments, and acknowledge your partner's way of expressing love and admiration for you. You may decide to turn on their favorite music when in the car and sing along with them on the rides home.

If this is a friendship, it can look like:

Your friend is always sharing your posts on social media and crediting your information. They are always excited to hear when you are working on a project and are the first to congratulate you when you share a success.

You can thank them for their support by sending a handwritten note to their address. Take out time to schedule facetime calls to check in with them. Or even the next time you see them, give them a sketch you made of her from what she expressed to you during the facetime call.

If this is a foster/ resource parent, it can look like:

Your foster/resource parent has taken you into their home. He is continually encouraging you to join a sports team because you've expressed how much you love basketball. Your foster parent makes sure to give you three delicious, hot meals every single day. Your foster parent makes sure to advocate on your behalf for you to see your siblings, because that's something that is important to you.

You can thank them for being so invested in your well-being verbally or in a note. Let your social worker know how much you enjoy staying in your foster parent's home. Ask your foster parent how you can show your appreciation for their generosity. Ask to play this sport with the foster parent for practice. You can write a song or poem to share with your foster parent at a later date (like their birthday). Regardless of what the title or age may be, we are all human. As humans, we make mistakes.

#IAM SUCCESS QUESTIONS:

+ How can you work harmoniously with your foster/resource parent(s), social worker, and GAL?

_____

_____

_____

+ Make sure to be honest with yourself about your current relationships in your life.

_____

_____

_____

+ Ask yourself "Are they feeding my flame?" Yes or no. And how are they feeding my flame?

_____

_____

_____

CHAPTER EXERCISE

Build Your Success Team

Begin thinking about who you want to include in your success team. Throughout your time in foster care, begin to develop a list of 10-15 trustworthy adults that agree to being in your life after foster care. If that seems overwhelming, start off with just one and go from there.

Establish what their relationship is to you and how you would like for them to support you. The adults are also able to establish how they will know that you are showing appreciation for their time, efforts and support.

Now use this sheet to actually contact them and meet up with them in person. Let them know you would like them to be on your success team.

I, _____have agreed to become a part of _____'s success team. This means that I will_____

_____

_____

_____

And when times get tough or I do not agree with a behavior, I will __

_____

_____

_____

I, _____, am excited to have you on my success team. I will show my appreciation for our relationships by_____

_____ *example: call you and update you on my progress every week/ month/ year

If I become frustrated with something you say or do, I will_____

_____

_____

My current goals are : (You can say this verbally)

_____

_____

_____

I would like to reach them by (give yourself a date)

_____

Please hold me accountable for this by: _____

_____

_____

If I do not reach my goals of _____

_____

_____

_____

Then _____
_____ (list consequence).

Together, we agree to voluntarily come together in a success circle and have a reciprocal nature of relationship so that I can continue to build myself up to become the best me that I can be.

** Adult supporter ** I am grateful that: _____

_____

_____

_____

Young person * I am grateful to have you on my team because:

_____

_____

_____

_____

We sign this agreement to affirm all the above to be true and valid. Our signatures symbolize our commitment to each other's success and as a step closer to furthering the strength of our relationship.

_____(young person signature)

_____(Adult signature)

FosterClub has this sheet, called Permanency Pact to help with establishing lasting relationships with people in the foster care system. It's imperative to know what each person is doing and how to support their work.

I am very much about reciprocal relationships and so I have expanded on that work to create a side where the adults are able to share how they would like to be supported as well. All relationships are a two-way street. Relationships in foster care are no different. This sheet will help you and your supportive adult(s) be clear on their roles and how they'd like to support you.

#FOSTERINGSUCCESS TIP:

When a young person is expressing themselves, do not always feel like you have to agree with what they say. Challenge them and ask them why they think what they think. Allow them to dive deeper into their ideas and maybe come to a different conclusion on their own. This is not to be in a chastising or belittling way, more so an invitation to express clear thoughts, opinions, and ideas.

| CHAPTER SIX

MAINTAINING A CONNECTION TO YOUR CULTURE

"Teach them while they're young, it starts at home with 'who' they are and raise them with the knowledge of self."

- MALCOLM X

"A people without the knowledge of their past history, origin and culture is like a tree without roots."

- MARCUS GARVEY

Have you heard of the Hashtag #ForTheCulture? What does it mean to you?

Some have used excessive marijuana smoking, drinking, and promiscuity to demonize the meaning of #ForTheCulture. So, other than plays on our egos, what does doing something *for the culture* really mean to you?

Throughout my entire life, I've struggled to navigate my identity. Part of that reason is because of the historical beliefs, ideas, and behaviors passed down to me from the older people in my family. I believe that some of these ideas were passed down to them from their parents, and so on.

As mentioned in chapter two, my mother is of Indigenous descent and my biological father is of African and Indigenous descent. At first, I identified with being "blaxican", a slang term for Black and Mexican. Later, I identified with being Afro-Latina and Hispanic, since my family was from a Spanish speaking country, Mexico. At the end of the year 2017, I began to readopt the Spanish pronunciation of my name Angela, changing it from (An-jel-ah) to (On-hel-ah). After nearly two decades of intense research, I've been consistently learning and unlearning who I am and the history of what happened to my people.

Why does my mother's side of my family, and many families of Indigenous descent, call themselves "Hispanic, Latinx, or Mexican"? And why does my father's side of my family call themselves "Black", when black is a color?

Yes, my grandmother is from Mexico, but what was the history of Mexico? How did it come to be? Was there colonization there, just like in America?

Why did my grandmother have pictures of herself living in adobe huts? I only saw pictures of adobe huts in my history books under the chapters about the Aztecs. Did that mean she was Aztec? I thought the Aztecs were extinct. And if she was Aztec, wouldn't that mean... I was Aztec?

I followed that rabbit hole and actually found answers. Yes, I am Aztec. However, Aztec is a colonizing term meaning "people from Aztlan." The true term for my people is Mexica or Tenochca and guess what? We don't speak Spanish. We speak a language called Nahuatl.

This realization actually sent me for a whirlwind that I am, honestly, still processing. When I was younger, I identified the Spanish language as an endearing and comforting language that I aspired to speak fluently one day. My grandmother would call me empowering and loving names in Spanish like, "mi cielito" which means little heaven, "reina" which means queen or "mi amore" meaning my love.

After moving back and forth across the country over ten times with my mother and step-dad (who I didn't know was my step-dad until I was thirteen) I ended up losing my ability to speak Spanish, since my mother would not practice or teach me. As the years went on, I was increasingly frustrated. On top of my own desire to learn, my Spanish speaking peers would not let me forget that I was not a part of their group since I couldn't hold a full conversation in Spanish. Although I attempted to use the internet when I had the chance, my living environment was far too inconsistent, and my surroundings were less than encouraging for me to maintain a habit of educating myself and becoming fluent.

Once I ended up in foster care, this track record didn't improve. My foster parents would become annoyed that I was speaking another language that they could not understand. Needless to say, I was not allowed to speak any form of Spanish or any other language in their homes.

Continuously redefining myself has brought many truths to light regarding those of us of the African Diaspora and of Indigenous descent that are not often talked about. I've traveled within my mind's memory and rely on my ancestor's guidance in order to unlock different levels of understanding as well as mindset and behavioral changes.

It also brought up questions like, why did my grandmother always tell me stories about my great-grandfather being a dark-skinned farmer and medicine man? Why did she have to endure an extremely impoverished lifestyle, forced into a strict Catholic school and beaten by nuns?

Was this just bad luck for hundreds of years down our line? Or is there hundreds of years of racial genocide, colonization, and forced culture at play?

The complexities of my identity are difficult to navigate, even today. I'm not sure why I've been called to have a deeper understanding of my identity. Sometimes, I wish I could just be blind to it all and live a superficial life. Not only because it is a lot to process and understand, but it can be lonely at first. The road to truth, I've found, is far less traveled. Most people would rather just get their information from school or someone they admire then never question it for themselves. They will take information for face value and not search for additional answers on their own. Corporations and other dominating systems are able to capitalize on this and other levels of ignorance.

I encourage you not to be such a person.

| LESSON 23

BLACK PEOPLE WITH THE EXPERIENCE OF FOSTER CARE HAVE MADE IT BEFORE ME

"I'm starting with the man in the mirror"

-MICHAEL JACKSON

"Self-esteem is the key to high performance"

-DAN PEÑA

As mentioned in previous chapters, there are many Black and brown people with the background of foster care who have and currently are navigating their identities. Some of them are in high positions of power, serving honorably.

I encourage you to look them up for yourself! And read some of their stories.

They are secure in themselves, taking calculated risks, loving themselves and others without being overly competitive and secretly jealous.

The year 2020 has been a rough spot for many youth experiencing foster care with the added global pandemic and uprising of Black bodies being publicized yet again across the streets of America. There has been so much revolutionary work done to support the improvement of racial inequalities and the foster care system, and I am definitely excited about it. However, there is still so much more to be done.

The fact that Black and brown people are still being publicly lynched in 2020 is appalling and yet, not surprising. Some are being masked by the media as suicides. And "Mexicans" are being detained and deported from a land that is historically ours by people rationalizing with, "Well, you should have thought about that before becoming illegal."

How ironic that the original immigrants of this country that created this "legal system" after raping, stealing, lying, and cheating whole generations of people of color are now making sure people, "pay for their crimes of being undocumented in this country." I understand the idea of safety and making sure that no other criminals are coming into our country, but what if the criminals are already in here? What if they are the ones who created this whole entire system?

On one hand, I cannot believe all that's going in the world, and on the other hand, I can. And either way, I'm mentally, physically, and spiritually exhausted from it. It feels as though it doesn't matter how much we scream, "STOP KILLING US!" or "We are not aliens. Stop treating us like scum! We are human!" because there is always some-one who yells back "But..." and that's the true reality of our world as it stands.

I invite you all to continue to research "Black history", "Indigenous history" and foster care history on your own so that you can decide what you would like to do to support the improvement and removal of these systems as a young person.

#IAMSUCCESS QUESTIONS:

- ◆ How do you define your culture?

_____

_____

_____

- ◆ What language(s) do you speak?

_____

_____

_____

- ◆ What kind of food did you grow up eating?

_____

_____

_____

- ◆ What are your top 3 favorite meals?

_____

_____

_____

- ◆ Have you ever thought about your history?

_____

_____

_____

- Do you resonate with Black history? Why or why not?

  _____

  _____

  _____

- What cultural identity do you identify with the most?

  _____

  _____

  _____

- Do you know the history of the ethnic group you come from?

  _____

  _____

  _____

- Do you have a desire to know this history? Why or why not?

  _____

  _____

  _____

LESSON 24

YOUR HAIR IS YOUR CROWN

"I am part lioness. No, I will not tame it. No, I will not slick it back unless I want to. Yes it does this on its own. No I will not conform to your idea of "professional" or "beautiful". I am unapologetically me. Deal with it."

-ÁNGELA QUIJADA-BANKS

"Do not remove the kinks from your hair-remove them from your brain."

-MARCUS GARVEY

"Owww! Owwww!" I remember screaming when my mother would do my hair. I'd sit on the floor while we watched TV with my head between her legs as she sat on the couch. Lots of comb slapping on my head as I wished the process would be over already. I'd squirm with each pull on my scalp. It was excruciating! Six years old is my youngest memory of getting slaps on the forehead or whacks to my skull. Why? Because I was moving too much and my hair was *too unmanageable* in the form that it grew out of my head naturally. My mother, I believe did the best she could with the tools she had been given. Her hair, her mother's hair, and her grandmother's hair was fairly straight or wavy, but not coily or curly at all. She did her best with her own personal challenges to understand this new dynamic of what curly hair is truly, and what it needs and wants to grow in optimum health and hydration.

I didn't know it at the time, but this would breed another level of self-hatred toward my hair. And years of confusion as to why it was so dry and even straw-like at some points. Two decades of pure havoc wrecked on my hair. The first few years were other people that I allowed to do my hair, but the rest of the time was all me. I didn't have a clue what I was doing. I just wanted my hair to be and look "pretty", "manageable", "effortless", and accepted.

I had internalized this idea that "straight hair" was what I should have had, but unfortunately due to "bad" genes... I had curly hair instead. Being in Anaheim, California at the time and going to predominantly Caucasian and Mexican centered schools, I often felt "othered". And having all Caucasian teachers, I didn't feel like I had anyone I could relate to. I was half Indigenous and half of African descent. There was virtually no one that looked like me.

Surprisingly, within that same year while I was in second grade my parents, siblings, and I moved to Augusta, Georgia. I was there for probably two months and I saw many African-American students which opened my perspective, and I felt very much at home.

For the first time, I was seeing people who looked like my dad in quantities more than three in one place, and I was greatly comforted by this. It was also a shock for me from being one of the "only" to somewhere where pretty much everyone was of African descent. The mannerisms and dialogue was very different. And I think this is where my whole inner social scientist self began to take note and analyze people and situations more consciously.

In this school, we had drumming classes with a man with locs and a calm demeanor. We had history that taught us in depth about Indigenous people and African culture and language. We wrote in hieroglyphs and painted images from wall carvings of our ancestors on brown paper to symbolize the dried buffalo skin used to immerse ourselves in the teachings. I realized that there was much more to myself than I ever thought.

At some point in my life, I remember watching a documentary by Chris Rock called Good Hair. It was a huge eye opener and I believe it sparked an awareness of what not to do to my hair in the sense of perms and relaxers. It also broke down why many other ethnic groups own businesses and product lines for people of color instead of our own people. I was in middle school when I watched this and began telling other students in my classes, family members, and friends to watch it as well. It's important to know why things happen the way they do and also, most importantly solutions to these problems.

"I think you should put your hair back... it might be a little too much", an organization leader in foster care warned. I was told multiple times during my plight in so called "professionalism" that my hair needed to be slicked back or that it was too much in its natural state. I do not think people realize the damage you contribute to when telling human beings that the way their hair naturally grows out of their scalp is not "professional enough" or "pretty enough".

Now, I'm not condoning "bed head" as professionalism, but if it is curly and has been styled then that is what should be understood as professional. I mean, who came up with this idea that "professional" meant hair straightened or slicked back into a bun or ponytail? Why should your hairstyle indicate your intelligence? Having curly hair, cultural clothing, and intelligence in the field in which they are representing should be professional enough.

On the other hand, family, I suggest that we should focus on supporting those businesses and organizations that welcome us in our natural state. We should stop trying to force our way into businesses that see our curl patterns as an equivalent to our level of intelligence. #SupportBlackOwnedBusinesses

In 2016, I began to dive deeper into my culture and heritage, and recognized that I had developed a very toxic relationship with my hair. One way I began to repair this was by ceasing all negative talk to and about my hair. Yes, I would talk to my hair... oftentimes, in the worst of ways. I'd have one sided arguments with my hair and even plead with it to "act right for once". And what did my hair do? The complete opposite. So, I realized (like in many other areas of my life) there was something that was missing... I had to be honest with myself. I really did not know how to take care of my hair and I did not really know where to start. And that was okay.

Here are some things to get you started in repairing and sustaining your relationship with your beautiful kinky, coily, curly hair.

1. Take the Buoyancy Test to determine your hair's porosity level.
2. Researching products that have mainly natural ingredients
3. Using the correct tools to comb and brush your hair
4. Develop a hair care routine that is at least once or twice a month
5. Begin to identify protective styles for your hair

Today, I do not think there is anything wrong with switching up styles and even straightening your hair. I think it depends more on your internalized perception of your hair. Is it truly a creative expression in your hair's versatility and beauty or is it something more sinister? That is going to take you being honest with yourself and choosing to make some changes to truly embody self-love. You'll need to dismantle the biases you feel or may hold against your own hair and others that look like you.

Our hair is not a bother. It is not "bad hair", and we certainly do not have bad genes and were supposed to have straight hair. Our curly hair is absolutely amazing and deserves to be treated with love, nurturing, and understanding. We must continue to seek understanding of ourselves, our bodies, our hair, our culture, and our history to build our self-esteem.

In many cultures, our hair is recognized as our "antenna", or connection to source energy/ God.

Our hair is our crown and an extension of our nervous system, and thus needs maintaining, nourishing, and protecting.

Our hair is beautiful, manageable, phenomenal, magical, and defies gravity. Our hair is a reflection of our ancestors, a part of our true identity, and the identity of generations to come.

FOSTERING SUCCESS TIP:

Be proactive about supporting your young person through the journey of hair care. If you are a person of a different ethnic background and do not know how to support your young person in their haircare, then learn! It is your responsibility to make sure this young person has the resources they need to support them in their optimal wellbeing. Part of this is with their hair. If you have straight hair, and your young person's hair is curly or kinky, watch free YouTube videos around how to care for curly hair.

Talk with hair care professionals on which products to use, how often they should be washing their hair and moisturizing their scalp. Look up on google different hairstyles that your young person may express she enjoys. Find ways to wrap their hair at night and encourage wrapping their crown during the day. If money is tight and you are unable to afford someone to do your young person's hair, reach out to local organizations and see if they know of a resource to support you. We can't keep giving excuses around different reasons why the support for young people of color's hair, body, and wellbeing is unable to be achieved. If we have made an agreement to be a support or resource in someone's life, then we must step up to the plate. Foster Youth's success in life literally depends on it.

LESSON 25

GOING BACK TO YOUR ROOTS HELPS YOU MOVE FORWARD WITH CONFIDENCE AND CLARITY

"You are strong enough to face it all, even if it doesn't feel l ike it right now."

-UNKNOWN

"Invest in knowing who you are. Know where your lineage comes from, and start there. Don't look back to anything that doesn't serve who you are becoming."

- ÁNGELA QUIJADA-BANKS

"We have too many people going to Africa and they're not coming back... they are stuck in a time warp. That's not sankofa. Does (sankofa) imply that we are supposed to go back to Africa, take everything that happened in ancient Africa and replicate it in the year 2017? Culture is not static. Culture is dynamic! Culture changes. Cultures that are not able to change and adapt, become extinct... (Sankofa) also implies that we go back and we fetch the BEST of our ancient African ways. Not everything. People are romanticizing Africa."

-UNKNOWN

"Just because you were brought up a certain way doesn't mean you have to stay the course. It's okay to break toxic traditions."

-UNKNOWN

Sankofa means, *it is not a crime to go back and fetch what you have lost.*

Many of us have embodied a culture that is simply coping mechanisms that have been passed down from generations. These are behaviors, beliefs, and ideologies used to cope with the effects of the various forms of micro and macro white supremacy. We were never meant to cling on to these concepts and behaviors, we were supposed to transition out of them once, as a people, we were free from enslavement.

However, we never had a healing period to do so. In America, we never had a period of true acknowledgement of what has happened to African and Indigenous people with clear, apologetic, reparational actions. After all, the best form of apology and showing remorse is through changed behavior. Not shifted predatory behavior cousins with the same creature we have identified as destructive and malice. Whenever the history of institutional racism and the current effects of the hundreds of years of oppression is brought up, many people become defensive, obtrusive, and angry. It's a topic that when addressed causes more chaos than recognition of the why, how, and what.

For several centuries, the topic of race and the history of race has been consistently difficult to talk through. In foster care, this conversation is expanded through the realization of that history as well. It will take several generations of proactive healing. It will take "white" people's recognition of the hard pill to swallow, digestion of the truth, and the passing of information to cease the false indoctrinations of who and what people of color are. It will take generations of changed behavior and proactive contribution to communities of color in order to begin to pay homage for the pain, strife, losses, and hard work our ancestors endured to build the United States of America under free forced labor. We have been expected to just pick ourselves back up after the rape, torture, humiliation, dehumanization, murder, removal of our true identities and culture, among so many horrific events and move on.

And yes, I'm sure many of us would love to get over it. However, with the current state of the world harboring it's biases, it's hard to do so. Whether it's police brutality, mass incarceration, or simply low statistics for specifically young people of color successfully aging out of the system, we cannot get away from the history of race and America. In order to be successful, you need strong support systems, tangible known resources, an understanding of fundamental life skills, and a high level of self-confidence.

Having high self-esteem is a form of self-love. And one way to cultivate this innate trait is to build trust within yourself.

It is important to study, practice and to be consistent with uncovering who you are and acquiring a skill you'd like to master. It is important to master something and not just see it as a hobby.

You enjoy doing hair and it comes natural to you? Amazing! You really enjoy teaching others how to sew? Wonderful! You are a math wiz and are determined to crack the code with pi? Phenomenal.

Now that you identified something you enjoy and that comes easily to you, begin to think through ways that you might master it. Talk with a supportive adult on what the steps will look like for you to master it. What kind of schooling is required?

You can be great in anything; however, it may not always be immediate...

We live in a world of instant gratification. We are learning at earlier ages that all we have to do is push a button, click a link, or say a demand and we will get exactly what we are looking for. A five year old could tell their Alexa to play their favorite song and instantly it will be played.

However, many of the most rewarding things in life require delayed gratification. For many concepts, the bigger the success, the longer the delay. Whether that's graduating from high school, writing and publishing a book, training for a sports game, or practicing on an instrument for the end of year orchestra.

What do you want to achieve? How big is your dream? Will it happen overnight? We have to start being okay with actively pursuing a long term goal. The art of being patient has been a virtue that has repaid me 1000x over. Delayed gratification is actually pretty amazing. You work hard for something over a period of time and get to reap a multitude of rewards!

When I graduated high school, I couldn't believe that after 20+ moves since birth, and switching to three different high schools, that I had actually made it. I walked up on the stage, shook my principal's hand, and received my diploma. As I walked back down to my seat, my mind flashed to the millions of obstacles that I had overcome. "Move your tassels from the right side of your cap to the left!", our valedictorian announced, bringing me back to the present moment. I smiled as I moved my tassel.

Graduating any program is going to require habits that affirm your alignment in who you want to become. You will have to add sweat equity and consistency to your work, current lifestyle, and your mindset about the long term will have to shift.

#IAmSuccess Questions:

◆ Defining my culture now that I have been to so many homes. What is my base?

_____

_____

_____

◆ What do you enjoy celebrating?

_____

_____

_____

◆ How do you identify yourself?

_____

_____

_____

◆ What skill comes natural to you?

_____

_____

_____

◆ What do you enjoy doing the most?

_____

_____

_____

◆   What are your thoughts on police brutality and mass incarceration?

_____

_____

_____

◆   How does it make you feel when you watch the news?

_____

_____

_____

LESSON 26

FINDING A HEALTHY COMMUNITY IN YOUR CULTURE

Toxic individualism is a white supremacy concept that has been indoctrinated amongst people of color, specifically those of us of Indigenous and African descent. We come from societies that are more community-based in nature which goes against American culture. American culture teaches us to only look out for one's self and one's self alone. To accomplish or acquire "success" and "wealth" even if you are stepping on someone else's neck.

Historically, we have been separated from our families, spouses and close friends to be sold off for far less than what we were worth. Our worth is not quantifiable. And while being in foster care, finding a healthy community that acknowledges and celebrates our cultures can be difficult, but not impossible. It's important not to quit because it may be difficult and decide to just assimilate instead.

Isolating ourselves in this world, as Black and brown people is not going to liberate our people let alone ourselves. The truth is we need people. We need everyone to do the work. White people, Black people, yellow people, brown people, and pink people! We need all people putting their minds together and developing actionable plans in the fight against institutional racism and false ideas about each other. Historically, no individual or small group of people has ever freed a nation of people.

So, we must work together in order to create lasting impact. Remember, no one expects you to save the world or do everything by yourself. Just start with you. We now have the internet so a simple search may prove to be helpful.

Fill your personal home libraries with authors of all ethnic backgrounds; however, to continue to support the connection to culture and self-esteem, it is imperative to include autobiographies, memoirs, and self-help books by Black and brown authors.

As young people of color, we need to see, hear, and imagine the strength, courage, intelligence, beauty, and brilliance of people that look just like us.

CHAPTER EXERCISE

BUILDING YOUR CULTURAL
CONNECTION THROUGH ART

Visit your nearest history and museums that showcase art and philosophies from Black and brown artists. Take lots of pictures and document in your journal about what you've learned.

Look up cultural events that will help you navigate your cultural identity. Hang out with people that make you feel like you're at "home". Be proactive in trying new ways of being and celebrating your culture. Let your supportive adult know what you are interested in doing. Even if they do not have the same ethnic background, invite them along! They might want to learn too!

Begin going to your local library to familiarize yourself with that environment. There are also free e-books all over the internet. Familiarize yourself with Black authors, your ethnicity of people's autobiographies, and stories that are uplifting and positive. Not just slave narratives.

Maybe even start a Book club!

Take a picture/ or draw something that depicts your historical roots and paste or tape it below:

Be sure to include a title and caption so that you can refer back to it in the years to come!

MY READING GOALS
Year:
Name:

JANUARY	FEBRUARY	MARCH	APRIL	MAY	JUNE

JULY	AUGUST	SEPTEMBER	OCTOBER	NOVEMBER	DECEMBER

FOSTERINGSUCCESS TIP:

- Create opportunities for your young person to learn more about their heritage.
- Provide feedback and affirmation
- Be supportive of their culture, belief system and navigating their identity.
- Be proactive about making sure they know who they are and where they come from
- Look through documentaries of history by people of color sharing their side of the story.
- You can download this sheet on :
  www.blackfostercareyouthhandbook.com

Congratulations!

You have just completed Phase 2 of the Black Foster Youth Handbook. You are half way through this!

How do you feel?

Before you rush to move forward, take some time to pause.

Reflect and record your thoughts and what you've learned in your notebook/journal.

Take a day to think through what you have been reading about and doing in your every day life thus far.

And celebrate!

How will you celebrate this incredible milestone?

You've been doing the work!

You've been showing up and taking steps (even if they seem small) to heal and process where you are to envision where you are going!

Congratulations on completing Phase one: Root and Phase two: Envision,

Let's Move Forward.

"You don't find peace first. If you do, Merry Christmas. More power to you.I found peace on the opposite end of finding myself. And no one really finds themselves without going through trials and tribulations, suffering, accountability. And accountability is suffering. Being accountable everday and doing right for yourself and for the people next to you is miserable. It's hard. " - David Goggins

Phase 3
Ascension

| CHAPTER SEVEN

YOUR EXISTENCE MATTERS

*"I am no longer accepting things I cannot change. I am changing the
things I cannot accept."*

-Angela Davis

"Self-love is not external, it's internal."

-Agyei Tyehimba

Having gone through childhood hell... I mean trauma, I learned
as I began to set into my early twenties that I was always in
my head. I would constantly numb the feelings of my physical
body. In 2016 when I was a sophomore in college, I became extremely
sick. My face was covered in nasty red, pimples and scratch marks
of the ones I would poke at. I would have a difficult time using the
restroom and my period was always 8+ days with super heavy cramps.
My feet became swollen. My body felt heavy.

By February of that year, my health continued to plummet. One day,
I awoke in my dorm room. What time was it? I turned to my left toward

the brown dresser near my bed to check my phone. Ugh. I forgot to put it on the charger. Luckily, I had my iPad in the compartment in the dresser. I double tapped the screen to discover that it was 3:23 A.M! Why was I awake? It was way too early! As I turned over to go back to sleep, I felt a sharp pain in my throat. I attempted to ignore the sharp pain. I tried but it became simply unbearable with each swallow. Within minutes, my cheeks streamed with tears. I rushed to the restroom on the other side of the dorm room, as quiet as I could to not disturb my sleeping roommate. I closed the bathroom door behind me and made my way to the mirror. I felt disgusted. My face looked puffy, I had pimples covering my cheeks and forehead. And now it felt like someone was repetitively stabbing the back of my throat.

I opened my mouth wide and leaned in closer toward the mirror. I tilted my head back so that I could see deeper down my throat to discover my tonsils to be enlarged, covered in white spots. I snapped my lips shut to contemplate what I had just seen. What in the world was going on with my tonsils?! I tried to convince myself that I was okay and just went to lay back down. The pain only grew as I tossed and turned all night long.

Eventually, I got up and decided to take an uber to the hospital. It was six in the morning and I had class at 8am. As I approached the waiting room, I felt my body tense as the pain kept pulsing in rhythm. It's like it was trying to create a beat in there. I began to hope and pray that it was just a sore throat and I would be sent back to class good as new. Tears continued to stream down my face as I suffered in silent agony. Eventually, I was called over to the nurses cubicle as she took my blood pressure and asked me several questions. I could barely respond due to the severity of the pain.

She looked at my tonsils and concluded that I just had a sore throat. I felt frustrated and relieved. I had never felt a sore throat like this before. She told me to gargle with salt water and I would be fine by the end of the day. I did not see a doctor and was sent back to class. Only, I made it back to my room and decided not to go to class. I was a mess. I could barely breath and every few moments I would groan in pain. I still hadn't stopped crying.

Ugh, what was different about the sore throat? Why did it hurt so bad? I rationalized with the fact that I hadn't felt a sore throat in years and maybe my pain tolerance had lowered. Days passed. Weeks turned into months and the suffering did not stop. Every now and then it would subside then come back with a vengeance. I was worried, but kept in the back of my mind that the nurse told me it was normal. My gut told me to consult with a few other health care professionals, just to be sure.

So, after meeting with several nurses and doctors, I decided to make an appointment with an ear, nose and throat specialist. Upon arriving at my appointment, I was notified that I had tonsillitis and my tonsils would have to be removed immediately. They also said I had an abnormal growth in my eye so they would also have to remove my eye. When they mentioned the removal of my eye, I laughed because I thought it was one of those doctor jokes that they tell to try and make you comfortable when it's awkward. However, I was only met with a serious face as to which I immediately thanked the doctors for seeing me, their diagnoses and took a one way ride back to my dorm room.

LESSON 27

LEARNING HOW TO LOVE YOUR BODY

"People with low self-esteem are more likely to sabotage themselves because they don't think they are deserving."

-UNKNOWN

Overtime, I created a very toxic relationship with my body. I didn't mean to. I actually thought I had really great intentions. But after some deep uncovering and healing, I discovered the truth to be that I didn't believe that I was deserving of love. I didn't believe that I was deserving of success. I didn't believe that I was deserving of a life. Most days I felt horrendously ugly and others I just would think about all the times I was abandoned, belittled or betrayed. I thought back to times that my mother left my siblings, my dad and I in the middle of the night to be with another family. Just abruptly disappearing for months at a time. Why did she leave us? Why weren't we good enough? Why wasn't I good enough? Why am I still not good enough for her to fight to be in my life? Why is it so easy for people to just hop up and leave my life with no explanation or thought about how it might affect me? Why don't they care?

One time, she abruptly left in the middle of the night while my siblings and I were asleep. My dad was at work so he came back to discover his wife had left him yet again. I was in high school at the time, and was expected to pick up the pieces she left behind. I remember us all in this hotel room. We were getting ready for school and my dad asked me to continue school but to get a few jobs to help out with everything. It felt like my mother didn't matter how badly I wanted to finish high school and attend my dream university. It didn't matter that I was just a young teenager trying to stay sane in a whirlwind of crazy and take care of my siblings. And why didn't it matter? Why didn't I matter? Why was it always about someone picking up after my mom's reckless decisions?

Ever since I was a young 7 year old kid I remember people saying that I was so mature for my age, that I was an old soul. As I've gotten older, I still get this. the downside to that is it became a part of my identity. I was grandma Angie in an internalized way. I believed that I was supposed to take care of kids and make sure everyone's needs were met even if it meant my own weren't. I didn't know what it was like to be or act quote "my age" or put myself first.

Historically speaking, it is only recently that we as, Black and brown people have had ownership of our bodies again. Add to this the premise of trauma that we may have experienced due to the actions of our loved ones, the picture becomes clearer.

Do not be hard on yourself about what you haven't done. We are in a marathon, not a sprint, with rediscovering and uncovering our brown and Black identities. White supremacy has been in place for centuries and we cannot believe that after a few self-love posts on Instagram, trendy videos on tik-tok, and taking bubble baths every other month that it will repair the damage that has been done. We are talking centuries of subconscious programming. Awareness of the first step.

It is your right to maintain a connection to your culture.

At this time, take a moment to go back to chapter one to review your foster care bill of rights. One of the rights, I wish I would have known was about church. I was not a religious person and grew up with church going as an option. In foster care, if a certain religion is not something you would like to participate in then it is your right to refuse to go. Your care takers are then obligated to discuss other ways to support you.

Although it is the 21st century, we still deal with colorism.

I have dealt with this in the "Mexican" (Indigenous) community as well as the "African" community. People in the African diaspora believe that I have privilege and are unaware of the plight of our ancestors due to the shade of my skin. I've had people tell me,

"You could never understand the full Black experience because you are light skin."

"You act white."

"I wish I was your shade, it's prettier."

"You talk like a white girl."

"You're an oreo."

I've had people purposely exclude me from African diaspora events because I didn't act, speak, or look "Black enough".

My "Mexican" counterparts have been no better. Between not being fluent in Spanish (which is a language we were forced to learn and adopt as our own during colonization and still passed down through the misconception of our history as Indigenous people) and not being light enough with certain determining facial features, people make it a point to tell me I am not a part of my own culture. Over the years, I have asserted my identity and shared with others that this is something that we cannot just ignore. If we do, it will continue to disconnect generations and pass down more confusion. I've led training around navigating your cultural identity and maintaining it through foster care. On YouTube (Consciously Melanated Queen), you will find an episode on specifically, "Are you Mexican or Indigenous w/ Citlalli".

In the Willie (William) Lynch Letter, one of the first documented colorism concepts promoting dark skin versus light skin as a way to separate enslaved Africans, I learned about how this colorism issue began. This ideology was used to help slave masters keep control of the human beings that they owned and to help the slave masters create a strong discord between each person of color based on whether or not they were mainly forced to work in the house with the slave owner's family or out in the field under the hot scorching sun. This was created as subconscious programming so they could focus on the quarrels they had with one another rather than the oppressor. They would not be sure who the fight was against. Was it really only the slave master who, although committed heinous acts toward them or was it also their lighter skinned son who seemingly received slightly better treatment and was mainly told to do house work?

I invite you to learn further about this concept if you have not heard of this.

We can no longer allow these generational racial systems to divide us whether its skin color, hair texture or political, religious beliefs and even dialect.

Diversity of Blackness and other ethnicities should continue to be seen as a positive addition. A "and" conversation not a "but" conversation. Simultaneously, we must release the idea that there isn't enough space for all of us to come together and that we all need to be the same. No, we are all different and that's okay. In fact, it's more than okay! It's amazing and what truly keeps the world interesting.

We must become proactive on decolonizing our Black and brown minds, bodies, and spirits. Ubuntu.

AFFIRMATIONS TO AFFIRM TO YOURSELF DAILY

My body is beautiful and it matters how I treat it.

I am confident in myself and my abilities

I will always stand up for everything I believe in

I respect myself at all times

I choose health

I choose Healing

I choose happiness

I am courageous

I am breaking generational curses

I am deserving of a wonderful life

I love my body

I respect and care for my body

I honor the power within me

I am very strong

My emotions are my power

I make my own choices in life

I am open to the fullness of this life

I am living in abundance

I have the power to manifest all that I desire

I am capable of achieving all that I dream of

I am powerful beyond measure

I used to be afraid of having children. When I was a child, I would tell my parents I wanted to become a boy. I thought maybe they had it easier. I wouldn't have to become a "woman" or deal with a period. I didn't want to have all the pressures I saw women around me having and I didn't want to behave in the ways my mother did. I saw my dad as strong and very smart. I thought to myself, "I want to be strong and smart!" Every other night, I'd toss and turn as I slept, dreaming of myself being a man with facial hair and glasses. I'd wake up confused and wondering if that meant I was supposed to be a man. When I finally got my period, which was a horrible experience that I will not be sharing in this book, I was mortified. What did this mean? Was I now expected to be a woman at twelve years old?

No one really prepared me for that journey or explained to me the importance of this and the connection it has to the moon. I wondered about how all of the women's period cycles would sync up. In my early twenties, I began to research the chemical and long term effects of wearing tampons versus pads. Then what birth control could mean for my body. I wondered why sometimes my period would last for 7 plus days although the doctors told me it was normal. Well, abuse in my household was "normal", people coming in and out of my life were "normal" and eating "chitterlings" (chitlins or shitlins) are all normal things that doesn't mean it is right. So, I dove deeper. I invite you, queens, to dive deeper to understand your womb wellness and see what may be truly going on.

LESSON 28

BLACKNESS IS PROFESSIONAL

At the beginning of 2020, I was invited to an event called Day at the capitol in Sacramento, California. Day at the Capitol is an event where young people who have experienced foster care, go and speak to congressional members in their district in California. I have done a lot of this type of advocacy in Washington, D.C and North Carolina but I had never done it in California before. I was excited to partake in this experience. During this time, I was told that California Youth Connection (CYC) had this "Clothing closet" with cool clothes and "professional attire". I was like "oh okay, that's dope but I came pretty prepared this time around."

So, then eventually I get this black and bright green shirt to wear for a group photo, I realize I have no shoes that match that shirt. I only brought gold shoes, brown shoes and white shoes. Naturally, I decided to go to the clothing closet.

Once there, a queen showed me this beautiful gold colored skirt and the rest of the staff told me that NO ONE wanted it because it's not the traditional, " black, grey, blue" you know the "professional "colors.

And I was like, *hmm... that's interesting. How can I make this work?*

The staff asked if I would consider taking the skirt. I checked the size, and how interesting, it was my exact size. So, I decided to go on a hunt to find things to match it.

I ended up being in the clothing closet for about 30 minutes and found a golden shirt and red jacket... I told the queen I wasn't going to make any commitments, but would try on all the pieces. I made my way to the bathroom that everyone was using as a changing room.

Once in the bathroom and after helping another queen out with her styling, I changed into the possible "professional" outfit to meet with congressional members the next day.

A group of women came in with amazement that I had "THAT SKIRT" on and wondering how I got it to come together the way I did. Moments later, a different staff member I've never seen came in the bathroom and was washing her hands when she glanced at me and said "Wow, that looks so good! But... are you thinking about getting something more professional?"

Instantly my spirit moved and I said, "Well, honestly, I've been doing this work for a while. I've been speaking with legislators, speaking events and meeting with some 'elite' individuals, and I'm tired of the black, white, grey, blue colors of so called professionalism. My hair in its natural state is technically not 'professional' either... Why should I have to conform to that idea of professionalism? My ancestors build this country and therefore I think, within modesty and elegant standards this is just as professional, if not more. And that's not even including the mannerism, information, and expertise I bring to the table."

I don't think she was expecting that, and a part of me wasn't either...

Either way, she smiled and told me she was proud of me, that I was absolutely right and she would like for me to model the outfit to show the rest of the staff and customers in the clothing closet at the hotel.

"Umm... yeah. OKAY! Let's do it!" I said even though I was disheveled. I thought this was just a pass-by conversation and that I was going to change and head to lunch, but I guess not.

So, anyway, she takes my phone to record the moment since this is the technology age now and says, "Alright, let me roll out the red carpet for you..." she leaves then pops her head in "Umm yeah the carpet is already red."

"Okayyy well guess it's meant to be."

Then she called me to come out. I came out strutting and took off my red jacket. The little crowd cheered in shock that I actually was going to where that colorful skirt. Compliments from all corners of the room exploded any doubt that I felt.

I had found my outfit for the next day for sure... and also a confirmation of my cultural awareness and confidence in my knowledge of self to stand my ground!

By the way, I never found those shoes to match the black and green shirt... and honestly, I don't think spiritually it was ever about them. I ended up wearing my white shoes instead.

#IAMSUCCESS QUESTIONS:

- Am I hydrated today? How can I begin to make sure I am hydrated today and every day?

———————————————————————————

———————————————————————————

———————————————————————————

- Have I moved and stretched my body?

———————————————————————————

———————————————————————————

———————————————————————————

- Have I connected with someone I love today?

———————————————————————————

———————————————————————————

———————————————————————————

- Have I eaten at least three meals today?

———————————————————————————

———————————————————————————

———————————————————————————

- What kind of clothes makes me feel the most confident?

———————————————————————————

———————————————————————————

———————————————————————————

- What are my favorite features on my body? Why?

  _____

  _____

  _____

- What are my least favorite features about my body? Why?

  _____

  _____

  _____

- Has there ever been someone who said something negative about my body? Who and what did they say?

  _____

  _____

  _____

- How have I internalized these words?

  _____

  _____

  _____

- Why do I feel the need to hold on to these words as truth?

  _____

  _____

  _____

LESSON 29

EATING PLANT BASED IS NOT JUST A COOL FAD

"Health is a human right, not a privilege to be purchased."

- SHIRLEY CHISHOLM

"Calm your mental. Center your third eye. Feel your heart vibrations."

-UNKNOWN

At the beginning of this chapter, I told you about being diagnosed initially with a sore throat and later finding out it was tonsillitis. After I went back to my dorm room, I began to look up ways to cure myself naturally. I thought to myself, well if my ancestors dealt with far worse things including curing whole nations with herbs and vegetables that grew from the earth without the internet, surely I can figure this out.

Within hours, I came across several soup and vegan meal recipes that promised to help alleviate tonsillitis. After making and eating the first soup recipe which consisted of only herbs and vegetables, almost overnight, I felt 1000x better. My throat began to open up and I could breathe clearly. I was skeptical and decided that I would continue to put these recipes in practice, slowly updating it with my own taste.

Within three months, I was back to normal. My energy levels had returned and my skin was clearing up. I couldn't believe it. Did I just cure myself with eating healthy and following Indigenous recipes?

"What are we ingesting? The body was not designed to be sick." -Dr. Sebi

Dr. Sebi explains in his teachings that mucus is the center of all the body's disease in different forms depending on where it is located in the body. He suggests that if you elevate your body's wellness to at least a 70% alkaline environment you will be free of dis-ease. Help your body to heal itself and prevent any foreign substance from entering your temple. Are you fighting disease or feeding it?

This is an area I am extremely passionate about for many reasons, so I will say, eating healthy is more than just a cool trend. It is something that will prove valuable to you long term. In the future, I do plan on creating a book that cover some basics of what we must know but for now, I suggest looking into Dr. Sebi and Queen Afua's teachings on health and wellbeing.

I created a #MelanatedKingsMonday video on my YouTube channel : ConsciouslyMelanatedQueen about Dr. Sebi, if you'd like to get a start on being better acquainted with who he is.

#IAMSUCCESS QUESTIONS:

◆ Did you know that each of your organs run on a cycle?

_____

_____

_____

◆ What are Dr. Sebi and Queen Afua known for?

_____

_____

_____

◆ Do you prioritize your physical well-being? Why or why not?

_____

_____

_____

◆ How will you begin to prioritize your physical wellbeing?

_____

_____

_____

◆ How is your current diet serving you in the long term?

_____

_____

_____

♦ Do you care about having physical health? Why or why not?

_____

_____

_____

LESSON 30

PHYSICAL CONNECTION WITH SELF IS KEY

"You don't make progress by standing on the sidelines whimpering and complaining. You make progress by implementing ideas."

- SHIRLEY CHISHOLM

Stress can take over our physical bodies. It's important to make the time to check in with our bodies.

How does your body feel right now?

You can do this in many ways. When your body feels tense, you'll know what to do. Our bodies are constantly talking with us. Sometimes, it nags us to pay attention to it and we don't. We neglect our bodies and try to shut it up with medication, alcohol or drugs. I will list a few ways that you can begin to connect with your body deeper below and invite you to try them out and see which ones work for you.

- Take a body scan
- Meditate
- Working out
- Going for runs
- Clearing the lymphatic system with face tapping
- Kemetic Yoga
- Qi Gong
- Breathing exercises

Watch your body posture. It will also tell you a lot about what is happening with your body. Skin lesions and breakouts can also communicate what you are needing in that particular moment. Respect and care for your body. It works tirelessly to keep you alive.

#IAMSUCCESS QUESTIONS:

• Do you pay attention to the signs and signals your body gives you?

_____

_____

_____

• Do you drink alcohol or take drugs/medication to numb the pain instead of addressing the root cause? Why?

_____

_____

_____

• What does your body posture say about you?

_____

_____

_____

• Do you deal with skin issues?If so, what kind?

_____

_____

_____

• What are you currently doing about aches, pains and skin breakouts?

_____

_____

_____

♦ Which way have you connected with your body in the past? What do you want to learn in the future?

_____

_____

_____

♦ How will you begin to connect with your body more?

_____

_____

_____

♦ What is one thing you learned that you can share with a loved one today?

_____

_____

_____

LESSON 31

WATCH WHAT YOU CONSUME

*"Energy is the currency of the universe. When you "pay" attention to something, you buy that experience. So when you allow your consciousness to focus on someone or something that annoys you, you feed it your **energy**, and it reciprocates with the experience of being annoyed."*

-EMILY MAROUTIAN

In this day and age of social media, it's almost impossible to not see the latest meme, celebrity gossip or random horrific bit of news. When I was younger, as a way to cope with everything around me, I'd immerse myself into social media or get lost in a drama filled show. I wanted so badly to escape my reality and for those moments, I did. I would lose countless hours drowning myself in another world. It felt good to worry about someone else's problems rather than my own. I mean, how wild is it that someone around the world is upset because their inanimate object boyfriend who happens to be a car may not want to indulge in sexual intercourse with them. Yeah, you read that right. Some of you may even know what show I am referring to.

On the other end of the spectrum, seeing Black and brown bodies lying on the streets day after day is not conducive to our health either. Scrolling on social media and constantly comparing our bodies, lives, and material possessions will only plummet our self-esteem. We can begin to feel jealous or envious of others. We may feel depressed or even like victims, falling right back into the, "they are so lucky!"

mindset, complaining about how we got the shorter end of the stick. We have to keep a healthy mind in order to be the best versions of ourselves and certainly if we want to create change around the bigger pictures of our world.

We need to be protective of what we allow ourselves to consume mentally, physically, and spiritually. Whether we would like to acknowledge it or not, what we consume affects our state of being. It affects our mental images of wealth, love, health, and success. All consumption is not bad. Mindless overconsumption is when it becomes a problem. The benefits of mindful consumptions can be some of the following; a place to share information, build community, learn more about various topics, engage in incredible conversations with people all over the world, building community, and even educating others.

FEED YOUR SUBCONSCIOUS MIND the nourishment it needs to 100X your chances of your version of success. You must understand that it truly is that deep!

#IAMSUCCESS QUESTIONS:

◆ What and who are you "paying attention to"?

_____

_____

_____

◆ What experience and quality of people are you allowing into your energy? Why?

_____

_____

_____

◆ Are you substituting overconsumption of media for happiness or love?

_____

_____

_____

◆ Is there an emotional whole that you need to heal?

_____

_____

_____

◆ What does mindful consumption look like to you?

_____

_____

_____

◆   What do you feel you need to forgive yourself for?

_____

_____

_____

LESSON 32

TRUE SELF LOVE TAKES WORK

"Don't let this tainted 'self-love' trend have you 50 and alone because you walked away from everything that did not 'serve you' instead of learning conflict resolution."

-NAMI

"Self-Discipline is self-Love"

-WILL SMITH

Allow yourself to make mistakes. Be honest with yourself that you've made the mistake. Then get back up and do better. Do not just wallow in your own self-pity and expect to reach success.

This is one of my favorite quotes from an interview with Will Smith. His words helped me detox from my ego's fragmented view of self-love. This change of view didn't happen over night, but instead slowly with subconscious programming from mainstream media and conversations with people who buy into mainstream media.

Have you ever been super hungry before? Like on a big holiday celebration and you have to wait for the food to be done and for everyone to come together and eat? For me, this was Thanksgiving (in my adult years I refer to this as #GivingThanks because we're not celebrating all of that genocide). My siblings and I would help my nana cook for literally the whole day for about 14-17 people, and we were not allowed to snack or anything! With all that good smelling food and spices around... smh, torture, I know.

One time, when I was about 7 years old, I remember telling myself, *I'm so hungry! I could eat a whole elephant!* In that moment, if someone gave me candy or an entire cake to eat for myself, I would not have even thought about the effects or that I was preparing this bountiful meal already. I would have later acquired a stomach ache and a chain of reactions to my body being exposed to the high amounts of sugar as well as my body attempting to digest a whole overload of JUNK aka DEATH food. And that's just with our bodies. How many of us ignore what we feed our minds?

Let's take a look at your social media. Is your "NEWSFEED" on social media uplifting or empowering you in your life? Are you learning something new from those you are following? Are you stuck in a dead end job, feeling hopeless with no end goal, just YOLO-partying and drinking every single weekend? Are you showing love to your mind, body, and spirit? How about your finances?

These are some the #SelfReflection questions I had to ask and answer MYSELF in order to begin a journey of clarity and understanding of where I came from, where I am and where I was going .

You have to discipline your behavior to be fruitful in what you exemplify. Otherwise you're stuck in survival mode and dependent on other people, situations, and your environment.

So, I ask you today, what are you eating physically, mentally, and spiritually? And how is it benefiting you? Is it benefiting you at all? Remember that the more you allow your mind, body, and spirit to starve from the elements that are in your OWN best interest, the more your mind, body, and spirit are feasting on all the things that do not serve you.

#IAMSUCCESS QUESTIONS:

◆ Do you have enough self-discipline to accomplish your goals?

_____

_____

_____

◆ Are you procrastinating with what you believe you can achieve?

_____

_____

_____

◆ Have you understood how to carry out your life purpose?

_____

_____

_____

◆ Are you making the most of your life?

_____

_____

_____

◆ Do you have a planner? Are you setting goals for yourself with plans and deadlines?

_____

_____

_____

◆ What is your definition of self-love?

_____

_____

_____

◆ What is your definition of self-discipline?

_____

_____

_____

◆ Who/What do you need to start following to see more of what you aspire to do and be? Who do you need to release to move forward?

_____

_____

_____

Loving your Blackness is decolonizing your lineage.

Loving your Blackness is a movement.

Loving your Blackness is revolutionary.

Loving Your Blackness is breaking generational curses.

Loving my Blackness is _____! (fill in the blank)

#FosteringSuccess Tip:

You can support a young person in this process by providing resources such as books, documentaries, movies or looking up events in your area that help young people see others that look like them loving themselves and each other. Find and put pictures around your home that are of people that have done incredible work to help dismantle systems and educate our people. You can even make it a family or neighborhood affair and invite others for a movie night. You can also do this exercise on your own as well and chat with them to see how you both feel.

CHAPTER EXERCISE:

Write a letter to your body. And or/ different parts of your body that you recognize you are not necessarily happy with.

Repeat this process with each part of your body that you feel negative about. Make the time and be sure to honor the commitments you describe and promises to yourself.

Then, while holding your completed letter(s), stand in front of a full length mirror. Notice the thoughts and emotions that come up. You may decide to do this with or without clothes. My most effective results were when I was naked in front of the mirror and having to confront all things I hated about my face and body.

As I looked upon my facial features and full naked body, I felt a sense of disgust and annoyance. Different parts of my body even made me extremely sad due to memories of past sexual assault. All emotions and thoughts are normal and apart of the process. Stick with it, and you will find it easier and easier to this will not be an overnight process to love your body.

Eventually, I learned how to accept my body for how it is and later was able to fall in love with my body as I have today.

Ex. of letter to your body:

Dear _____ (ex. Curly, coily hair)

When I wear you natural, you make me feel _____
_____ because _____

_____. I hope to feel
_____ about you, curly, coily
hair, because that would mean _____
_____. The reason I
currently feel this way about you curly, coily hair, is because _____
_____. My first memory feeling
this way is _____
_____. I was with _____
_____. I apologize for treating you like _____
_____ and will now work on loving you
wholeheartedly by _____. I realize
that no one is coming to do this for me and I must make loving you
a priority in order to stay on my path toward success and leading a
purposeful life unapologetically. Knowing this, I promise I will begin
to _____ because you are a part of
me and you are worth it. I am worth it. I love you.

Signed,

Full Name

CHAPTER EIGHT

PROTECTING YOUR SPIRITUAL CONNECTION

*"I define spirituality as the fundamental relationship with self.
Nothing in life will be in true harmony until you first align with your
soul's mission."*

- ÁNGELA QUIJADA-BANKS

*"And one day, just like that... you'll rediscover your light. You'll
embrace your inner warrior. You'll snatch your power back. And the
whole game will change."*

-UNKNOWN

How is your connection to self? Do you establish boundaries between yourself and people, things or events that can be or are harmful to you? Do you stick up for yourself when someone disrespect you?

Do you stand in your truth even when no one else is on your side?

Do you constantly apologize for just being you ?

Are you willing to make others uncomfortable by asserting your self-respect when they make you uncomfortable or feel unsafe?

LESSON 33

SPIRITUALITY IS YOUR RELATIONSHIP WITH SELF

"Plant seeds of happiness, hope, success and love; it will all come back to you in abundance. This is the law of nature."

-STEVE MARABOLI

RELATIONSHIP GOALS:

To be merged with my higher self, to maintain the highest vibration ((love)) through adversity-being patient and remembering my oneness with my ancestors, this multiverse and connection to God. I am what I am... at all times.

Many people lump spirituality and religion together. And I've learned that it creates confusion about who self even truly is and how to maintain this fundamental relationship.

Spirituality is not crystals, yoga, sage, and incense. Spirituality is not talking in codes, wearing all black, or anything that is outside of you.

Spirituality, or at least the way I define it, is a relationship with yourself and the connection to the power that lies within you. After all, the main person that you will be around your entire life is none other than you. So, why not prioritize this relationship above all else?

Crystals, sage, meditation, and having a personal altar in your home are simply ways in which you express your relationship with yourself. It should not be seen as a force outside of you that has all of the answers and if you don't have a particular stone or herb that you are not connected to the source of all energy or as many call it, infinite intelligence/God.

Affirmations to raise your consciousness:

1. "I Let Go Of ALL attachments and set myself free."
2. "I envision my life in perfect bliss. I love my freedom."
3. "More and more WONDERFUL things are coming to me."

Tip: Repeat these as many times as you'd like. BREATHE deeply, and envision each statement. Feel that emotion of it already happening, smile.

Declare that from today forward you will indulge in HEALTHY LOVE ONLY .

Are you in a healthy and loving relationship with you? Or are you critical and judgmental of your own damn self and when someone tries to come around and love you... you're just looking for a reason to dismiss them?

Our inner work, or lack of, affects every part of our lives...

So it's time to take a look in the mirror... because what you're subconsciously manifesting. It may be YOU in the opposite gender with all of the traits you cannot stand about yourself... well until you truly love yourself, then that won't be the case. Have you done a #selfreflection lately ?

If YES, wonderful! What did you do? If not, how will you start? It's time for you to be honest with YOU. Are you a partner worth being manifested beyond your "good looks"?

LESSON 34

DON'T RUSH THE PROCESS

"You are allowed to be a masterpiece and a work in progress, simultaneously."

-UNKNOWN

Most people have the focus of getting instant gratification as discussed in previous chapters. Sometimes, we want to bypass the steps and order of the process to get an outcome. However, many times that is just not the way life works.

After finding out that I have siblings on my biological father's side of the family when I was thirteen years old, I instantly wanted to fly out and meet everyone. I'm very much a family and community oriented person and so I wanted to meet the people who shared blood with me. Over time, I realized that many of my new-found brothers were much older than me and going through some extreme poverty situations. Also, I was only thirteen and it would not have been a good idea to jump up and travel on my own to people that I honestly did not know although they were blood. Many years passed and over time I was able to speak with some of my siblings via Facebook messenger.

At the beginning of 2020, I ended up moving to San Diego, California with my husband and to my surprise, one of my new-found brother's was just moving to Los Angeles. He called me for the first time on a Wednesday and we were shocked on how similar our conversation style, jokes and even laughter was. On a twist of events, we ended up coordinating a time and place to meet that same weekend since I was planning to visit a friend for her birthday in Los Angeles anyway.

February 2, 2020 at midnight, my husband and I met up with my new-found brother, RJ at a park in a park nearby his current residence. As he walked toward the car, I felt a sense of euphoria and excitement! I couldn't believe it ! It had been over nine years and I finally was seeing one of my siblings on my father's side. When we were face to face, all we could do was laugh and say how wild everything was. My husband, Michael just looked at us both and covered his mouth at the similar gestures and vocal patterns. It was like I had a twin brother that I was meeting for the first time. I was so happy and tears streamed down my face. I could not have predicted the moment to be as blissful as it was. As we drove back to San Diego, around 2am that same night, we just marveled at the amazing evening we had. I was so grateful to have my husband accompany me in such a beautiful experience and knew that this was one of many. My brother, RJ and I still communicate regularly and before COVID-19 interjected itself, had planned a barbecue. In fact, this experience pushed me to reach out to cousins, uncles, and aunts on the other side of my family that I barely know. And it has been a wild, and enlightening journey within itself.

During my long nine-year wait, I would moan and cry about not being able to connect with my family that I did know. And if I'm being honest, at times I still do and it's frustrating. However, in divine timing I was afforded a life-changing event that enhanced my view of family and my own identity within this current human experience. I understand my family to be very complex and different from many other families. This understanding used to bring me a lot of pain and frustration because I just didn't understand why my family was this way. Why wasn't my mom naturally loving and aware of her actions affecting others? Why did I have a step dad and a biological father and both are not as consistent as other fathers are in my life? Why was I so different from the rest of my family? Why was my step dad's family, my mother's side of the family and my biological father's family all segregated? And why do I have so much family and yet feel so alone and disconnected?

Overtime, I realized that my families and how they currently disassociate with each other is part of the effects of generational colonization, enslavement and perceptual beliefs and behaviors that have been continuously passed down. Knowing this, has eased my frustration and alleviated my need to compare my family dysfunction to other family's connectivity. It still is painful because well, I would still like us to come together, however I recognize that this may never be my reality.

It is important to not measure yourself in comparison to others or other seemingly favorable circumstances. You never know what they are dealing with behind closed doors. For all we know, some families could seem incredibly happy and connected and have a world wind of hell beyond the reach of our eyes. And secondly, there are families that truly are connected and recognize that the past is the past. They recognize that all they can do is focus on how to heal from the past and focus their attention on creating a beautiful, prosperous reality now and in the future.

Whether it is family or you individually, we all go through hardships. Some feel simply unbearable and that it will never end. It may feel like a spiral of never ending suffering. I used to feel this way as a child, teenager and young adult. After a while, I felt like that was just the reason for my life to suffer. I told myself that perhaps I deserved it and that God was punishing me for things I had done that maybe I knew nothing about. I allowed myself to just continue in one cycle to the next of pure pain, agony and what felt like- an everlasting hell.

What I know now, is that is not true at all. I as well as no one else is put here to just suffer. It is when we hold this idea as truth that we begin to attract thoughts, people and events to us to affirm this "truth". What I've come to understand is that we must detox our minds, body's and belief systems of this notion that we are bad and deserving of pain, even if it's on a subconscious level. When this idea is held at a subconscious level, we begin to permeate this even when we say that we do not want to suffer. Because there is a gap between what our subconscious programming is vs our conscious awareness, we end up self-sabotaging our experiences.

In other words, we are going up stream and making it difficult for us to live out our life's true purpose, being in a joyful state and releasing the ideas and thoughts that no longer serve us in the new of who we desire to become.

To achieve a state of flow, we must define what we truly desire and alter our subconscious programming to match that which we define as what we want then trust the process. Attempting to rush the process will only cause anxiety, pain, frustration, and even anger. We may even begin to fear what is happening because we do not trust ourselves or the higher power that is beyond our thought process of how something should go.

When I was thirteen years old, I wanted to meet my siblings that before that time had no idea they existed. I had a perfect scenario of how things were supposed to happen and when that perfect scenario did not happen with the specific timing and specific place, I felt pain, agony, and frustration. If I had understood and trusted that everything that we desire happens in our highest good, requires patience or pivoting and is in alignment to my divine assignment, I may not have felt the way I did.

Sometimes, we forget to marvel at the progress and not the perfection. The progress that was made from being thirteen and not knowing much about life, my siblings or having stability in my life to being twenty-three, had been getting to know them for over nine years, understanding holistic stability and meeting one of the five that I know of, is invaluable. However, if I chose to look at it in a different frame of mind, I would say, "it was too late to meet him. If I was supposed to meet him it would have happened a long time ago." or "I didn't grow up with those siblings so what's the point now that I'm in my twenties?" This frame of thinking could have very well sent me a completely different frame of events that never afforded me the opportunity to meet with my amazing brother, RJ.

Once I got the call from him, although it was sudden, I trusted that it was divine timing and my gut allowed me to stand in a park in the middle of the night and actively participate in a blissful experience. It did not happen the way I thought it would. It did not happen when I thought it would and I'm glad it didn't. Truth be told, I was not ready at thirteen to experience discernment, understanding and gratitude opening the doors to my biological side of the family. My emotional intelligence was underdeveloped and I was in a perpetual state of victim mode. So, for all I know after a few hours of conversation, I could have asked to live with him. And beyond my perception, my brother might not have been in the right place either. I was living in Tennessee when I found out he existed so at thirteen, I wouldn't have even been able to cover the transportation expenses. I am now grateful of the timing and feel blessed to know I, now have an older brother (something I always prayed about) that is less than three hours away from me.

Seek to make progress, not perfection, in your personal life journey. Even if it seems like you're just taking a baby step. It's a step in the right direction toward your ultimate goal. Release yourself of the expectations of it coming it perfect every single time. You are not a machine. You are human. And progress beats perfection every single time. A completed project outweighs an incomplete project that is perfect.

And above all, work on yourself continuously while trusting the process. Do not rush the process. Believe that you are on the right path toward your desired outcomes. Trust your gut. Trust your intuition. It is simply a communication alongside reasoning, logic and emotion to support you in this journey. Do not ignore it. If something feels bad, look into why it does and see what you can do to alter your perception to it. Begin to unravel it like an onion. Tears may fall due to certain realization or releasing of a fixed paradigm and that's fine. It's a part of the process. The important thing is that you cry then wipe tears, get back up and see what you can do to move forward on your path toward leading a successful life.

To help you understand your path, you may want to head on over to japrofile.org and take the assessment. The results were astounding when I took this test because many of the career fields were things I was already pursuing and had already done.

You will learn the deeper understanding of what to look for in your career fields, affirm what you enjoy and even questions to ask your employer (or yourself if you are entrepreneurial spirited) to help you make sure it will be a good fit.

LESSON 35

DIFFERENTIATING BETWEEN INTUITION AND SELF-SABOTAGE

Them: Why are you so quiet?

Me: Something about you just isn't resonating with my spirit.

IS IT REALLY YOUR INTUITION... or is it something ELSE? This is another form of imposter syndrome... aka self-sabotage. It will have the same tone as your ancestors, spirit guides/God, but it really isn't.

It's your lower self trying to protect you from an evil that truly doesn't even exist... Or does exist, but it makes you forget that you are way more powerful than that "bad" thing or even a so-called "not as important" task.

Has this ever happened with you?

I've touched on this in previous chapters, and as I said before, I definitely still deal with it but not to the extent as it once was.

What do you do when it comes up?

Sometimes, self-sabotage can leave us lost and confused and even in a dark place.

What do we do when this comes up?

Well, I've learned to feel the emotions with an exit plan. When I was a freshman in college and I began to notice how badly my depression was taking over... I started timing myself to feel however I felt and after the timer went off, it meant I had to let it go. This eventually forced me to think of ways to get over the event or situation and move on.

I allowed myself to feel upset, pissed off, deeply hurt or nothing but only for about 5 mins. In extreme cases, I gave myself thirty minutes and allowed myself to just feel it but not over take me. I observed the thoughts that came up, some of them very dark and depressing but I did not allow myself to attach to them. I felt them, I reviewed them, and I released them.

I asked myself, " What would punching a hole in this wall do for me in the long run?"

Yes, I might feel better at this time, but what is it really accomplishing?

Oftentimes, this alone would bring me to a more positive state as I realized that in the grand scheme of life, my goals and who I am becoming that issue or circumstance was not that deep and I needed to let it go.

What emotion and focus could I replace it with instead?

After this blip in my mood or negative event in my life, what would be the next step?

How was I going to begin to move on from this situation?

#IAMSUCCESS QUESTIONS:

- How can you begin to differentiate the two?

  _____

  _____

  _____

- Why is it important that you recognize self-sabotage when it shows up?

  _____

  _____

  _____

- When you begin to feel "off" what do you do, say or think about?

  _____

  _____

  _____

- It's important to ask yourself, " What am I feeling right now? Why am I feeling this way?"

  _____

  _____

  _____

- Where in your body, are you feeling this?

  _____

  _____

  _____

◆ What are three words that can describe this feeling?

_____

_____

_____

◆ Is there a lesson to be learned from this circumstance? You may have to dig deeper, it may not be surface level. What is the lesson?

_____

_____

_____

◆ What do you need right now to alleviate this feeling?

_____

_____

_____

◆ What small step can I take for mankind... lol... couldn't resist. But no, seriously. What small step, today or this week can you take to meet your needs?

_____

_____

_____

LESSON 36

MAKE #SELFREFLECTION A DAILY HABIT

"Don't be afraid of what's going on in your mind... deal with it and face it head on. Begin to heal it and move forward. Understand that this is a marathon, and not a sprint."

- ÁNGELA QUIJADA-BANKS

I was watching an episode of Divorce court one day with Judge Lynn Toler, one of my favorite people on this planet, by the way, and it really had me thinking around the stigma of "therapy" and how that language in African-American as well as Hispanic households is perceived.

Now, there's so much to this topic and there's only so much space on Instagram, but I'll be diving into it throughout the weeks to come.

People of color have experienced extreme trauma for very long periods of time. I was watching Dr. Joy DeGruy Leary the other night with my husband and she was talking about how not only did we not get reparations but we also didn't ever get a space to "heal" from any of the slavery, lynching, rape of our men, women, and children behind closed doors and in front of our faces, selling of our family members and so on... so much pain and no time allotted to reflect, mourn, grieve, or heal. And she said "Do you think that actually went away?" No. Of course it didn't... we just kept carrying not only the pain, but also the behavior that was created to endure that pain and push on. We couldn't afford to stop. And so we have many challenges mentally that we will barely even "want" to scratch the surface on.

I remember as a small dark brown child, being raised by a Mexican (Indigenous) mother and African-American father, having lots of questions about my own thoughts and actions.

To my surprise, my parents didn't have many answers. When I began to learn about African-American history in 3rd grade, I was mortified and shamed all at once; however, it seemed that the more I began to speak out about these feelings and true events that had taken place-everyone's reaction was to keep me quiet with comments like, "Oh, it happened a long time ago." and "Isn't it time to get over that?"

I remember one time attending a school in Kalama, Washington. It was actually the same school featured in the Twilight series. I was pretty ecstatic about it because I was a Twilight fan, #TeamJacob. (Author's note : If you've been counting than you will see that I attended three high schools from Washington, Tennessee, and graduating in North Carolina.)

My English teacher, we'll call her Ms. C, told us we would be reading a book with more culture to it, or something like that. It ended up being a slave narrative type of book where the text was openly using the "n" word from different character angles. There were times where the enslaved person would refer to himself or herself as the "n" word, and other times were it was used in a derogatory manner by white slave owners and common folk. Needless to say, I was not excited to read this book.

My white classmates, on the other hand, seemed to be excited. Why? Was it because they were going to be able to say the "n" word aloud? Would they dare try to gesture to me with it?

During this time, I was very quiet as I tried to understand the anxiety building up within my body. Between my internal dialogue and attempts to excel in this class I made it a point not to draw too much attention to myself.

As the only brown person in the class and cohort for that matter, I didn't realize that in the moment this book was chosen, none of my good intention would have prepared me for what happened next.

"Ms. Quijada?" my teacher called.

"Yes, Mrs. C?"

"Would you lead us in reading the introduction? Please be sure to speak clearly and loud enough for everyone to hear you."

Startled and frustrated, I opened the book and flipped through the first few pages of the title and copy right info. I came to the page where the top read, "Introduction" as I coached myself in my head to just say it and get it over with.

I struggled a lot trying to understand myself, my identity, the world, and how I fit in it. What was I supposed to be doing with this information?

This created the start of my anxiety that would haunt me for years to come. My mother, at the time, didn't know how to celebrate me or my color. She was taught a different way and resulted in creating my own self-hatred that followed me into adulthood.

As a child, I remember speaking to my friends and asking them about therapy. They replied with, "Therapy? Esta Loca or something." I didn't know how to respond. But it got me thinking harder and I recognized... that not only was I dealing with a lot that just wasn't right internally, but there was the huge stigma on even talking about it.

How do you see yourself?

And how will you begin to #SelfReflect?

LESSON 37

UNAPOLOGETICALLY EVOLVE

"Faith comes by hearing and hearing and hearing."

-LES BROWN

"You teach people how to treat you by what you allow, what you stop and what you reinforce."

-TONI GASKIN

How are YOU treating you? A lot of times, people blame others for how they treat them time and time again. I was definitely one of these people. Untilllll I asked myself, "Okay Ang., but what are you allowing?" I noticed that I was allowing a lot.

1. When people had a whole lot going on that they hadn't processed yet, I volunteered to basically process it for them... well I learned the hard way why you shouldn't enable a person by doing that. And that there is moderation in what/ how you assist.

2. I wasn't confident in myself, and acted surprised when complimented, like what?

Them: Oh wow! You are so beautiful!

Me: Really? You think so?!

Like damn it was the most awkward thing when people complimented me and I just didn't know how to receive the compliment.

3. Not knowing when to walk away.

I gave wayyyyyyyyy... ayyyyyyyy tooooo many chances. I wanted that person to live up to the potential that I clearly IMAGINED, so I allowed them to talk to me a certain way, or have actions toward me that I was strongly against. It was even more difficult to maneuver around this when it was family or even close friends that I felt should KNOW me already and RESPECT me... so why would I have to blatantly show the line and the standard of my expectations?!

Well, because everyone doesn't think or move like you. So, no matter who they are or how tight you think that relationship is... you HAVE TO set boundaries and show them how to treat YOU.

Be unapologetically you and don't allow ANYONE to think it's time for you to dim your light !

People may begin to think you are "acting funny" or switching up on them once you decide to pivot your sights and focus your intentions on success. Do it anyway.

CHAPTER EXERCISE

CONNECTING WITH SELF

Go into a room that's quiet and close your eyes. You can have music or no music. Smile. Now, without moving your lips, say the words " I am safe."

If the world is just a physical plane with no substance, just a bunch of bad things happening with no way out... who just said that?

Was it you?

Was it god?

Who is speaking when your mouth is closed?

How can you hear the voice without it coming from outside of your body?

How do you relax?

What have you tried?

What will you try to connect to yourself further?

Have you heard of the 12 Universal Laws?

What are the 12 Universal Laws?

CHAPTER NINE

LEVEL UP, LEVEL UP, LEVEL UP

"If you're serious about changing your life, you'll find a way. If not, you'll find an excuse."

-JEN SINCERO, *YOU ARE A BADASS*

"Genes do not determine your destiny. They determine your areas of opportunity."

-JAMES CLEAR, *ATOMIC HABITS*

LESSON 38

DON'T JUST HUSTLE, BUILD A LEGACY

"Are you building a legacy or still hustling?"

- ART STEELE

Many of us are taught to just go out and make money. This can be translated in many ways that are not only destructive to our health and well-being but also the health and wellbeing of the relationships we are connected to: romantically, platonically, familial, and otherwise. We have to shift our ways of thinking to a more long-term thought process...

And from a scarcity mentality which is a main focus on finances to abundance which is in alignment to wealth. Chasing money will only take you down a road of "quick ways to get rich" and leave you vulnerable to scammers and " schemes" so that way you can finally catch a break in a "once in a lifetime opportunity".

Look, you don't want to go down that route. It's not pretty or profitable. I purchased a "one in the life time opportunity" scam to try and make a lot of money quick and almost ended up on the streets because I attempted to put my trust into people who were just trying to get a quick buck out of me. Les Brown says, "You don't get in life what you want, you get in life what you are." At that time, I was someone with a scarcity mentality chasing money and reflected that back into my experience. And unfortunately for me, I didn't have anyone to tell me not to do it or why not to do it. So, I blindly gave my money to them and listened to the whole " don't research us because there's a bunch of people that didn't put in the work who are mad and wrote reviews." And so, I did look the companies up and saw the bad reviews and took their word for it. I told myself that I was different, I was smart and a hard worker so I wouldn't end up like those people.

Hey, you can do what you want. You can make your own decisions, but I will say do your research. Not just surface level... in-depth research where you find at least three people that are making six figures with what they are doing. Learn from them and study what they did. Don't fall for the hype.

Don't just be a hustler all about money. That's bad juju fam. Be a wealth seeker. Be a legacy builder in holistic health, finances, and healthy loving relationships.

#IAMSUCCESS QUESTIONS:

• What are the ways that I will begin to build a legacy for not only my life but the lives that will come after mine?

_____

_____

_____

• Will it be financially, health wise or will I change the way I structure and maintain my relationships with people? Perhaps, you'll decide on all three.

_____

_____

_____

• Are you already doing this in your own life?

_____

_____

_____

• What is one way you will begin to build your legacy?

_____

_____

_____

• What are you already doing to build a legacy?

_____

_____

_____

‖ LESSON 39

YOU DO NOT HAVE TO REINVENT THE WHEEL

I used to believe that no one has ever done what I wanted to do and therefore, I had to figure it all out on my own. I would have to find the cure to cancer. I would have to push myself to figure out how to create generational wealth. I would have to figure out by myself, how to own a home. What I have come to learn is there is not much that hasn't already been thought about or done, I just didn't know that it existed. I was not attuned to the frequency in which this information played out. In other words, I was listening to a heavy metal radio station searching for contemporary jazz music. Of course, I wasn't going to find it there! I was looking and tuned in to the wrong station.

Once I heard the quote, "In order to get what you've never had, you must be willing to do what you've never done." I recognized that a shift needed to happen. Clearly, there were things I just did not know. So, I began to focus on How to get myself tuned into the right frequency to begin to uncover what I did not know. One of the things that I noticed that was not making any progress was my finances. One day through a meditation, I was led to a book. And then that book got me to a YouTube channel. And that YouTube channel, led me to this real estate investor named Jay Morrison. And Jay Morrison helped me feel empowered to know that there were people of color making millions of dollars and teach others how to do the same!

Step 1: Establish a goal that you would like to achieve.

Step 2: Establish a deadline for that goal

Step 3:Begin to look at WHO has done what you want to accomplish already. (That will give you clues on the HOW.)

Step 4: Establish with yourself why you want/ need to accomplish this goal.

Step 5: Appoint at least one person to be your accountability partner. (If you are not sure of anyone you want to take this spot, allow it to be social media. Post on social media your goal and your deadline)

Step 6: Identify what the first step is and do it.

Step 7:Make a vow that you will never quit on yourself no matter what!

Establish role models in your circle, even if they are celebrities or don't know who you are. That is not important. What is important is you being able to recognize who your role models are, their characteristics, and their why. What was the first steps they took to accomplish their big goals?

Learn the behaviors of successful people by studying them. Pick up a copy of 7 Habits of Highly effective people by Stephen Covey. This is one of the books that I consistently recommend to my clients in my coaching program and personal life. You have to start somewhere. The more you put it off, the more unhappier you will become and life will pass you by. Start now.

LESSON 40

LOVING BLACKNESS IS ALSO LEADERSHIP

Loving Blackness is also leadership.

Then teaching others how to love themselves as well. We must continue to identify problems that you are connected and committed to solving.

My definition of a leader is not someone who is perfect or has all the answers, but rather one who steps up to the plate to define or better understand the person, people or given situation and how to best alleviate and solve the matter.

A leader is someone who shows accountability, respect, and responsibility. This person is accountable for their faults, mistakes and is able to provide accountability for those that are being led. Respecting oneself is extremely important in leadership because if you don't respect yourself than how will you show others how to?

And how will you effectively respect those that you may or may not care about. Being a responsible individual, is a strong characteristic of a leader because it establishes trust and it creates a strong reliable rapport. A leader is one who assumes the best intent of every and any situation. And if the impact regardless of the intent is negative, owns up to it.

A leader is one who acknowledges a challenge and then is able to find something to learn from it as well as teach others incredibly valuable lessons. A leader is brave when no one else will be and paves the way no matter the cost to create a better tomorrow for others. A great leader leads when necessary and follows when clueless. Someone who perseveres through adversity and may have some down -falls but does not allow them to buckle under pressure. This person will take the experience and grow from it while moving swiftly in the success lane.

Leadership is essential in revolutionizing systems because without it-everyone would remain clueless or stagnant and the issue would remain an issue. With leadership, people can be assembled, ideas can be formed and actionable solutions can be executed. Leadership is an important tool to motivate the unmotivated and uninspired to carry out what needs to be done with balancing empathy, honesty, integrity, and transparency with those being led.

Find the problem you want to solve, then do something about it.

Maybe that's starting a business around it. Maybe it's donating to a worthy cause. Maybe it's volunteering your time at nonprofit or charity events.

#IAMSUCCESS QUESTIONS:

- What is the definition of a leader?

_____

_____

_____

- Am I a leader?

_____

_____

- What is the problem you would like to begin to solve?

_____

_____

_____

- Why is it important that it is solved?

_____

_____

_____

- What can I do to support solving this issue?

_____

_____

_____

- What business already exists that solves that is actively working to solve this problem?

  _____

  _____

  _____

- Who can help me solve this problem?

  _____

  _____

  _____

- What resources am I lack that could be in the way of me being able to solve this problem?

  _____

  _____

  _____

LESSON 41

FAILURE IS NOT AN ENEMY

"It's not over until I win."

\- LES BROWN

A lot of times we have beliefs about failure. We internalize failure as a final concept. And sometimes that is the case but majority of the time it is not. Most of the time, all we have to do is learn the lesson that the "failure" had to teach us in order for us to be better prepared the next time.

I grew up in pockets of extreme poverty. There were seasons within my life where sis was not doing so hot. I was barely a teenager, sleeping in a one-bedroom hotel room on a pallet on the floor with my siblings as we fought over who was going to be covered by a small blanket. We ate microwaved watery white rice, slices of fried bologna, and expired weight loss meals that the local homeless shelter would drop off at the motel. My parents would constantly be arguing and take their rage and discomfort of our reality out on us. I don't blame them for all of the pain and suffering that I had to endure. In fact, I really do not blame anyone because it is not the fault of just one person. The truth is what I endured as a child, teenager and even the lack of support from my family today is all symptoms of systems and incredibly destroying behaviors that have been passed down from my mother's mother and my father's father. It dates back several generations. But I do know one thing, all of that wild and toxic mess ends with me.

I always knew that was not the life I wanted to live. And over the years, once taking responsibility for my life and no longer remaining a victim, many things began to change. Once I realized that I could be in control of my mindset, surroundings and able to dictate the quality of people I had around me, I vowed to myself that I would never be in that type of predicament again. Poverty is not your destination. Illness is not your life sentence. Pain is not in your future. Choosing who, what, why, and where you want to be in this life becomes a matter of the sum of answers to the "How's and when's" of our reality.

Questions like *how* will make sure that I do not behave in the way my mother did when she got triggered about something in her childhood?

How do I begin to hold myself accountable and not be quick to explain away my coping mechanism that I once needed and now need to release in order to elevate my consciousness, wellbeing, and finances?

How do I become a better person each and every day?

How do I begin to build generational wealth within my family?

How do I prove to myself that obtaining $10,000 a day is possible for me?

How will I show others that I love and care for them more often?

How will I make sure that I'm not working so hard that I forget to eat?

And *When* do I want to hit my daily income goal of $10,000 a day?

When do I want to release my limiting beliefs about my own ability to succeed?

When will I begin meal prepping so that I can make sure I have healthy meals ?

When am I going to starting taking financial literacy seriously?

When am I going to look into the process of buying my own home?

Poverty was never meant to be your reality. So, stop using language and behaviors that are telling yourself and other people otherwise.

When I tell people, I will be a multi-millionaire, they look at me like I have three heads. Some people even laugh. Look, if you feel some type of way because my goals are making you uncomfortable, check yourself, sweetheart. It feels like some people just go ahead and hold on to certain marry narratives about themselves.

"Girl, I wish I could, but I'm broke." or "Bruh, I only have about $5 in my bank account."

It's not like you don't end up having the money at some point to put away or save, but it's the habits you have that do not allow you to do so.

Some of you all need to divorce the BS you've been holding on to, because it's really keeping you back. Failure is not a sign for you to stop. It's literally just a bump in the road. You don't see ants turning back when something is in their path. Nope!

They will either start talking to each other and proceed, go around the obstacle, or move it. And that's the way we need to see "failures". If you started a business and it failed, go back and retrace your steps. Regroup, then relaunch. Maybe you had the wrong target market. Maybe you weren't being authentic due to feeling you might not be recognized as professional, not knowing that your target market isn't looking for Mr. Perfect in a blue-collar suit and a politically correct demeanor. Maybe your products were actually trash and running your business to the ground. Maybe your customer service could use less attitude. Maybe you need to throw the whole business away and start over with something new. Lean into that discomfort.

Beyond foster care, life will send you curve balls. The challenges of life do not stop because you turn a certain age, become an adult, or age out of the foster care system. Shit will happen. Crazy circumstances will hit the fan!

LESSON 42

LIFE IS A SUM OF THE BELIEFS AND HABITS WE FIGHT FOR

In past chapters, we covered the importance of dreaming big. Dreaming big is a big piece of success, but it also includes taking time to plan, strategize and create actionable goals.

So, have you considered attending a community college? Perhaps a historically Black university? What about a trade school? Or do you want to jump into entrepreneurship?

Whatever path you are considering, it's important to look through what your options are. Many young people that have the experience of foster care who are interested in going to achieve a secondary education may have the opportunity to go for free. In many states, they have options for young people to have chafee funds, scholarships, and grants to cover their education after high school.

Check with your supportive adult(s) and online to see if you are eligible. Foster Care to Success is a great resource to get started. Open your browser, and type in www.fc2s.com to learn more about your options.

Another great resource that not many people know is that you can take courses from some of the top Ivy league schools across the U.S! Check out the free courses from schools such as Harvard and Yale university.

In life, we have to level up our mentality and seek the resources we need to succeed.

For a long time, I thought I was an introvert, but it turns out I just had underdeveloped social skills. Once, I challenged this limiting belief by putting myself in uncomfortable situations, like speaking in front of hundreds of people, I slowly began to grow these skills and get out of my shell.

In order to reach our big goals, we need to level up our beliefs and behaviors. We also need people to support us. Not just any type of people but those that want us to succeed.

Why goals matter:

-Allows you to dream BIG

-Gives you something to look forward to

-Gives you a sense of motivation

-Opens up the doors of possibilities toward the end result that you want in life

-Gives you a clear sense of what to focus your attention on

-Gives you the opportunity to act wisely toward a desired end result

-Helps you take one step closer to achieving your highest potential

ACHIEVING GOALS :

- helps you believe in your ability to get something done
- helps you measure your progress by taking one step closer to achieving your highest potential
- Build your self-esteem, your ability to trust your words and actions
- Build credibility in what you say once you complete each one

DISTANCE

BY ÁNGELA QUIJADA-BANKS

Believe in the success of Foster Youth, no matter the age.

Breaking statistics and overcoming suppressed rage.

Not the easiest thing to do for many
  but that doesn't mean give up on them... for a few more pennies.

Give foster youth hope.

Don't assume that if they mope
That somehow it's personal..

Think before you speak

Don't poke and pry into a foster youth's life
Then tell all your friends
And not expect them to cry.

Because the next thing you ask,
Foster youth may lie or
Begin acting shy

Don't say they're acting funny
And exchange them for another

And by the way,
Did you think that maybe they should see their brother?
Or sister? NO. Perhaps not.
You told them to get their grades up- and they did not.

So as a punishment..
You dangled their sibling relationship?

Ha. Yeah, Like that helped a lot...
"Mo money, Mo problems"

But if this one acts up, just send them away.
You'll get a new one, like cattle- and oh the incentive?

More money ,new face and new hair
They call it "Therapeutic foster care"

I've seen many horrendous lives
Destroyed beyond my eyes

Too many meds and way too many lies
Do you hear our cries?

People misunderstand us because they choose to
Focus on our reaction to pain.

Then wanna give us the boot.

But how about we start examining the roots.

We are moved from one pot of soil to the other
While through the transition,
Still trying to process why "after 15 years, why can't I connect to my birth mother?!"

Never the less, constant thoughts of
" why us?"
And " why now?"
"Will it ever end?"
That constant need to be "strong" and "bend"..

It's exhausting ...

And we need more support.
Believe in the success of foster youth...

Even with a 25 to 1 as our score on the court.

And foster youth never give up hope.

Even though, we've been given the slippery side of the rope.

We can still find healthier ways to cope.

Like singing and dancing, writing poetry and sports.

And I know, life is rough especially thus far ...

And some people haven't made the weight of the world any lighter

But maybe that special someone, that new family has good intentions. So let's not write them off
After just one or two unfavorable mentions.

Or Maybe it's a shift in your perspective
Even an idea that has yet to be uncovered ...

It could all just be in the distance, waiting to be found
Or maybe it's right there in front of you

Silently waiting around

#FOSTERINGSUCCESS TIP:

Listen through a trauma informed lens AND create space for accountability and correction.

Hold your young person accountable by being understanding about their past but making it clear that is not an excuse for poor behavior.

One way to do this, is to follow up with something a young person has said they will do. Help them grow up to be someone that is upstanding, and honors their commitments.

This not only will help develop a reliable adult in the future, it will also build trust within the young person's own ability to say and do as they say they will.

Self-esteem is the confidence in one's self and holding a young person accountable will help them rise from victim mentality to victor. And for them to know that they have supportive people in their corner when they need assistance.

They must build confidence within themselves to know that they can get something done and to reach out if it will take more than just them.

If a young person needs to study, rehearse, review or commit to something for a period of time, become their accountability partner.

One way to do this is by streak tracking to sustain habits that will pay off in their journey through navigating foster care and beyond.

Brainstorm a list of rewards and allow them to choose what they're reward will be if they remain consistent for (x) days or months. Whatever you both agree to, be sure it is honored.

❚ CHAPTER EXERCISE

HABIT DEVELOPMENT

What Ideas have you married?

_____

_____

_____

Are they causing you joy or grief?

_____

_____

_____

It's easy to fall off on habits that you are not used to having. I still fall off from maintaining proper eating routines.

What are your current habits?

_____

_____

_____

What are some things you would like to start doing that you've been putting off because you don't think you can do it?

_____

_____

_____

Talk with your adult supporter and see how you all can work together to get you another step closer to your goals.

_____

_____

_____

Below is a Habit tracker that I created so that you can print it out at www.blackfostercareyouthhandbook.com and begin using it each and every month! Hang it somewhere you can see and make sure to let your adult supporters know so that they can help you stay accountable to your goals! Maybe they want to join you!

My Habits to Success
The Black Foster Youth Handbook

THIS MONTH OF _____, I PROMISE TO:

	MON	TUE	WED	THU	FRI	SAT	SUN
Habit:	○	○	○	○	○	○	○
Habit:	○	○	○	○	○	○	○
Habit:	○	○	○	○	○	○	○
Habit:	○	○	○	○	○	○	○

WHEN IT GETS TOUGH OR SCARY, I WILL DO IT ANYWAY!

Author's Note: If you are assigning chores to a young person, sit them down and explicitly share why having a sense of responsibility and giving examples of reciprocity in a relationship is important.

This will help the young person understand what is happening and why it is important for them to do this. Young people in foster care are often always told what to do by complete strangers. It's important to take time to explain why, even if you think they should know this already, they may not. How could they know certain basic concepts if no one taught them?

Then begin with one chore for the young person to begin implementing. After a while, you can create a list of chores that a young person can choose (2 or 3) as their responsibility on certain days and at certain times. They may not be consistent at first. Patience and repetition will be needed until they have something that will remind them to do it on their own.

Maybe type up a Responsibilities agreement between you and your young person. In this agreement, you list out the days and times you and the young person has agreed to complete chores. List the rewards for completing these chores and how often. Perhaps make some of the rewards being able to spend time together to get to know each other.

If you become frustrated, speak to your social worker, therapist and other seasoned foster parents that are not quick to remove their young person from their homes.

If you'd like to take it further, begin connecting with other like-minded foster/resource parents in your community and hold weekly or monthly meetings. This can be virtual or at a local coffee shop. Not just to talk about what is not going well with your new young person, but all the exciting new concepts, behaviors and ways that you are looking to support them with. Ask questions on how everyone can begin to support each other's young person. Maybe coordinate times for everyone and your young people to hang out together. It's important to note that many young people in foster care self-isolate as a coping mechanism they learned throughout their lives.

Take time to get your young person out of the house and around other young people that are also on the path toward success. Begin scheduling to go on interactive personal development events to get your young person to think bigger than their current situation. Have space to just hang out and invite others who have young people over to join in the fun.

Congratulations!

You have just completed Phase 3 of the Black Foster Youth Handbook. You are a 3/4 of the way !

How do you feel?

Before you rush to move forward, take some time to pause.

Reflect and record your thoughts and what you've learned in your notebook/journal.

Take a day to think through what you have been reading about and doing in your every day life thus far.

And celebrate!

How will you celebrate this incredible milestone?

You've been doing the work!

Continue to build your success team, maintaining your connection to your culture and strengthen your connection to your physical body !

Congratulations on completing

Phase one: Root

Phase two: Envision

Phase three: Ascension

Let's Move Forward.

"Every day you may make progress. Every step may be fruitful. Yet there will stretch out before you an ever-lengthening, ever-ascending, ever-improving path. You know you will never get to the end of the journey. But this, so far from discouraging, only adds to the joy and glory of the climb."
- Winston Churchill

Phase 4
Liberation

| CHAPTER TEN

YOUR VOICE MATTERS

"Our Lives Begin to End The Day We Become SILENT
about Things that Matter"

-DR. MARTIN LUTHER KING JR.

W e shouldn't be mute about what matters. We shouldn't be silent when signs of injustice come around and flaunts itself in our faces.

We must own our voices and speak out even if we know no one will be clapping in the end. It's the UNPOPULAR opinions that truly change the world. Dr. Martin Luther King Jr's Dream was an unpopular opinion. Foster Care reform, reconstruction and revolution is an unpopular opinion. Black and brown lives still need to be spoken up for. We need more people speaking up about the issues that matter. And educating people about the correlating history of institutional racism and the different ways it rears its ugly head.

Take the history of melanated people and police brutality. What people fail to realize is that #BlackLivesMatter is not saying because you're a "white" person and a cop that it's a problem. Nor are they saying that no one else experiences hardships but Black people. No, if you were an African-American cop and killed someone... actually multiple people of the same race, gender, hair color, or even height for no moral reason, it would still be wrong. There would be riots and people demanding justice for that as well. The #BlackLivesMatter movement is explaining a truth that should not be a form of debate. Yes, all lives matter. However, we are specifically talking about the Black and brown ones right now. All lives are not being disproportionately targeted through mass incarceration and police brutality. All lives have not had the centuries of colonization leading up to the continuous ways white supremacy shows through today. So, if you hear someone saying that Black lives matter... Why argue? Unless they don't matter to you...

What will you speak up for ?

LESSON 43
YOUR STORY IS NOTHING TO BE ASHAMED OF

"Your story is what you have, what you will always have. It is something to own."

MICHELLE OBAMA, *BECOMING*

Decide today that you will not be ashamed of your story! It may not be one you're proud of, and trust me, you're not alone. But what about the fact that whatever it was, YOU ARE HERE TODAY! You are living, breathing, you have a roof over your head each night and you have people who care about you. And that... is something to be proud of yourself for.

Change the way you see yourself in your story. Maybe your childhood was hard and your parents didn't validate your accomplishments or maybe you didn't feel heard when you had something to say. Guess what? You're not there anymore! And you definitely don't need your parents to validate you... truth is, you never did.

Reprogram your mind to find the "why is this happening FOR me" answer to each and every situation vs. "why is this happening TO me?"

What is this situation trying to teach me? And has this happened multiple times?

If it has, what is the lesson that I have yet to have grasped?

YOU are the author of your own book, the CEO of your own life, the painter of your own masterpiece, and you decide how you see yourself today and every day. You decide how your life will pan out. You decide when you will own who you are unapologetically and shine your brightest! So why not start today? Why not have started yesterday?

Your story is yours, and it matters.

Write it, sing it, paint it, live it, and own it!

LESSON 44

MIND YOUR OWN BUSINESS BEFORE SPEAKING ON OTHERS

"They need to mind their own business! Why are they all up in my kool-aid for?!" I would say. Looking back, I find this funny because well, one... they didn't have a business to mind and neither did I.

If we really think about it, if you are someone who wants to be successful in your career or business... you actually want people to be all up in your business. It wouldn't be of your best interest if they are not interested in what you've got going on in order to support and share what your business is up to.

In foster care, adults would make assumptions about me before even meeting me whether that was – because I was in foster care or because I was a young black teenage girl. They automatically assumed I was promiscuous and that I was hungry for sex, which was not the case at all. Or that I didn't value family. Some of these adults vocalized this to me and others showed me their biases with their actions. It really hurt me to know that this is what they thought of me, but the truth is that what they thought of me was still none of my business. I could have very well internalized this idea of me and said, "well, since they think this of me anyway...I mind as well act just like what they are saying since I'm damned if I do and damned if I don't", but at what cost? My future? My dignity? My values?

At this point in life, I let other people's opinions of me roll off of me and just focus on my own business. I focus on how I want other to talk about me and "my business". I recognize that most people will not stop talking about you, however, you can be the best you can be and influence the conversation.

Otherwise, how would your business be profitable if no one is talking about your business?

It wouldn't be. So, we have to get more focused on how we want others to speak about our "business" when we are not in the room? What are some of the words we would want them to say about us?

How can we be clearer about who we are and what we stand for?

We do not need to be so focused on the negativity that people spew about us. It can be a huge distraction on the purpose we are here to realize.

A lot of times, the people who have a problem with gossiping about you and others, don't have much going on themselves. If they did, they would not be utilizing their free time to talk about others.

Protect your peace of mind and focus on who you are becoming. Trust me, I know this is easier said than done but the more energy you give to others shenanigans, the less you will have to create the reality you desire.

It's important to keep an open mind to the fact that there may be some truth to what is being said. And if there is, how can we take it in and learn from it?

One time, my dad told me I had a problem with apologizing when I did something to hurt others. He would tell my siblings that I was someone who always felt like I did no wrong even if I was shown the facts to my face. At first, I would be extremely defensive about it. Over time, I realized he was right and began checking myself.

Take responsibility for your faults and be proactive in growing into better versions of you. Mind your own business before pointing out the gaps in someone else's.

Now, excuse me while I go mind my own business and finish writing this book.

#IAMSUCCESS QUESTIONS:

Instead of explaining something off or trying to turn the situation back around on another person, it may serve better value to acknowledge what is being said and see how we can face the reality, without covering it up of the words or action we have used. Do not disown it or change the subject. Do not flip the script. Before you respond, listen and accept what is being said.

+ When someone tells you that you've done something to hurt their feelings or betray their trust, how do you react?

_____

_____

_____

+ Do you compassionately try to understand why you said or did what was done?

_____

_____

_____

+ Do you recognize the person or people involved and convey a clear knowing and understanding of the damage done?

_____

_____

_____

♦   Do you sincerely apologize and try to find ways on how you can reconcile with the person or people who were affected?

_____

_____

_____

♦   Do you commit to changed behavior after going through the previous questions?

_____

_____

_____

LESSON 45

I CAN SAY NO TO AN "OPPORTUNITY"

I know that it may seem like common sense, but for a while I didn't know I could actually say "no" to an opportunity.

There are many things that my husband has taught me and shown me. And so here are three of them:

1. Patience:

I always thought I knew how to be patient until I got into this relationship with someone who is in the military. I had a completely different negative connotation about the Marine Corps and I could have never indulged in this opportunity to even have a conversation that sparked this amazing union between Michael. We're exactly two years into our relationship and July 24th marks the day that I officially realized that our friendship was much greater than what I thought that I wanted at the time.

We thought that barriers like distance and different time zones and horrible connection with phone service would be too detrimental to our relationship to even begin one. Although we never discussed these periods before we actually started officially courting, we did talk to our friends about them and at first tried to use it as a way to brush off our connection. Little did we know that we were both contemplating the same barriers and ultimately, they were nothing compared to what we shared and what we planned to share together. Patience has shown up in every aspect of our lives while being together and apart. Each time I knew exactly what was happening and the lesson that was being taught but it didn't make it any easier.

One full year after agreeing to be courted, I look back at my past self and see so much growth in my patience for people, situations, and the future that we are building together. Most of our initial time in our relationship was apart. The first six months of our relationship we didn't see each other because he was in Japan and I was in the states. Through our love, greater vision, and LOTS AND LOTS OF PATIENCE, we made it through. Same with each time apart that has followed since. I used to say that I don't know how people do long distance relationships and that I could never do one but the truth is: once I found my special person, a man that is an understanding, compassionate and natural leader such as myself-the rules of the game changed.

2. Standing up for myself:

I never really noticed that I had a problem with verbally standing up for myself. I usually would say things politely and repeatedly explain myself to people that would try to pursue me romantically even when I was single. I have always thought about the other side of my feelings like how would me abruptly telling someone to F off affect them in the long run? However, Mike has taught me to stop putting all my effort into what's happening with the other person and look at how the other person's actions are affecting me.

From his own way of communicating his boundaries, he has inadvertently helped me see what I needed to work on and I had a lot of work to do. So each time someone would disrespect me or a guy would try to holler at me I sought that as an opportunity to then show myself as well as Mike what I've learned. It's been difficult. I can say that I am now more aware of where the guilt of standing up for myself comes from. I was taught as a young child to be nice to people even if those people weren't nice to me. As an adult, realizing that I have the power to change the way I deal with those disruptions to my peace has been liberating. I no longer feel like I have to say yes to anything. When organizations or corporations would ask for me to speak or be featured on something I'd jump on it even if it went against what I wanted to share. I would disregard how I felt and told myself, "oh people need to hear about my trauma in order to get through their situation." Although, that may be true, that doesn't mean it had to be at the expense of my own well-being. It didn't even have to be *me* all the time. And especially if these same organizations are really just using my story in order to gain profit(millions) for themselves and then leave me high and dry to figure out what to do with the reopened wounds. To be barely compensated, with a $25 dollar gift card made me internalize that was the worth of my story and time. No way, my stories are valuable. I am valuable. And I am learning how to reclaim and communicate my self-worth in my own graceful way...

3. Challenging my past trauma:

I think a lot of us deal with some really rough trauma. There have been things that would come up because of my experience as a woman, an Afro-Indigenous (Mexican) woman, extreme poverty in some areas and all the intersections in between.

First off, I do not think people are used to seeing a multidimensional, multicultural woman consistently doing well. It's not as popular as it will be in the future. And for now, I am going to continue to speak to others and empower others like me to motivate and spike that shift. It has been rewarding for me to speak life into my king and to have that reciprocated. And life-changing is an understatement of how I now see my past trauma. Michael has supported me in seeing my trauma as not only stepping stones but no longer as an excuse. We will both recognize when we are experiencing something from the past and hold each other accountable for not only acknowledging the behavior but also healing and correcting it. I believe being informed about trauma affects one another is powerful and helpful but without accountability and correction, it can create a toxic cycle of reliving the hard parts of our pasts.

This is not an easy process at all and I don't want to make it seem like this is a cakewalk because it's not even close. But this is exactly what we signed up for and is exactly what I will continue to do if that means breaking generational curses! If that means we are re-creating and redefining what it means to be in a loving and healthy relationship for our future generations and family that currently surrounds us-then this fight is well worth it and beyond both of us. Michael empowers me to be my best self every single day that I wake up and inspires me to never quit anything because it may seem too hard. I've been intentional about growing my own self determination and self-discipline to continue our path because my "why I'm doing it" is stronger than any jurisdiction of my past.

Foster care is not your identity. It is where you are right now. Not where you will always be. Be mindful of who you tell your story to and in the ways you tell your story. Not everyone is deserving of knowing what you've been through. Know your value and triple it.

Tokenizing is a real thing out here in the advocacy world and can wreak havoc on your mental health. Your story is more than foster care.

Your identity is more than foster care. There is a world of limitless possibilities! Speak up and speak out about the issues that matter to you but do not do it at the expense of your own mental well-being. Protect your ideas (legal action), your mind, body, spirit and energy!

Focus on prioritizing your own healing. The world will still need saving tomorrow.

A LIFE IN SILENCE

BY ÁNGELA QUIJADA-BANKS

Ever wonder why that kid is so quiet?

Maybe they even have a different kind of diet...

So quiet that it makes you think they have a secret... But even if

they did, what makes you think you could keep it?

An individual that creates mystery about themselves... Are they

really this silent? Or is it a mask that disguises their defiance?

The other kids... they flock together in an ignorant alliance.

They pick and they tease...

Even act like introversion is some sort of a disease...

But little did you know that same kid that you kicked in the knees

and ignored even when they scream please... don't

Are dealing with far more worse things

and coming to school is the only thing that keeps them at ease...

Even if it's walking to school at 3 in the morning in the rain...

And you say you've experienced pain?

A pain so deep, even if you soaked in love... it would be a lifetime

before it would seep

When the air is so cold & you have no heat...

and you realize all there is to to do is freeze?

Or not having anyone that wants to cook you mac and cheese?

Just the simplest things we often take for granted.

That kid did not have their parents to cook for them yet you moan and groan about the cheese not being on the grits...

That kid doesn't have the new Jordan's that make you throw fits...

Instead $4 flip flops for the rest of the year and a grilled cheese sandwich can make them cheer

That kid is walking two miles to school

From somewhere that doesn't even have an address

And you're worried about who you can Impress and how better you can dress

And yeah I know you can careless...

About what that kid even went through to have those clothes you snicker to others about...

You get tucked in every night with a kiss on the cheek

That kid sees their parents MAYBE once a week

Every night their head is filled with negative thoughts of reality and they can never sleep...

And yet they don't weep ..because they know that one day it'll end.

A life in silence is never by choice.

I mean sometimes you just feel like you don't have a voice.

You watch as everything around you just happens and you wonder to yourself

"When will this crap end?"

But It's all for a reason.

That kid knows that God will prevail, no matter the season.

You must be patient and remain focused.

The temptation may be great and you'll feel like you're broken.

But don't give up, stay positive because I have a token.

A token of not only forgiveness but resilience.

No matter the cause

No matter the struggle

If this sounds like you, don't be alarmed, don't give up hope...

There's always success even if you got the slippery side of the rope.

If you're feeling down and think there's no one around...

There always is.

Believe in yourself because you matter.

Close your eyes and picture something greater...

Just think who and where you could be ten years later

CHAPTER EXERCISE

SHARE YOUR STORY

"Get in good trouble, necessary trouble."

CONGRESSMAN JOHN LEWIS

I met Congressman John Lewis in 2017 with a leading organization in child welfare. He was one of the leading social activists for the well-known sit in movement. He has been an incredible African-American leader and among those who laid their entire lives on the line to create the necessary changes for people of color to gain access to the basic necessities of life, have a voice and be treated like human beings.

I encourage you to watch his film, Good Trouble.

Connect with other young people currently experiencing or have experienced foster care through Facebook groups and in your local organizations. A simple google search may be all you need to help you find your next friend!

Look for opportunities to speak out about the causes that matter most to you.

Think about how you would like to share your story. There are many different types of advocacy and many ways you can get involved in your community. Figure out which ones work best for you.

It is also important to keep in mind that you and your story is valuable. Just because you believe it will help others to share it, doesn't mean you need to do it at the expense of your own mental, physical or emotional health.

Think to yourself, is the return of the investment for me sharing your story worth it?

If you believe it is, then move forward with it. Be cautious, and know your worth.

#FOSTERINGSUCCESS TIP:

It is imperative that you look out for your young person's story. Their story is theirs to tell, no one else's. I've learned that many times adult supporter's may mean well when sharing how a young person is progressing or expressing how they feel about something a young person is struggling with. It is imperative that you be cautious and aware of WHAT you are sharing about your young person and WHO you are sharing the information with. How would your young person feel about that particular information being said to others? How would you feel if someone told a complete stranger about something you were struggling with? And then you meet that stranger and they being to act weird around you or make snarky comments.

Be especially aware of people "othering" your young person.

Othering could be saying things like, "You are not a part of this family, but you can jump in the photo." Although, that may be technically true, the statement can be more harmful to the young person's self-esteem and further alienate them.

Every young person is different. So, the overarching message here is protect your young person's story and be mindful about what you are sharing about them without their permission.

CHAPTER ELEVEN

CULTIVATING AND SUSTAINING INNER PEACE

Worry is a misuse of your imagination.
Don't allow your worrying to be your crutch. Don't allow the "What if"s to spiral into self-doubt. Don't allow your vision to be stifled by your inability to see who and where you are in life! Worry will have you walking slowly toward your goals instead of chasing your dreams . Worry will make you fall on your face before you even really have been able to take a step, self-sabotaging by tying your shoelaces together then driving your nose in the dirt and convincing you to stay there because "what if when you get up it's worse?"

No no no, honey! You are utilizing your wonderful mind's eye all wrong! Worrying about a "what if " and catastrophizing each and every situation is not just a misuse, but a whole waste of your imagination!

Instead think of all the reasons why you should. Now what if... you don't have to get your nose in the dirt in the first place. Matter of a fact, do the work to put your heart, mind, and soul at ease. Study how to tie your shoes correctly, lace them up and run after all you desire! It doesn't have to be all bad.

Get excited about where you're going and what you decide to get into! Remember the reason you're doing this! Your why has to be bigger than the "naysayers"... even if the naysayer is YOU!

Change the way you use your imagination. Your future self is waiting on you .

As an adult, I focus on what I truly want to do with the inner peace that I don't have to rush to do it all right now! I challenge my own story that I allowed myself to internalize and paralyze my own ability to live my dreams and root in purpose.

Yes, and it's hard to accept this sometimes. I think we create this idea of what family should be like and when they don't fit into that frame-we somehow begin to internalize inadequacy. This is a big piece of healing, recognizing that we do not have to be a part of this fabricated misconception and release the stigma around what a family should be, just holding them closer no matter how toxic because we would love for them to be in our lives... but at what cost ?

LESSON 46

KNOW YOUR WORTH

"Girls you know you betta watch out... some guys... some guys are only about..that thang that thang that thannnggg Guys you know you betta watch out... some girls some girls are only about... that thang that thang thanngggggg..."

- LAURYN HILL

"Stress is the trash of modern day life and we all generate it, but if you don't dispose of it properly, it will pile up and overtake your life."

-TERRI GUILLEMENTS

Gather Your Substance. Have more value than just THAT THANG. There is so much more to the human experience than just THAT THANG... EDUCATE AND ELEVATE YA SELF.

You have one life in this human experience, make it count.

Don't just follow your ego as if life is simply physical. Life is also metaphysical, spiritual, emotional, psychological, and unlimited with various realities. Explore the possibilities of your life! Not tomorrow, not next week, not next month, not next year, but today... RIGHT NOW. That is the only unit of time that we have for certain, right now... in this very moment.

Stop playing with your life! Last year flew by and the next year is on its way. It's time to stop surviving to the next pay period or waiting on the weekend to let your hair down and smile. It's time to start dreaming big and planning to THRIVE and live your life to the fullest. No, it is not too late.

No excuses. You've put it off for long enough.

Start making your days count instead of just counting your days. In my personal experience, I know what it's like to have "family" and friends drop off from your life, leaving you in a constant state of grief. It hurts, especially if they're still alive.

My mother has consistently disappeared from the face of the earth, leaving me confused. Why did I have to have someone like her to birth me into this world? I've had colleagues that say BLACK LIVES MATTER or Black Foster Youth Matter, block me once I began sharing that I was writing this book. Perhaps, they didn't believe me when I said I was going to write it? I've tried to collaborate with other Black and brown people who hold degrees doing similar work and instead got left on read. Maybe they didn't like the fact that someone was doing something they wanted to do. Either way, as covered in previous chapters... that's none of my business. I'd love nothing more than to come together and create incredible solutions to the issues that our communities face. I've learned that some people just have a crabs in the barrel mentality due to years of fighting for the spotlight. Maybe they feel like there can only be one?

The truth is that is a scarcity mentality and thinking that way won't get you far. Whatever their thoughts or motives are, it still hurts. Whether it's family not trying to support what you're doing or friends pretending like your successes are invisible, it can all feel extremely painful and can knock you off track.

Something that has helped me is knowing what the stages of grief are. When times are rough and someone passes or someone does something to change the paradigm of what I believed things to be or who I thought they were... I revisit the stages of grief to assess where I am in these stages.

It's important to understand that it is all temporary and you will feel better again. Do not waste so much of your time trying to get people to be on your side, on your success team or to support you. Instead, I suggest beginning to reach out to complete strangers. You'd be surprised who has the power to bless you but just has no idea you exist. Remember, there are over a billion people on this planet. Never feel confined to the little circle you have around you.

You are powerful beyond what you ever thought possible.

▌LESSON 47

WE NEED TO RELAX MORE

How often are we stressed?

Probably more often than we would like to admit, right?

The truth is, it's more natural for most of us to stress than to relax. And taking time to relax can have an overflow of rewards because it allows us to unplug and recharge. But with the hustle and bustle of the world and all of its demands... it can be increasingly hard to do so.

Between work, school, and all we desire to accomplish outside of that... when does relaxing fit in?!

In the beginning stages of my purpose and productivity coaching program, I surveyed 100 women of color and asked them a series of questions. One question was, "How do you like to relax?" I found that many queens were stifled by this question. They shared that this was actually a hard question to answer. Either they did not know what relaxation really meant or they did not know how to do it. Others felt as though they just didn't have enough time to relax. This was ground breaking news to me because it was something I knew; however, to see concrete evidence and hear it from others was confirmation that we really had some mindset shifts to make.

So, how do we begin to "fit in time to relax?"

Well, it fits in when we begin to prioritize it. Our mental, physical, and spiritual health aren't going to be maintained on their own. We have to be proactive and prioritize it as a necessity. The answer lies within your belief. So, The question becomes:

Do you believe relaxation is being lazy? Why? Where did you get that ideology from?

When I was a child, I'd be called lazy and in the way when I'd take a seat and watch television. When I came home from school, I was told to help with something and that I shouldn't be as tired as I usually was because I didn't have a job. I was told to stop being lazy and find something to do.

Now, as an adult I'd run myself rampant whenever I'd have a free moment to myself because I just had to be doing something or rather I just couldn't be seen as lazy... even if it was just to myself.

Start relaxing without the guilt that you should be doing something to stay busy. Do you believe your health is a priority? Or running yourself ragged with stress? What do your actions say?

I've found that the more you decide to prioritize your health-the smoother the rest of life seems to be. With less stress = less mess... of a life.

9 NEW WAYS TO CONNECT TO SELF:

1. Ask your closest friends and family what your strengths are. This will give you insight into things you may want to improve and give you a major confidence boost.

   Ask them what they see you doing in this life-it may be rewarding and even bring some humor into this journey...

2. Continue to Self-Reflect and ask yourself questions periodically to track your progress and assess your accountability.

3. Determine what is a problem that you want to solve.

4. Purpose has little to do with passion and more to do with how you use your life to serve others. In many cases, however, people experience both! (seasonal purpose -micro and macro)

5. Unblock your Chakras/Arits/Energy Centers in our bodies
6. Have a growth mindset not a fixed mindset. You don't know it all
7. Take time for just you-go outside, take a relaxing bath, spend time in nature. Educate yourself on what others do to connect with self and try it for yourself
8. Just Breathe. Try meditation/kemetic yoga. Look back into your past and see what stands out to you-are they good things? Bad things? What were the lessons? What happened for you to understand or speak up about a specific issue? Is there a specific demographic of people that may be struggling to find answers on what you have achieved? Are you currently happy?
9. Define what joy and success means to you and how do you see yourself in the future?

Again, recognize you don't have to do it alone.

What will you prioritize doing to take care of your health?

#IAMSUCCESS QUESTIONS:

♦ What kind of conversations are you having?

_____

_____

_____

♦ Are they mostly enjoyable and life giving or negative and gossiping?

_____

_____

_____

♦ If you find yourself in a verbal altercation, challenge yourself to ask questions like : "Why did they do that?" and " Do I need to respond to this person?" "How can I respond in a way that will deescalate the situation while getting my point across?" "What will help solve this issue- silence, a response, giving space?"

_____

_____

_____

♦ Before engaging in any activity (bad or good) ask yourself, what is my goal? What am I trying to accomplish with participating in this behavior/ event?

_____

_____

_____

- What are the possible consequences to this word choice/ action?

  _____

  _____

  _____

- Is it really worth it right now and in the long run?

  _____

  _____

  _____

- Will this action bring me forward or drag me toward the past?

  _____

  _____

  _____

LESSON 48

INCREASING YOUR FINANCIAL EDUCATION

"Money...Money management, understanding money, making good financial decisions, is pretty much psychological. It doesn't come down to how much money you have or how much you know. Some people think, "well I don't have any money because I don't understand money. I can't make money because I just don't have any money to invest." There are people who think they can't afford to invest in the stock market, but really the stock market has plenty of stocks that cost $1, $10, $15. Those same people, in many cases, will go to NIKE and they'll buy some $150 shoes that could have been used to buy a share of stock."

- DR. BOYCE WATKINS

"You wanna know what's more important than throwin' away money at a strip club? Credit. You ever wonder why Jewish people own all the property in America? This how they did it."

-JAY Z

"There is gold everywhere. Most people are not trained to see it."

-ROBERT KIYOSAKI ,*RICH DAD POOR DAD*

BASICS OF FINANCIAL LITERACY

Being poor minded pushes you in a state of scarcity which awakens the ego.

I've been reading Rich Dad, Poor Dad, a book by Robert Kiyosaki that I HIGHLY recommend and will be a part of my personal library! Absolutely love this book with very detailed story telling infused with financial literacy. In his book, I've learned very valuable ways of thinking about money that I otherwise may not have stumbled upon. Robert Kiyosaki's information is more geared toward teaching the fundamentals between an asset and a liability. As well as, how the reason most people continue to be poor or stuck in the "middle class" is the confusion between the two. We don't have the mental training to see the gold right in front of our faces and instead choose drowning in debt over and over again.

Reading this book continues to invoke the thoughts of my mind of "what is my WHY for obtaining Financial Freedom" and "How can I afford to retire early". A controversial topic, yes. However, there is an answer to every question we seek and with financial literacy this is NO different. I thank Robert Kiyosaki, and all of those financial literacy authors that have been taking time to pour their information into a book. The knowledge that they have shared has aided me on my quest to address and educate others about the financial education disparities and how we all can revolutionize our family generations to acquire wealth.

Begin to learn and understand the BIG 3 after making a habit of budgeting and evaluating your debt to asset ratio even if you are not interested in entrepreneurship or homeownership. The big three are:

TAXES: because we cannot keep being afraid of the IRS. Learn how to keep your receipts clean and organized.

CREDIT: because it is a currency that is not seen as something to learn about. How credible are you?

REAL ESTATE: is the real estate. One clear way wealth can be passed down from one generation to the next. (watch Jay Morrison on YouTube)

And if you are interested in learning about how to start a successful business, I would recommend reading the E-Myth Revisited by Michael Gerber to start you off. Remember over 90% of small businesses fail within their first year. I think part of that reason is due to poor preparation and a lack of understanding of what business entails. People want to seem like they know it all without putting in the work.

The best way I can explain the concept of money is it is a currency, just like energy and time. You exchange money for (x) in return. The goal is not to stay in a certain financial bracket. It's kind of like a video game. You are supposed to gain certain skills and you go through different challenges (bosses) in order to test your abilities. Through those tests (boss levels), upon winning you acquire assets. The assets allow you to become wiser and move on to the next level. Each level will inadvertently show you what you've been missing. You acquire what you are missing then you level up.

I was not taught this when I was growing up but as I am educating myself, I'm learning to see things more clearly. Being poor is to stay on Level One. The focus must be increasing income and lowering debt. As your level up on certain high-income skills and your income level reaches a certain bracket, you may need to start considering a business. Why? Because your income will be greatly cut by taxes. Going to the next level may require a new skill set. Most people struggle to ever get out of level one.

I am not a finance or tax professional; however, I have read a whole lot of books on personal finances, have been talking with multimillionaires, and am actively learning and growing right along with ya. Consult with a lawyer, CPA, or tax professional to assess what will be the best choices for your particular situation.

#IAmSuccess Questions:

+ What is money's purpose?

_____

_____

_____

+ What is the purpose I want to give money in my life?

_____

_____

_____

+ What is my yearly/monthly/weekly/daily income goal?

_____

_____

_____

+ How do I begin to save it?

_____

_____

_____

+ How much do I want to save by the end of the next 3 months? 6 months? A year?

_____

_____

_____

- Where will I house and invest my money? What options are available?

  _____

  _____

  _____

- How can I utilize it as a tool to create the life I desire?

  _____

  _____

  _____

- How will I begin to use money to support others in my community?

  _____

  _____

  _____

- What causes am I interested in supporting?

  _____

  _____

  _____

- What is the purpose of credit?

  _____

  _____

  _____

- What skills am I missing in order to level up?

  _____

  _____

  _____

LESSON 49

LEARNING SELF-DEFENSE

Self-defense can mean many things. And we need ways not only to create peace and well-being but also to protect it. We need to feel safe mentally, physically and spiritually in order to survive and thrive in our lives. Mentally we need to protect our ways of thinking and making sure to filter out what we allow ourselves to consume. Physically, we need to feel as though we can protect ourselves if there is a threat among us. We can enroll into some type of physical self-defense course to support ourselves in feeling safer. I have found kung fu to be one of my favorite ways to learn self-defense since the culture is holistic. Spiritual protection is another big one that many do not talk about. Look into different ways to protect yourself, spiritual warfare is no joke.

Many of the things I've mentioned in this book has helped me alleviate a lot of the anxiety and depressive episodes that once kept me in bondage. I encourage you to try them out, even if it is new to you and it seems difficult at first. Keep at it.

This one helped me a lot when I was learning about different coping mechanisms.

FIVE things you **see** around you.
FOUR **things** you **can** touch around you.
THREE **things** you hear.
TWO **things** you **can** smell.
ONE **thing** you **can** taste.

Then say look at the time and date then say it aloud. See, in your mind's eye the world. Then narrow down on your specific continent where you live. See the oceans surrounding it. Then zoom into the state that you live in and finally the current space that you are in. Say aloud the place you are in and the position your body is in. Complete this with a smile and say, "And I am safe."

Ex:

Today is... September 24, 2024

It is 3pm on a Wednesday. I am sitting in a chair with my friend. It's a beautiful day, and I am safe.

This is called grounding. It can help when you feel like you have lost all control of your surroundings. It may help you remember where you are and in the immediate moment, are okay.

LESSON 50

HOLISTIC HEALTH IS WEALTH

I've learned that money or even material possessions are not the only definition of wealth. Many of us get caught up in it but it's simply not the full story.

Money, cars, clothes, sex, alcohol, drugs, more men, more women... These are not the keys to happiness. Not even close. This is not to be mistaken for a life goal.

Think about your life.

Think about what you do every single day.

Is it the same old routine? When people ask you how you are... Do you always give the same answer?

What motivates you to get out of bed every day? Is it that blunt you're going to smoke later? Is it that girl or guy you wanna "smash" after work? Will you ever have enough of what you are desiring?

Take some time to reflect because if you continue to follow something that doesn't feed your flame or align with your personal legend, you will never feel whole. The reason you were created to be here was NOT to have the latest Prada this or the most expensive Gucci that... you can't possibly truly believe that. You must find what your purpose on this earth is and make a life out of the cards you've been dealt!

It doesn't matter where you come from, it doesn't matter how many setbacks you've had-all that matters is you knowing where you're going. You may not know exactly how you're going to get there, but as long as you know where your destination is you WILL MAKE IT!

Now is what you're chasing truly worth it? Or is it an endless loop that comes with instant gratification, fake happiness, fake friends, depression, and just a whole lot of meaningless "things"? Things will never make you happy... whether it's 100 pairs of shoes and 20 new crystals. Whether it's 50 pairs of earrings and 3 new cars. And what if you lose it all? Does your happiness go away with it? Pay attention to the person you're becoming. Pay attention to the company you keep. Pay attention to the thoughts that pass through your mind... and really ask yourself:

1. Why am I truly here?
2. What do I want out of life?
3. What am I going to do to achieve it?

Soooo, if you think about it, you cannot fully enjoy financial or romantic wealth if you're not mentally, physically, spiritually, or emotionally aligned, right?

It's difficult to have a great time taking trip to Disneyland in Paris, France (which is pretty fun by the way) if you have the flu and are upset about something that happened in the past that you just can't stop thinking about.

You can easily allow these things to overcome you in all the different avenues that will cripple your spirit. When you are in a good space in all areas of your life than you can also identify and celebrate the monetary and social areas of your life. Your health is part of your wealth and it is so extremely important to stay on top of this!

One way to stay on top of your physical health would be to do an exercise for 30 minutes every day, for emotional and mental health, to find some way to calm your mind with meditation, deep breathing exercises, or watching an interesting show. As for spiritual, prayer, meditation, and/or finding a hobby that helps you to connect with yourself is certain to heighten your sense of self thus secure your wealth... in your health that is.

Are you paying attention to your health? What is one way you make sure to #takecare of yourself ?

▌CHAPTER EXERCISE

Prioritize Relaxing and Protecting Your Peace

Begin to prioritize relaxing and protecting your peace into your schedule. Here is a Soul Care Checklist to help you check in each week. If you are not feeling well, see if you have done any of these. You may find that you have not and may need to do one or more of these tasks on your schedule! Consider even taking a 7 day social media or food fast. Take care of your peace, family. We cannot give from an empty cup.

SOUL CARE
CHECKLIST

The Black Foster Youth Handbook by Ángela Quijada-Banks

- Taking time to deep breathe
- Staying Hydrated
- Getting good amount of rest
- Did atleast ONE exciting thing
- Using essential oils
- Took a spiritual bath
- Got a massage
- Entertained my creativity
- Laughed every day
- Moisturized my skin
- Not entertaining drama
- Beautified my space
- Eating a well-balanced meal
- Watched feel-good content
- Hanging out with amazing ppl
- Monitored my social media intake
- Retail therapy
- Participating in physical activity
- Meditating regularly
- Plans for a vacay
- Rooting in purpose
- Released negativity
- Spent time in nature
- Did something that wasn't comfortable

NOTES

| CHAPTER TWELVE

BE IN A CONSTANT STATE OF TRANSFORMATION

"You CANNOT rush the process. You CANNOT skip the healing. You CANNOT brush past processing the pain. You CANNOT fast forward the time and investments. There are no shortcuts. Find your path and follow it-even when it's hard, even when it hurts-even when it's not as clear anymore. Give yourself time to become who you truly are."

-UNKNOWN

"Every day I wake up, I can't move without a purpose."

- ÁNGELA QUIJADA-BANKS

Sometimes, we look at our experience from only one angle. We subconsciously ignore the other possible perspectives of others. And when the wound is fresh, we decide not to care about the other perspective. But if we want to heal and truly relieve ourselves of deep anguish, we must continuously step out of the situation and look at it objectively. It's not simple or something done overnight, but once you begin, I promise many aspects will begin to clear your line of thinking.

I've had to do this countless times with my parents and at first, lots of anger came out. Knowing that anger is a secondary emotion, I challenged myself to dig deeper for the primary one. It did not happen overnight for me as it is a continuous marathon that I push myself to heal. I have decided that this generational perpetuation of pain will end with me. And for that statement to hold weight; I can, I will, and I must do the work.

LESSON 51

KNOWING YOUR PURPOSE IS LIFE CHANGING

"Purpose and fulfillment coexist when we try to meet someone else's need rather than our own."

-CLAY WATERS

"When we self-regulate well, we are better able to control the trajectory of our emotional lives and resulting actions based on our values and sense of purpose."

– AMY LEIGH MERCREE

Just curious, when was the last time you felt truly joyful?

Me? Every single day... so about 5 seconds ago and oh... right now!

I remember when I didn't used to know what it felt like to be truly joyful... but oh how that has DRASTICALLY CHANGED. Over the years, I have really completely shifted my paradox and it's only going to get better from here.

Yes obstacles may come but it's important to know ways to combat them so that we can see them as just a little bump against the road instead of a massive wall that is impossible to get over. I learned that NOTHING is impossible... there's just a "certain way " of overcoming each "hardship" and you MUST shift your mindset and be open to consistent growth and change.

One major key, is to KNOW your purpose because without a defined purposeful life... one may become trapped in their own belief of "nothingness" and condemned with their own personal "hell" filled with the spirit of complacency.

A life rooted in and full of purpose is full of joy, fulfillment, and excitement regardless of the circumstances! And because it is forever evolving, you are able to transmute your energy to marvelous ideas to support the people, communities, and issues of the world that matter most to you.

So, I ask you again... when was the last time you truly felt joy? When was the last time you lived a life full of purpose?

"I don't know my purpose."

"I'll just wait until the time is right."

"Maybe only some people get to learn their purpose."

"Maybe I just don't have a purpose to be uncovered..."

These are the words I hear with my clients when we first have a conversation about uncovering their purpose. I've learned that a lot of us hold our limiting beliefs close to our chests, cradling it like a delicate baby. As soon as we notice that this baby is not delicate, but more so leeching off of our psyche, it's understandably difficult to let it go.

I mean sometimes we think, who am I to be an incredible, gorgeous, and intelligent world renown chef or mathematician at 25 or #1 singer on all the charts at 29? We rarely give ourselves the credit we deserve. Our brains get scattered and our hearts get scared.

But today, I dare you to dream.

I dare you to dream bigger than you ever have and completely see who you could become in this world! Who are you and who do you want to become? Is it a zoologist? Or a holistic health practitioner? Are you a mystic or energy worker? Do you want to become a community organizer that helps get activists together to start a revolution? Do you want to start your own garden and help feed the communities around you? Do you want to learn finances and help others overcome poverty all over the world? Do you want to travel the world and speak to billions of people?

What would you need to sacrifice in order to make that happen? Your fear? Your BS excuses? How about your toxic relationship that hasn't improved in over a year?

We have to stop telling ourselves lies and snuffing out our own candles. Because the truth is we ALL have a purpose, and it's absolutely possible to uncover it. I've done it. And the women I've coached have done it. Women and men all over the world are living in their purpose and gaining a deeper understanding of who they are. They are playing full out and happily, healthily, enjoying their lives. So, when will you ?

5 MAJOR STEPS TO UNCOVERING YOUR PURPOSE:

1. Know thyself

Know your strengths and develop your weaknesses. Know what brings you joy and what brings up fear for you... and find out why.

Know your core values and never sacrifice them for anyone or anything.

Know who you are and what you stand for.

2. Know what you desire

Know what you desire in this life romantically, socially, in your career, and within yourself.

Know your purpose in life... so that you may order your steps according to that knowledge and wisdom.

3. Know your worth, then 10x it and add tax!

Know that you deserve everything you desire but you must align yourself to it.

Know that you must have boundaries in your relationships and even with yourself and your energy...

You must never settle for less in this life... or any life...

Playing small is not self-love or self-care, stop short changing your potential. And stop belittling yourself internally. Uncover your divine purpose and take steps towards it each and every day.

And if you happen to get stuck, don't hesitate to reach out with an email or message me... because helping you just so happens to be a part of my purpose.

4. Discover and learn from the ones who are doing what you want to do

Learn how they did it and what their reason for doing it was.

Learn how they viewed and handled fear

5. Take action

Take fearful or fearless action and do it without making excuses for yourself.

It won't be a cake walk every single day.

LESSON 52

MY ONLY COMPETITION IS WITH MY PAST SELF

"STOP underestimating yourself. You are your own limit."

- ÁNGELA QUIJADA-BANKS

"Never be a prisoner of your past. It was a lesson, not a life sentence. Life goes on..."

-UNKNOWN

"Jealousy's the ugliest trait."

-KERI HILSON

Your competition is not other people's version of success. Check your ego.

Your true competition is your procrastination, your scarcity mentality that makes you envious of others success, the unhealthy food you allow into your body more than the nourishing food, the knowledge you neglect to learn, the inner shadow work you ignore to heal from, those negative behaviors your nurturing, your lack of consistency in your greatness. Your competition is with your past self and current attributes that you'd like to alchemize.

Take each day as an opportunity to create a better you. Be authentic. Be original. Not a copycat. And embrace all the beautiful "imperfections "that have grown into who you are. You are amazing in so many wonderful ways. Believe it. Be it. You got this! It's always time for a better you. No one knows it ALL. So, learn, grow, and change. This is the journey of the competition between you and your past self.

If you find yourself being jealous of someone else's success, begin to check with yourself. Why are you feeling jealous? And maybe instead of being better, perhaps it's sign that you need to do better. You should feel happy about someone else accomplishing their goals. If you do not, then that may mean you are not happy with where you are and what you're doing. Start putting more focus into your business and well-being.

If you see someone doing something that you wanted to do, what's stopping you from still doing it in your own way? That person has now shown you that it is possible to be done. If anything, you can learn from them!

Stop comparing, and start connecting!

‖ LESSON 53

ALCHEMIZING PAIN

"There's never a true destination to healing...
Just milestones along the way"

- ÁNGELA QUIJADA-BANKS

A common way we alchemize pain negatively is through the over consumption of drugs and alcohol. Jason Christoff says,

The word "alcohol" is said to come from the Arabic term "Al-khul"
which means "BODY-EATING SPIRIT" (also, is the origin of the
term" ghoul").

In alchemy, alcohol is used to extract the soul essence of an entity.
Hence its' use in extracting essences for essential oils, and the steriliza
tion of medical instruments. By consuming alcohol into the body, it in
effect extracts the very essence of the soul, allowing the body to be more
susceptible to neighboring entities most of which are of low frequencies
(why do you think we call certain alcoholic beverages "SPIRITS?").
That is why people who consume excessive amounts of alcohol often
black out, not remembering what happened. This happens when the
good soul (we were sent here with) leaves because the living conditions
are too polluted and too traumatic to tolerate. The good soul jettisons
the body, staying connected on a tether, and a dark entity takes the body
for a joy ride around the block, often in a hedonistic and self-serving
illogical rampage. Our bodies are cars for spirits. If one leaves, another
can take the car for a ride.

Essentially when someone goes dark after drinking alcohol or polluting themselves in many other ways, their body often becomes possessed by another entity.

We must be careful on what we can consume and how we choose to alchemize pain. One way I alchemize anger or pain is through writing poetry and performing spoken word. So, here is a poem I wrote about the relationship I have with my mother. This was during the time I was planning my wedding. I was processing the pain of the deep realization that my mother broke my heart far before anyone else knew I existed.

Many times we hear about the daddy issues, but we rarely hear about the mommy issues...

SANDS OF TIME

She called me, I ignored it
Excuse me of my insubordinace
But I don't expect the respect anymore
Just the blatant disrespect from her
Cause
It hurts deep down,
down right to the core

I smell your pain
And I'm just trying to stay sane
Keep my head in the game
And all you wanna do is
talk about YOUR pain
Or ask me if your own happiness will last
Stop dwelling on the past

I don't always wanna have the answers for you anymore
This is my time and I'm not trying to be rude
But

I can't even understand you half of the time
Looking back
My childhood feels like a
Unsolved Crime
You know, Something off of NY Times
And I...

know you got yours for your dirt but
Shit

It still fucking hurts and
Yeah
what about you ?
Still in those same shoes
Flirting with the same fools
Using the same manipulation tools

But I'm not mad
Don't wanna bicker, be petty & fight
But the mood you have me in
Is like
A dark whole trying to suck
The life out of me

What's your goal?
Do you know your purpose ?
Have you noticed that this wormhole
That you're calling a life
Is really a cry & shit fest ?
I mean really
How many times will you fail this test ?
How much longer are you willing to sacrifice your rest ?

Or
The rest

Of your peace of mind and mine ?

And maybe you don't get it and maybe you never will
but
stop
Pulling me back
Matter fact
Don't touch me

I've had enough of listening to this sad, endless track
I pour into you and you take it all
No love back

Stuck in a loop
I'm taking shots and
Your cutting my hoop
Almost my wedding day
And still no heirloom?

I mean
What do you want ?
I can't help you
I'm pouring myself into an empty test tube
Damn

How far are you trying to take this ?
Because
Either way... I'm going to break this

Generational curse
They don't tell you but...
The process is really the worst

But I know MY VISION
I KNOW MY PURPOSE
AND I KNOW IM WORTH IT
I'll take the painful journey in my mind —
Sprinkle some seasoning on it
With a squeeze of lime
& Turn back The sands of time

To create my new reality
A life that's so fresh with no fatality
A place where the love is true
Where you ask the meaning of "excellence "
And your people scream back "YOU"
Wealth for generations
As we all take sacred libations
On lavish around the world vacations

Because if it's not now then when?
And if it's not me, then who?

Yet
I wish you could come with me
But
Ya know

I'm not your savior

I gotta cut the tithes off with self-sabotaging behavior
Maybe one day you'll realize
You ARE your OWN savior

I love you
Wish you the best
But I'm done settling for less

Be blessed
Peace

I was talking to a friend a couple days ago, and she made sense when she was saying how I can't expect myself to heal within a specific time frame. See, I'm a fairly structured person and I thought I could just put my healing in a box... like okay, Wednesday at 3pm for an hour I will focus on healing, literally trying to schedule my trauma. And wait, before you write that off-it worked! It works; however, that can't be the ONLY time I "allow" myself to acknowledge it, understand it, or just be completely devastated by the truth. The universe is on its own time. I can only choose to flow with it in those moments... I know that now.

I'm 24 years old and I'm going up against 24 years of trauma, plus the trauma in my DNA from generations and generations of shit.

And it's okay to admit that sometimes you just don't know what you don't know. There is NO "okay, by 5pm today allllll of my internal stuff will unpacked and handled." It's more so: whatever comes up today, I will care for myself with love, compassion, and understanding. What a game changer!

I think it's even more bizarre that I had known that answer and yet still shied away from it. There are so many layers, so many stages, so many levels that patience is the true virtue at play here.

Because you cannot rush the process! And you cannot time the process-for time is a mere concept that your soul doesn't abide by let alone acknowledge. So never be discouraged with yourself and your process. Just do the best you can and show up for YOU every single day. Honor yourself, your ancestors, and your future by continuing to reach the next milestone that fills your being! You are more than capable! You are enough.

Although, we have this power to alchemize our pain, it is important not to subject ourselves to more of it, in spite of the fact that "we can handle it" or subconsciously trying to prove to ourselves that, "we are strong enough this time to endure it." We end up torturing ourselves this way. And it definitely does more harm than good. It can numb your ability to feel genuine joy or even sorrow. Feelings make us human. Emotions hold power.

LESSON 54
THERE IS A CHAIN OF COMMAND IN FOSTER CARE

Upon my travel across the states, several foster/resource parents and social workers have openly expressed to me that it is not an obligation for them to make sure young people are happy since they are being paid regardless. They claim that it only matters that their basic needs are met. These kinds of statements are troubling for many reasons. And it's important to note that this still happens and to know what to do when people like this are in control of our wellbeing.

You must learn the chain of command in foster care.

Most people believe family is just blood related. Others think of a normal family as a mother and a father with a baby or several children. The corresponding definition for family or families is two or more people who regard their relationship as a family and assume the responsibilities and obligations that come with membership in the family. However, I believe that a family can also be defined as any group of people that agree amongst themselves to take on the roles of family due to their emotional bond, reciprocal nature, expression of love, and admiration for each other's wellbeing.

The purpose of a family is to be invested in one another's mental, physical, and spiritual development. As parents or caregivers in a family, they should supply the basic needs since young people are still learning how to navigate life to grow into responsible, interdependent adults. Young people have a choice to learn attitudes and embody a core value system, to develop acceptable behavior, and to cooperate with their parents and other caregivers invested in their well-being and success. Community obligations take the form of protecting young people through regulating and licensing day care, prohibiting child labor, and providing opportunities for quality education.

Although we want to create the best expectations for the adults in our lives, it is imperative to recognize that sometimes things may go wrong. All the way wrong, and you may not feel like you are safe. If that is ever the case for you, I want you to know that you are not alone and are able to figure out the best way to handle that situation.

At the beginning of this book, we talked through what roles different people in your life have through foster care, your Bill of Rights, and your Sibling Rights as a young person in foster care. If any of these rights are violated, first engage in an open dialogue about these rights because your caregiver or social worker may not know that they exist.

Seek to educate them first. I know you may be thinking, "well shouldn't they already know this stuff?" And I'd say yes, but many do not know because it hasn't been implemented as standard training within your state or the agency your placement is licensed through.

When something goes on that isn't right and you have already tried to bring it up to your social worker, CASA, and/or foster parent, it may be time to consider other options.

The adults in your case plan are here to work for your overall well-being and happiness. So, we need to begin to hold them accountable and know when it is time to advocate on our own behalf.

Self-preservation is key, and I think we forget what that truly is in times when we do not understand the new system that we are in. I recognize that it's tough to be in congruence to this ideology, but we have to stay focused.

In this aspect, we have to continue to find other people that can help us move forward in our own personal goals and aspirations. Hopefully, it will be our circles that include our foster/adoptive families, but in times that these needs are not met... we have to:

1. Advocate on our own behalf
2. Recognize that it isn't time to be shy and silent about things that matter most to us

Whether that is visitation rights with your siblings, making sure you have a good, nutritionally balanced meal every single day, or having a sense of normalcy. All of these aspects are valid and they matter. They matter enough for you to not only speak up about them, but to build a team that will support you in voicing how you feel!

It's imperative that you have a tight knit support system that will not only carry you through the hard times, but also celebrate with and for you when you win.

If you ever come across an issue with someone in your closest circle, know that there is a chain of command, and what is said is not always final.

You have an ombudsperson and can go along with the comfort that there are people in your corner and willing to go to bat on your behalf.

Do you have a CASA or Guardian Ad Litem? These are individuals that do not get paid to support you. You should continue to develop and nurture the relationship between these people.

It's important to know who these individuals are and how to keep in contact with them. Keep a digital file of contacts and a physical copy of all the people in your case file as well as people that you would like to have supporting you.

This is something, when I was going through hard times in foster homes, I wish I had taken the time to organize. I had the best intentions and expectations about my placement; however, something inevitably hit the fan, and when it did I was not prepared.

It's better to have a database of individuals to pull from then to have to scramble and figure something out in the moment of despair. Emotions can be high and can cause you to think irrationally. Be cautious in who you allow into your inner circle . It took me several years to understand the concept of boundaries and also that not everyone is here for your highest good. Not everyone has your well-being in mind when they meet you. Many people are curious about what you have and can be in their life and only care about the opportunity that you give to them.

The truth is, there may be many times that you feel alone.

It is your responsibility to speak up about the things that matter most to you.

If you are unclear of who your command is, you can ask your social worker and your case manager and ask them to provide you with a list of the individuals so that you can keep with you as a physical and digital file.

You can also go online to your local DSS or DHS website and locate your chain of command.

#IAmSuccess Questions:

◆ How do you view family?

_____

_____

_____

◆ Are you open to having support from the supportive adults around you?

_____

_____

_____

◆ On a scale of 1-10, how safe do you feel in the home?

_____

_____

_____

◆ What could be done to make you feel more safe?

_____

_____

_____

◆ Who are the top three people that you trust right now?

_____

_____

_____

◆ Are you willing to grow your list of trustworthy people? Why or why not?

_____

_____

_____

◆ Are you a trustworthy person?

_____

_____

_____

◆ What is the chain of command in my case plan?

_____

_____

_____

◆ Who are people you can talk to when you feel down or frustrated about something?

_____

_____

_____

LESSON 55

AGING OUT OF FOSTER CARE DOESN'T HAVE TO BE LONELY

Too many young people, aging out of foster care can be extremely frightening. It means that you will be given a week or up to 30 days to find somewhere else to stay and possibly, if you are so fortunate, a financial amount to help support your decision of total independence up to $800. Most youth do not have a car, their license, or any skills as to how to be a productive member of society. To other youth, it's a moment that they dream of, finally being free.

According to Yahoo News, "Approximately 20,000 kids who age out of the system each year age out with no permanent family connections. About 25 percent have no high school diploma. Nearly 40 percent have been homeless; 33 percent have not had enough food at some point within the past year. 60 percent of young men are convicted of a crime; and about half struggle with substance abuse. Less than will be employed by age 24, while 71 percent of women will be pregnant by age 21-and one individual in four will experience posttraumatic stress disorder (PTSD)," not to mention the suicide attempts. Aging out of the system does not necessarily make things any better.

In 2014, North Carolina had something called a "C.A.R.S. Agreement" that youth were required to sign if they chose to remain in their current foster home. C.A.R.S. stands for Contractual Agreement Residential Services. When this contract was relevant, there was an increase from less than 1 percent of foster youth graduating from college about 3%. That particular agreement allowed youth to remain in foster care beyond their 18th birthday if they remain in a licensed placement and attend school full time.

This was with the intention to give youth in the C.A.R.S agreement the ability to have somewhere to stay during holidays while pursuing their education. However, there were some real complications with this contract.

For instance, if the foster parent for any reason decided they did not want to care for or allow the youth to remain in their home then the agreement was terminated and in many cases documented as some fault of the youth. If the foster parent is retiring and moving then the foster care agency is not obligated to find the youth another placement and instead, the youth will be given a certain amount of days to leave the home. Youth also had the option of signing themselves out of the C.A.R.S. Agreement on their own, at any time.

Unfortunately, this was something that happened to me. I was having some real safety issues within the foster homes I lived in, and every single time I reported it, there was negative backlash and I later found out the social worker documented my experience in the viewpoint of the foster parent, although I was the one requesting to be removed.

In January 2017, North Carolina launched their eighteen to twenty one program for youth aging out of foster care. This coupled with a piece of legislation, I assisted Senator Tamara Barringer to write and advocate for, which was finally passed as a law in July 2017. This was monumental in increasing trauma informed, evidence-based, and culturally competent practices to the radical transformation of the child welfare system in North Carolina. I did not benefit from any of these new practices, but it made me happy to know that we truly are able to make a difference for young people going through the system after me.

I didn't have to be a person with a fancy label with multiple letters after my name. I was just me, with my story and a basic understanding of my right to share my personal experience within a system that needs change. Freedom of speech is an incredible liberty that we are all afforded and should continue to seek understanding on how to effectively utilize. We must unapologetically advocate about the issues that greatly affect us and can increase the likelihood of more foster care improvement policies, practices and studies. Although these laws and many others such as the Family First Act are being passed there is still a ton of work to be done. In the political realm just because a piece of legislation gets passed into law... doesn't mean it will be implemented. That's a whole other battle.

As a young person getting close to aging out of foster care, I wasn't sure where to go or what to do. I felt very anxious about it but thought, "I still have time to figure it out." since I was supposed to stay in until I was 21 years old. Unfortunately, that did not happen. In my last foster home, I felt very unsafe. It was the summer of 2016. I tried to make it work despite mine and my foster parent's (we'll call her Ms. M) differences. Ms. M wanted me to drink and party, but that wasn't me. She wanted me to work at a fast food restaurant like she did when she was younger, and sabotaged my chances when I got a job for a political campaign.

Ms. M wanted me to wash her and one of her boyfriend's dishes and clean her house as if I was some sort of form of foster slave. Many times, foster parents would order me around to wash their clothes, dishes, scrub their toilets, etc. When I was younger, I would just do it to appease them and hope that they wouldn't want to send me away. At twenty, I wasn't going to clean after other grown adults and certainly not after a whole adult man that I didn't even know.

Something that really bothered me was when she would give other men the key to the house while she was at work. She wouldn't even tell me men were going to be coming by or that they had a key! I'd have days where I'm coming out of the shower, only to find a random guy sitting on the couch waving at me or a guy working on the carpet with her nowhere in sight. I still tried to stay there because I did not want to leave and be faced with something worse. I didn't want there to be any issues, but I think we were not on the same page regarding each other's expectations and boundaries, among other factors.

I attempted to talk to her about it but she seemed to always be in a bad mood. Eventually, I decided to talk with the case manager and tried to get answers about what to do next. I phrased the scenario as a hypothetical question because I did not want anything negative to happen to Ms. M. I just didn't think it was conducive to my wellbeing to keep going as it was. I went out of town for about a week and when I returned there was a new girl living with us. She was in foster care too. Upon meeting her, she told me how our foster parent was saying so many negative things about me while I was gone.

I immediately thought back to what happened when I first came to live with Ms. M. There was a middle-school aged younger girl who was living there first. In fact, she had been with Ms. M for over a year. A couple of weeks into me staying there, Ms. M began to speak negatively about her and within the month she was removed.

I follow patterns, and I knew what that meant. My time was about to be up. I began to question if it was the right idea to notify the case manager about what was going in the way that I did. A few hours passed and I tried to call the case manager. She kept forcing my call to voicemail. As I waited for Ms. M to return to the house from work that day, I became increasingly anxious. Was she going to kick me out?

Eventually, she burst through the door, slamming it behind her. Days prior, she had been talking about how much she was hating the new principal at the school she worked for. And I guess they still hadn't ironed out the issues. I wondered if my case manager had told her anything. How was the information presented? I quickly went to my room and closed the door behind me. To my surprise, she knocked and asked me to talk.

I came out and we stood in the kitchen as she scolded me for telling the case manager about what she had going on in "her house". She told me I had no right to open my big fat mouth and tell them anything. She began to verbally threaten me that she was going to make sure I was sorry. She said she would make sure I'd pay for trying to ruin her career. I told her that was never my intention. I just didn't think me living there was a good fit. She then started to threaten me about putting hands on me and honestly, anything else she said I zoned.

I zoned out as her voice began to raise louder and louder. Her gestures becoming more and more aggressive. I zoned into a dark place in my mind. The feelings of abandonment and being misunderstood crept back up. The pain of someone wanting to harm me for trying to protect myself burst out of my eyes in forms of tears. She stormed out of the kitchen and slammed her room door. I could hear her little dog, that she'd lock up in the bathroom yelping as who knows what was happening. The other girl who was living there, came to my room. We talked all night as I tried to text someone, anyone, to talk to from the adults I knew in my circle. No one picked up. No one responded. Eventually, I cried myself to asleep and told myself that the next day

I would be talking to some other social workers in hopes of getting answers on what to do.

Upon waking up the next day, I was sent an email that I had seven days to figure out where I was going to move to. It was an emergency removal and my foster parent, Ms. M had requested that due to her state of safety, it would be best that I be removed immediately. My chest began to tighten and I tried to breathe slowly. I thought, "How come no one even heard my side? Am I being kicked out of foster care?"

My social worker's supervisor sent the email based on false accusations my foster parent told her about me. My social worker had retired earlier than anticipated, the week before after getting into a car accident with my brothers as she was bringing them to a sibling visit. We did not get a visit that day. And I didn't have my guardian ad litem (CASA) because she was removed from my case a year prior due to her supporting me beyond what she was supposed to. They shared that my guardian ad litem had crossed her boundaries by allowing me to stay at her place at a time where I had nowhere else to go. If she hadn't stepped in, I would have been sleeping at an airport for a couple of days since my social worker didn't see anything wrong with that while I was transitioning placements.

After reading the contents of the email, I attempted to reach out to my social worker's supervisor. She did not respond. I tried to reach out to a well-known social worker in the triangle area and he actually did respond. However, that did not go how I thought it would at all. Once he answered, I asked him if he knew what was going on with my case. He said he did and I was going to have to learn my lesson. I had a previous CARS agreement and it didn't work out. He said they were being lenient and gave me another try with this placement. Since, I couldn't make it work, I was going to have figure something else out on my own.

I tried to take deep breaths and instead my face flooded with tears. I asked how I was supposed to figure out where to go in seven days and he said, it was no longer any of their concern. We were on video chat and his face was very firm. I asked if we could at least have a meeting since I wasn't given a chance to tell my side of the story. He told me that was not a part of protocol and the decision was final. He wished me luck and got off the phone.

Ironically, it was my birth family who provided the most assistance and emotional support. If I didn't have my dad come pick me up from an emergency removal from my last foster placement, I don't know what would have happened. He helped me move into a place I found on craigslist to meet my 7 day notice deadline and he was the only one to help me get settled. My dad, who I was removed from, was the only person to visit me for the week to come and ensure I made it to my classes. He tried to check in for the months to follow. Although I am grateful for his efforts, due to his own personal struggles, this wasn't consistent and overtime I began to feel alone and isolated again.

I realized that for the most part I was on my own. Within a few months, I became homeless because my lease ran out with the craigslist place and I had no idea how I would have a stable apartment. I attempted to ask others to cosign or if I could stay with them, but everyone told me that they'd love to help me but they couldn't take the risk. I was working a tutoring job and attending North Carolina Central University. Most of my money went to transportation and food.

Many youth aging out of foster care seem to have a similar story and it can become increasingly difficult to see the finish line and achieve graduation in post-secondary education. Acquiring a stable place to live is something you can stay stuck in a loop in if you are not prepared before aging out. Thus, keeping you from laying a foundation to reach self-actualization much less soulful liberation.

What I've gathered is whichever path a young person chooses can still be difficult if they do not prepare themselves. And if the supportive adults do not make their holistic stability and success a priority. Whether it is low self-esteem, underdeveloped communication skills and emotional intelligence, or even the lack of permanency and support. There have been new policies in place that state that each youth that is in foster care has to be enrolled in some sort of "Independent Living" or "Transition" program prior to the youth's 18th birthday. Since these implementations within the past five years, the numbers of youth who reported not knowing what to do at all when it comes to adulting has lowered. More than 20,000 youth admitted to knowing of some type of resource to assist them with furthering independence and seeking support. So, let's keep going in this direction.

Normally, most people have their family throughout their entire life from eighteen and beyond. They have at least one place that they can stay even if it is not with their biological parents. Yes, one is considered as an adult when turning eighteen, but why do we keep on pushing "independence" when that is not realistic? That is creating an idea that to be competent and considered an adult, you must know how to do everything on your own.

In foster care, at age eighteen, a young person is considered an adult and expected to do and handle life all on their own without any help whatsoever. However, how many people that are truly "successful" have done it all on their own? The privilege in a "normal" home is that you never quite "age out" of a family or lifelong support, so why should foster youth?

We need to start preaching and teaching interdependence instead of "independence", otherwise, we are instilling within youth and constituents within the system that youth with lived experience in foster care are not being successful adults until they are doing everything on their own. And that's just not fair. We do not ask youth without lived experience in foster care to do this so why foster youth? The truth is we need each other and lifelong support. We need community. Not as a crutch or to be solely dependent on one another, but to support, love, care for, and celebrate each other. We need to learn how to allow others to help us and appropriate ways to help others. Our mental, physical, financial, and spiritual wellbeing depends on it.

CAGED IN CARE

Smile when you are mad.
Take these pills when you are sad.
If you act too bad...
they'll send you away.
Don't be emotional about your trauma.
Don't cry even if you miss your mama.
Shut up.
Sit down.
Don't complain about their food.
And Don't complain if there isn't any.
Wash their dishes.
Don't leave a mess.
Don't tell them too much about your past.
They'll judge you.
And for Christmas, no one will grant your wishes.
No you cannot see your family.
No visitation unless mandatory.
No friends over.
No you may not leave this house.
It does not matter if you're
making friends and just want to be normal.
Shut up.
You're talking way too much.
Tell the social worker what's going on?

Wow. You're just asking for a punch.

Don't yell.

Don't scream.

Don't write it out.

Don't wanna eat 3 times a day.

Don't stay to yourself.

You're selfish.

You're stuck up.

You're ungrateful.

No wonder your parents didn't want you!

Life?

Just trying to make it

All on your own

Without having to fake it

Do I have what it takes?

How much longer before I age out?

Whether or not it was true... it doesn't make it okay to have been said to you.

What they say doesn't matter.

They didn't know your story. Only bits and pieces through a distorted perception. They don't know your heart and all you're destined to be. And maybe you don't either but that's okay if you don't. One day you will.

Just focus on healing and know that we all make mistakes! It's not a big deal. The biggest resolution is to learn from your mistakes, read lots of books, and ignore all the dirty looks. Life is harder and harder if you're a foster youth with limited supports. That doesn't mean give up. It just means we have to try a little harder to build ourselves up and create a healthy circle for ourselves. Continue to persevere through any obstacle that life throws out at you. Go to conferences. Maybe even go to therapy, talk with some trusted people and meditate on past traumas you have yet to heal from. It will get better, it always does. I know it may not seem like it, but everything is temporary. Your fate is in your hands. Do what you can to fix it and disregard what you cannot because it will only make you stressed and sick. You are the CEO of your own life. It's time for you to own it! You got this! I believe in you!

You can listen to this poem and many others on the *Soulful Liberation* podcast.

A free resource to support your journey through navigating this system and other challenging factors to come.

#FOSTERINGSUCCESS TIP:

My dad and other birth family members helped me tremendously in gaining closure about what happened in my childhood as well as showed up for me when I was in dire circumstances that the errors of the child welfare system created. Secondly, financial literacy, a basic understanding of credit and maintaining stable housing is imperative to young people's success. Please make time to understand it and help them see the value in creating a plan to execute and prepare them for what is to come.

If possible, I encourage you to leave a window open for birth families. There are several articles and research done that explains how imperative it is for young people to be connected to birth families. And no, it may not be easy to navigate at first. However, I believe it is worth working towards extending the social capital spectrum for your young person, especially if that is what your young person is craving. It doesn't have to be that the young person is spending the night at their birth families house, maybe it starts off with one hour fun time at a public restaurant. Include siblings, aunts, uncles and other parts of the family in your young persons' life. Be careful not to isolate them. I do not understand the whole concept of demonizing the birth family. Get to know the birth families. They are human too. This may not be possible in all cases, however for those that it is-it's worth it.

Also, check out Foster Youth to Independence Initiative and share the resource with all you are connected to. This is a new federal program to help young people aging out gain housing stability.

CONCLUSION

LIFE IS FEEDBACK TO WHAT FREQUENCY WE ARE VIBRATING ON

"It is not easy healing yourself, transforming your mind, building new habits, observing reality without projections or delusions. This is work that takes effort, but when you continue trying, it creates significant results that have an immensely positive impact on your life."

-YUNG PUEBLO

By now, you should have a clearer understanding of your definition of success and be at peace with your journey toward holistic healing. It's important not to focus so much on the negative because whatever you choose to focus on, energy will flow to and amplify.

It's imperative to check what you are rooted in. Every decision we make in life is either rooted in fear or love.

Take a moment to look back at your decisions from the past six months. At the core, have they been rooted in fear or have they been rooted in love? Be brutally honest with yourself. Whether it is the fear of losing love, losing an opportunity, losing finances, losing a mental state of being etc... have your decisions been made out of fear or have they been made out of love?

Perhaps, it is time be clear about what you are rooting in. Do you need to pull out the weeds? Maybe you just need to switch out the quality of soil. If you are unsure, look to what the fruits of your roots are bearing. What quality of life are you reflecting? Life is feedback. It will show you through the people you have around you, the results you are producing and the feelings you consistently feel each day that may need tweaking or if you are on the right path.

Once you have a clear, safe, and secure base-it will be easier to truly envision and see your next steps in making that vision a reality. And don't live a small life. Stop being "realistic". It's not about being realistic. If I was "realistic" with my goals....well honestly I would not be on this earth anymore and I would not have written this book. It's important to consider the financial investments, emotional return on your investment in your dreams to make them a reality, however don't be so "realistic" that you stifle your ability to dream big! And to think big!

From there, it is time to level up and ascend to your next steps in life. It is important to recognize that foster care is not an isolated issue. It is a complicated system that is entangled with multiple factors leading it to be what it is today. And you do not have to untangle it all by yourself and definitely not all at once. In order to improve this system, other systems and your personal outcomes... we must visit the past, self-reflect and progress. We must challenge ourselves to be vulnerable and begin to share out stories to shed a light on the realities of what's going on within these systems.

One of the biggest factors in healing will be forgiving yourself for things you've done in the past due to not knowing better. Forgiving yourself for the way you handled a certain situation. Forgiving yourself for not doing (x) when given the chance. Forgiving yourself for allowing a certain caliber of person into your space.

Make sure you are not allowing your circumstance to become your death sentence. Life is never meant to be your own personal hell. If you feel that way, I hope you now know what it may mean that it's time for you to get out of your comfort zone!

It may mean that you need to go back to your younger self and remember what you used to love. Maybe you loved drawing and you now feel like too many years has passed and you shouldn't try anymore. Perhaps dancing or when you were ten you wanted to become a scientist. Revisit those desires. It's not too late to pick it back up and get back into the groove of it.

You may have days that you can't stand looking at your face or hearing your own voice. That's okay. Many times, we speak highly and uplifting to others but we do not keep that same energy with ourselves. Be gentle with yourself. Know that self-love and self-acceptance is a journey. Building wealth and holistic health is a journey. Aim for progression, not perfection. You are exactly where you are supposed to be.

Breathe.

Today is the first day of the rest of your life. A life that you can create without heartache and strife. A life you deserve and have the choice to root in your purpose and holistically heal. Thank you for awakening to the possibility of Soulful Liberation. May you continue to learn and grow into who you have been predestined to become. May you move forward making choices rooted in love instead of fear.

Peace, family.

Congratulations!

You have just completed Phase 4 of the Black Foster Youth Handbook. That's all of the phases!!

How do you feel?

Take some time to pause.

Reflect and record your thoughts and what you've learned in your notebook/journal.

Take some time think about your takeaways! Then post a picture or your reflections with the #IAmSuccess if you are a young person and #FosteringSuccess if you are a supportive adult.

And celebrate!

Congratulations on completing

Phase one: Root

Phase two: Envision

Phase three: Ascension

Phase four: Liberation

You are well on your way to achieving success and holistic healing. May you continue with divine guidance and clarity in who you are and why you are here. I hope to meet you on the other side. Much love, light and healing energy,

Ángela Quijada-Banks

"Self-realization is liberation. Liberation is self-realization."
-Fredrick Lenz

RESOURCES

Visit www.blackfostercareyouthhandbook.com for resources

California:

https://jitfosteryouth.org/

https://twinspire.org/

https://calyouthconn.org/

Colorado

https://www.elevatingconnections.org/

North Carolina

http://hopecenteratpullen.org/

https://www.saysoinc.org/housing-resources

https://www.facebook.com/atrisk4great/?ref=page_internal

ABOUT THE AUTHOR

Ángela Quijada-Banks is an American best-selling author, Founder and C.E.O of Soulful Liberation (a Book publishing company and podcast), Program Director and Holistic Health & Purpose Coach at Consciously Melanated Queens, Decolonizing educator and transformational artist. On the Soulful Liberation podcast she aims to empower foster youth by day and break generational curses by night. Through her everyday work with helping young people uncover their divine purpose, performing spoken word events, workshops and political advisory to legislators across the nation, she aims to aid in revolutionary change in holistic health, economic injustices, child-welfare disparities, cultural competency and identity within low-wealth communities of color both on a micro and macro level.

In her most recent best-selling book, The Black Foster Youth Handbook she sheds light on a taboo topic through her own personal experience highlighting 50+ lessons she learned in order to support young people's journey and equip them with necessary tools to successfully age-out of foster care and holistically heal.

Born in Anaheim, CA her reach has spanned across the nation and in several countries. Since the age of three years old, when she was first introduced to swing dancing she has always come back to it even in the most unstable of circumstances. To this day, Ángela is still open to learning new things that excites her including Kung Fu and drumming. Between her day to day adventures, Ángela enjoys traveling the world and adrenaline rushes at amusement parks with her husband, Michael. She is lovingly called a "graceful powerhouse" by all who know her, as she lives by the quote, " If not me, then who? If not now, then when?

WORK WITH ÁNGELA

1:1 and group Purpose coaching www.consciouslymelanatedqueens.com

For speaking engagements/workshops and trainings, visit www.original soulflower.com and fill out the form on the website or send an email to mrs.banksofficial@gmail.com

Looking to publish a book or want to tell your story, feature your music or poetry? Send an email to mrs.banksofficial@gmail.com !

Bulk orders of books, www.blackfostercareyouthhandbook.com

Learn more about the work I've been doing, check out www.original soulflower.com

Thank you !!

Thank you for joining me on this
journey toward Soulful Liberation!

I cannot wait to hear from you!

Wanna help spread the word
about this book?

1. Be sure to leave an honest
review on Amazon!

2. Tell someone about it!

3. Encourage your local foster
care organization to purchase
bulk copies.

CPSIA information can be obtained
at www.ICGtesting.com
Printed in the USA
LVHW031520260221
680020LV00002BA/10